Public Policy and the Family

Wives and Mothers in the Labor Force

Z.I. Giraldo
Center for the Study of
the Family and the State,
Duke University

LexingtonBooks
D.C. Heath and Company
Lexington, Massachusetts
Toronto

306.8
G516p

Library of Congress Cataloging in Publication Data

Giraldo, Zaida Irene.
  Public policy and the family.

  Includes bibliographical references.
  1. Family—United States. 2. Family policy—United States.
3. Mothers—Employment—United States. 4. Public welfare—United
States. I. Title.
HQ536.G57   306.8'0973   80-7692
ISBN 0-669-03762-1

Published simultaneously in Canada

Printed in the United States of America
81-4505
International Standard Book Number: 0-669-03762-1

Library of Congress Catalog Card Number: 80-7692

Public Policy
and the Family

Contents

Contents

List of Figures

List of Tables

Acknowledgments

All of the chapters of this text were prepared while working on the completion of a National Institute for Mental Health Post-Doctoral Fellowship at The Center for the Study of the Family and the State in The Duke University Institute of Policy Sciences and Public Affairs.

Carol Stack, director of the Center, reviewed, edited, improved, and guided all of these papers through their various stages of preparation.

Fellow research associates at the Center, Jack Weatherford, Sarah Ramsey, Robert Kelly, Eli Zaretsky, Jan Brukman, Karen Sacks, and Elizabeth Friedman, also read and helped edit these papers.

I would particularly like to acknowledge my debt to Jack Weatherford, who shared in the writing of both the introduction and part I and to Sarah Ramsey, for all of her work on the research and writing of part III.

I would also like to thank Colin Blaydon and John McConahay, faculty at the Institute, for their help during the research stages of the project.

In addition, the following persons and organizations were essential to the completion of the Employment and Family Survey in Mecklenburg County, North Carolina: Robert Kelly and Susan Gabbard, my associates in the project; the Junior League of Charlotte, Inc., particularly Bettie Buck, Cynthia Marshall, and Lynn Murray; the Mary Reynolds Babcock Foundation; the Family Impact Seminar, Washington, D.C., particularly Halcy Bohen; Heidi Hartmann of the National Academy of Sciences; and the Charlotte Public Library and its staff.

Finally, I would like to acknowledge the contributions of Mari Clark and Lanier Rand Holt, staff of the Center, and Susan McDonald and Catherine Mishler of the Duke Documents Collection.

Acknowledgments

Introduction

The American family today is a thriving institution although it has changed from the era of our grandparents. At a time when the public schools are moving away from their traditional role as socializers, when elected officials are no longer looked on as models of behavior, and when the churches are retreating from an admonitory role over the personal lives of the general population, the family continues as one of the most persistent, if not the strongest, molding and modeling institution in society. It is still the primary residential unit, basic consumer, means for reproduction and socialization, major personal support system, and primary social-psychological network available to adults and children.

Yet despite all of its persistence and strengths, the family of today is beset by a host of problems. Many of these problems are caused by social or economic developments beyond the control of individuals, so government agencies often are held responsible for dealing with them on a systemic basis. Too many times these problems are completely ignored by the government or, even worse, the regulatory solutions enacted are overloaded with so many restrictions that new problems are created while the old problems are being remedied. In this book a number of these situations are examined, and many of the governmental solutions attempted or proposed are evaluated and judged on the basis of their effectiveness. The major focus of the work, however, is on patterns of family life that emerge when viewed through the perspective of the different phases of the family life cycle and the various pressures that have changed or reshaped family life during the course of history. There is only a secondary emphasis on public policy.

The reason for following this approach is that the U.S. government does not have a national policy on families or anything clearly labeled "Family Policy." Therefore any attempt to analyze the impact of the U.S. government on families can be determined best by focusing on the changes that have occurred in family life and then measuring the role public policy played with regard to those changes.

The chapters which make up this book were written independently and are not intended to be a complete and comprehensive analysis of public policy and the family. The subject is vast, and a great deal of in-depth analysis needs to be done in specific areas before it can be brought together in a satisfactory manner and treated as a unified whole. All writers on the subject agree on the need for more research to provide insights that will eventually discern overall patterns. The impacts of employment on family life, tax policy on employed women and their families, and the Equal Rights Amendment (ERA) on families are examined here to determine how varying approaches to dealing with families affect individual and aggregate numbers of families in the United States. The belief that there are patterns that will contribute to a greater understanding of the dynamics of the subject is the premise for this book.

Prior to the Industrial Revolution, for the majority of the population the home and workplace were one. There were no hard and fast rules that gave the major responsibility for child care to mothers and the provision of economic sustenance to fathers. These roles tended to overlap and interchange according to circumstances. With the growth of industry and urbanization, in addition to the separation of the family from the wage earner's place of work, the idea became fixed that these two basic conditions of human existence ought not, could not, and should not be combined. These biases and prejudices formed what has been termed "the myth of separate worlds" by Rosabeth Moss Kanter.

As the myth of hard and fast delimitation between the worlds of the family and the employer became an accepted fact of human existence, people, in turn, were conditioned by it. This was actually only a middle- and upper-class prerogative since poor females could never be exempted from productivity by their families. But because of the association with the privileged classes, this ideal began to be viewed as the norm to which all aspired. Men were socialized to believe that their natural sphere was the workplace and that somehow this was the superior sphere of existence in that it demanded more difficult accomplishments. Women, or rather that segment of womankind who could be spared from wage earning, were conditioned to accept their homes as their domains, along with all of the resultant restrictions that this form of existence imposed. By the twentieth century the belief in the essential separation of employment from the family was so widespread that is has permeated the fiber of modern American society and governs all of our institutions and attitudes.

It has long been known that a man might bring home some of the frustrations of his job and that this would have detrimental effects on the family. Similarly, employers have been aware that unstable familial relations can lead to alcoholism, absenteeism, and low worker efficiency. Yet despite this commonsense awareness of the interrelation between home life and work life, for the most part these aspects have been treated as minor factors hardly affecting the larger reality of separation. Even the obviously fundamental impact of work on the family of an employed mother has not destroyed the accepted belief in the myth of separation. It has served to bolster it in fact. Because women did not belong at the workplace and since, until recent studies disproved it, public opinion held that an employed wife and mother damaged her family by sacrificing their interests to the demands of her job, the need for a separation between the two worlds was confirmed.

This attitude remained widely prevalent during the 1970s in spite of the fact that women comprised 42 percent of the labor force in 1979. Women's participation is projected to continue growing at a faster rate than that of men. In 1979 51 percent of all married women worked for a living. Obviously the myth of separate and incompatible worlds cannot continue to exert influence on people's minds as fewer and fewer families live in conformity to it. Yet until this myth is thoroughly explored for what it is, an unhealthy state of affairs will exist. People's lives will not conform to what they have been taught to perceive as truth; that is, working men will continue to feel forced by the modern work situation to behave as though paid labor was their rationale for living, causing them to undervalue the other dimensions of their lives. Few of them will have wives who stay home and assume full responsibility for the family's home life. Working wives will continue to feel guilt for leaving their families while working to provide them with their material needs, and nonworking wives will feel more and more that they are given insufficient respect and admiration for performing what they see as their duty.

The same attitude that raises the question of the presence or absence of a female from the home to the plane of a moral issue also governs the debate over the proposed ERA. Fear that guaranteeing women equality of legal rights will cause them to abandon their roles within the family or legally force them out of their chosen family roles dominates a great deal of the debate on the pros and cons of enacting the amendment. While many believe these fears are irrational or even trumped up for a sinister purpose, I take the fears seriously and have made an attempt to look into what impact the ERA might have on American family life. Since I view the role of female heads of families as equal with that of the male heads of families, my findings indicate that it is beneficial for families to have courts base their decisions on the concept of legal equality between sexes. This attitude is consistent with the present-day reality and represents the one development in the area of public policy that is truly responsive to the needs of individual families. I found that the ERA enables the courts to make decisions that are flexible enough to accommodate the individual life styles of all families without imposing unrealistic governmental norms. The ERA, therefore, represents a model of how public policy should be built in order to address the needs of today's families. The reason the ERA works when other policies do not is that it is based on a modern concept of equality between all parties as opposed to the older view that whenever governmental interference was required by a situation it was because government had to deal with dependents needing a protector or with situations involving pathology.

Governmental attitudes toward social problems have historically taken a paternalistic mein. Since the early nineteenth century policymakers in the United States have adopted a consistent attitude toward anyone in need. Too often the remedy of first recourse has been that of institutionalization because the problem was interpreted as stemming from an illness. Whether the problem involved orphans or the mentally ill, the response of the bureaucracy has been to build an institution to literally house the problem. In that way the children of parents who were too poor to support them, the mentally ill whose families could not afford to provide private care, and juveniles with behavioral problems were all removed from the family and placed in institutions where the state exercised total control over them. Fortunately, that notion of helping the needy has been modified in the twentieth century. Large numbers of lunatic asylums have given way to community mental-health facilities where the mentally ill are cared for while living with their families. Now families are encouraged to use a variety of counseling services to help them cope with difficult children without having the children removed from their custody, and families with inadequate resources are given monetary aid so that they can rear their children at home. This transition has been brought about by the realization that not all problems can be resolved by using indelible definitions of healthy and sick, good and bad, normal and abnormal. Individuals, unlike machines, are products of homes, not factories, and the majority of these individuals are best helped within their own individual families and not in factory-like institutions. And unlike products of a factory, differences among individuals do not necessarily mean that there is something wrong with the system.

Despite considerable progress in changing attitudes toward those who need help, a residue of the institutional mentality continues to pervade public policies regarding America's families. The poor may no longer be fed in poor houses or soup kitchens, but the Department of Agriculture still tries to regulate which necessities poor people should be able to purchase with food stamps. One might also wonder how much effort has been expended by a bureaucracy trying to decide whether bathroom tissue should be paid for with food stamps or whether that item falls under the mandate of some other governmental agency. While this may be as much a product of bureaucratization of government as it is a result of the remnants of an institutional mentality, the willingness to accept the position that the government has the right to regulate in this fashion stems from earlier attitudes viewing the poor as pathologically incapable of making sensible economic decisions concerning their own welfare.

In this book I deal with the specific problems faced by families with inadequate resources and the view that these families must be helped on their own terms and without recourse to sterile, conventional stereotypes. The problems of the poor, like those of women, are often assumed to be special problems of particular economic groups or a specific social stratum in which a certain number of unfortunate members live all of their lives. This model of poverty has persisted despite the fact that we have long been

aware that the poor are primarily the very young and the very old. The specter of poverty, furthermore, is not confined to urban ghettos and the agri-
cultural back country. It is a problem that large numbers of middle-class
Americans might have to face at the beginning and again at the end of their
family cycles. It is true that a minority of the population does seem to be
permanently trapped in the ghetto or in rural poverty, but to focus on them
only blurs the fact that poverty is a general socioeconomic problem found
throughout the United States. The mother on welfare in the city and the
migrant worker's family on the farm epitomize the plight of the impover-
ished, but they represent only a fraction of the entire gamut of financial
distress in America. The young family struggling to establish a decent home
for its young children, the middle-aged couple trying to cope with high tui-
tion bills to provide their children with some form of advanced training,
and the retired couple living on a small, fixed income all face years of great
financial strain and conceivably could find themselves in the statistics of
poor families or view themselves as poverty stricken. On the face of it their
problems appear quite different, and certainly less immediate than those of
the mother on welfare who is trying to feed and clothe her children. But
basically all of these families are attempting to deal with situations in which
the resources available to them are inadequate to meet their needs at particular junctures in their family cycle.

It has become clear that government policies must be updated to
acknowledge and support the growing number of families who do not fit the
traditional pattern and who are healthy but afflicted with specific problems,
often inherent in the family life cycle. These families must also be recognized as legitimate and viable units that are providing for the care and nurture of a large proportion of society's children and adults. In every way
government policy should reflect concern for the serious economic responsibilities of the family and the fact that these responsibilities now weigh
heavily on the shoulders of both the male and female heads of families.
Families in any stage of poverty are entitled to receive the kind of help that
will enable them to continue to function as viable units of material support
without forcing them to reshape themselves to conform with norms of eligibility. Families not needing direct government subsidies should be able to
depend on supportive policies in regard to day-care needs, reasonable
medical care, and protection from the ravages of inflation. There should be
policies to encourage employers to acknowledge and address the family
needs of their employees. The needs of the elderly should be addressed
within a family context, and governmental policies should encourage family
bonding and provide incentives for families attempting to keep generations
together. Petty intrusions on family life, like the marriage tax, should be
eliminated and disavowed as an unfortunate by-product of short-sighted

governmental policy that did not acknowledge the primacy of the family within the American social fabric and the need for governmental flexibility in dealing with all types of families.

The social climate of the nation is ripe for such a new focus. America may be entering a new era in respect for familial values. When the children of the baby boom passed through the *Sturm und Drang* of adolescence, the very fabric of family life and society seem frayed and in the last stages of decay. Homes were torn by generational conflicts magnified by the unprecedented numbers of adolescents, communities experienced surging rates of increased crime, the public school system was on the verge of collapse, and the nation itself was divided by the generation gap. Now that this very large cohort is well into the young adult years, the social milieu of the nation is beginning to reflect the new status of the population, and a large part of the new emphasis is on family life. The same young people who seemed to be at the point of bringing about the destruction of their own families a decade ago now are marrying, having children, buying homes, coping with two-career marriages, and paying the taxes. The integrity of the family as a primary social unit has been preserved. A renewal of faith in that institution is blossoming in conjunction with a recognition of the great variety of styles and forms available to family units.

While it is true that American families today appear to have ridden out the storm and continue to be relatively better off economically than many others in the world, that picture seems to be changing. American families will be facing a new set of economic challenges based on lowered standards of living brought about by lessened productivity and a shift in economic clout to different portions of the world. Public policies can be brought into line with these new challenges if they are endowed with adequate flexibility to address specific and changing conditions and needs. Revitalized policies may be needed to help families deal with changing world conditions, but dramatic shifts in policy can be avoided if all policies are designed to meet both the changing needs and the changing population of families. Most of the credit for the endurance of the American family should go to individuals themselves, however, this does not mean that policymakers should stop attempting to improve the state of American families, particularly in the light of the new challenges and threats that loom for families in the 1980s. Policymakers must learn from the past when planning for the future.

Part I
Life Cycle and the American Family: Current Trends and Policy Implications

Z.I. Giraldo and
J.M. Weatherford

1   Overview of Part 1

In recent years a number of policy analysts have focused more attention on the relationship between the family and the state. Important questions are being asked in order to better understand the role of government vis-à-vis the American family. What constitutes current American policy toward the family? What should that policy be? How can policies already in force be improved and made consistent with an overall policy toward the family? In this section these questions are addressed by looking directly at families. Who are they? What are they like? What is their composition, and how are they changing? The emphasis is on families and family problems in order to better focus attention on how government policies affect families through explicitly ennunciated positioning or implicitly in subtle, and not so subtle, ways.

Within the restrictions of this approach to the question of the family and family policy, there are two possible approaches. One is to emphasize the pluralism inherent in American society demonstrated by the unique aspects of particular economic, ethnic, or social groups within the population and to stress the particular needs of these groups and the families comprising the groups. The second approach is to search for what is common throughout the various groups within the society as a whole, seek the dimensions of the basic structure of the family, and discern the problems common to all or most families. This section takes the second approach and concentrates on the general characteristics of the entire population with occasional emphasis on specific or particular ethnic, racial, or class differences. In opting for this methodology, however, we are not trying to minimize the differences in order to deny their importance. Many of the problems often attributed to only small groups of the population are in fact problems that affect almost everyone at some point in the life cycle. Many of the problems of the poor are, to a different degree, the same problems faced by the middle class, and the problems of working women have become the problems of all American families in much the same way that the problems of working men have always been assumed to be those of the majority of the population. Although there are problems peculiar to the poor or to the particular racial groups, by and large many of the problems of one group fall under rubrics that apply to numerous other groups as well. The implications of the shared problems for government policy are examined also.

Because of its focus on the nation as a whole, data for this study are taken primarily from U.S. census reports and the publications of government agencies such as the Departments of Labor and Health, Education, and Welfare. The use of the term *family* is consistent with the U.S. census definition of a household of two or more individuals related by blood or law. This definition has the advantage of making units that are easy to quantify and amenable to statistical analysis and comparisons. It has the disadvantage of missing or burying much of the richness of family systems in America today. For example, it omits from families the daughter who is at college or in the armed services, just as it excludes many of the elderly who no longer live with their families, or the young man who has taken an apartment nearer to his work. These people are more often than not intimately connected with their families. They too are part of the strengths, liabilities, problems, and merits of American families. But in spite of the limitations imposed by this definition, census data provide a necessary starting point from which to begin any assessment of the modern-day family in the United States.

In order to evaluate the family and its problems in contemporary society, chapter 2 begins with an overview of the American population. It examines the total population of families, compares people living within families with those not living in families, and looks at the major changes occurring in family composition and organization in the second half of the twentieth century. Chapter 3 examines the flow of life events that compose the family life cycle. As an adjunct to the major changes isolated in the chapter 2, chapter 3 contains a more focused analysis of the various stages of the family cycle as a way of locating particular problem areas that all families must face at some point in their existence. Taken together they present a static and dynamic portrait of structure in the contemporary family and the major stress points that strain that structure over the course of its existence.

Chapter 4 begins with an analysis of the most radical change to overtake American families in recent years, namely, the dramatic increase in the number of wives and mothers in the labor force. After presenting the basic dimensions of this phenomenon, chapter 5 examines the factors that underlie female employment and the impact it has had on the family and its individual members. The entire question of female employment is bound up with the changing economic position of the American family in the last two decades, and chapter 5 deals with it in these terms. From the analysis it is evident that when viewed in terms of the family life cycle, many of the problems being examined are common to a majority of American families. As such, the solutions for these problems must be devised in terms of the larger population; the problems of the poor cannot be solved by restricting measures to alleviate poverty to a part of the population. A much broader perspective is necessary if effective remedies are to be applied.

2 Family Structure

The Family Structure of the U.S. Population

In order to make an assessment of the state of the family in contemporary American society, a series of questions about the numbers and types of people living in families must be asked first. What percentage of the total population lives in families? How has the familial population changed in terms of membership and composition over the course of time? What are the distinguishing characteristics of the population not living in families?

As of 1977 approximately 90 percent of the American population resided in a family household. This represents over 190 million persons living in over 55 million family households (table 2-1). Therefore when the American family is discussed almost the entire population of the country is involved.

Between 1940 (the first year for which such data are available) and 1977, there has been a net decline of 3 percent in the total population living in families. Much of this decline seems to be a result of the fact that the baby-boom cohort (those born between 1946 and 1957) has now reached adulthood. These young adults have left their families of origin and are in the process of forming their own families. As these new families form, it is quite possible that there will be a slight increase in the percentage of the population living in families.

Table 2-1
Household and Family Population, 1940-1977

	1940	1950	1960	1970	1977
Household population	128,300	146,800	175,800	199,100	212,000
Households	34,949	43,554	52,799	63,401	74,142
Families	32,166	39,303	45,111	51,586	56,710
Family population	121,000	139,100	165,600	184,700	191,000
Percent of population in families	93	94	94	92	90

Source: U.S., Bureau of the Census, Series P-20, no. 313 (Washington, D.C.: Government Printing Office, 1977).

Note: Household population equals noninstitutionalized population.

Yet whether or not that increase does occur, the family-population ratio of the United States is high when compared with other societies. The reasons for this are the numerous social, political, and economic factors that have prevented large segments of the world's population from forming nuclear families of their own or from being counted as members of a family. Three of these reasons are large standing armies, which remove a disproportionately large percentage of young men from the family for long periods of time; economic depression or chronically depressed economic conditions, which force young people to delay marriage and often precludes the building of an adequate supply of housing for families; and large religious institutions supporting large numbers of priests, monks, and nuns excluded from living in families or from marriage. In relation to the total population, these factors are not significant in the United States. Individuals are not in the military or priesthood in numbers out of proportion to the population nor are the conditions of the economy such that large numbers of people are prevented from forming or living in family units. Today almost all Americans spend the majority of their lives in the family.

Characteristics of the Nonfamily Population

Of the 10 percent of the population not living in family units, it might be asked where and how they are living. As indicated in table 2-2 15.5 million Americans were living alone in 1977. Slightly over half of these people were composed of young adults (under age twenty-five) or the elderly (over age sixty-five). Less than 1.5 million young adults live alone. They comprise 9 percent of all people living alone. An additional 2 million young adults live in households with other adults and therefore are not counted as members of families (table 2-3). On the basis of past trends it is obvious that most of these young adults are in a transitional phase of their lives between their families of origin and the families that they themselves will later establish. Similarly at the other end of the life cycle, the 13.5 million people over age sixty-five who live alone are not people who have opted out of family life so much as they are remnants of their former families. The 7.7 million people between the ages of twenty-five and sixty-four living alone are not completely outside of the family since some of them are likely to be temporarily outside of the family because of divorce or death of spouse. Some of these people are widowed and divorced and may reenter family life at another point in time.

So, even the 10 percent of the American population not residing in family units is not necessarily representative of dropouts from the American family structure. Most of them are simply in temporary situations that make family life impractical.

Table 2-2
Primary Individuals Living Alone, by Age Cohort, 1970 versus 1977
(*in thousands*)

	1970		1977	
	Number	*Percent*	*Number*	*Percent*
Total	10,900	100	15,500	100
14-24	600	5	1,300	9
25-44	1,600	15	3,500	23
45-64	3,600	33	4,200	27
65+	5,000	47	6,500	42

Source: Compiled from U.S. Bureau of the Census, Series P-20, no 313 (Washington, D.C.: Government Printing Office, 1977).

Table 2-3
Primary Individuals Living with One Other Primary Individual,
1970 versus 1976
(*in thousands*)

	1970		1977	
	Number	*Percent*	*Number*	*Percent*
Total	1,000	100	1,500	100
14-24	270	27	500	34
25-44	260	26	580	39
45-64	230	23	250	17
65+	230	24	150	10

Source: Compiled from U.S. Bureau of the Census, Series P-20, no. 306 (Washington, D.C.: Government Printing Office (1977).

Note. Approximately 2 percent of all primary individuals lived in households of three or more persons in 1976.

Characteristics of the Fragmented Family

With the rapid rise of divorce, one might assume that even though a high percentage of the population is still living in families, an increasing number of these families are only fragments. It is a well-known fact that there has been a great rise in the number of single and divorced women maintaining a household with their children. This leads to the question of what percentage of families are headed by a husband-wife couple in the traditional concept of a conjugal family.

As indicated in table 2–4 almost 84 percent of the 56.7 million families in America are headed by a husband and a wife who are living together. This represents a national total of 46.5 million families. When compared with previous trends, the proportion of families with an unmarried head is, surprisingly, the same in 1977 as in 1940. In the intervening years there have been minor fluctuations, but in both 1977 and 1940, 16.2 percent of all families had unmarried heads while the remaining 83.8 percent were headed by a married couple. In terms of aggregate figures there has been little change in the proportion of families with married and with unmarried heads.

When broken down by sex of head of household, some significant variation is evident. There has been an increase in the number and percentage of single-parent female-headed families and a corresponding decrease in number and percentage of those headed by a single-parent male (table 2–5). Families with single-male heads declined from 4.9 percent of all families to only 2.6 percent in 1977. Even though the total percent of families with an unmarried head has remained constant, there has been a marked increase in the proportion of these families headed by females. There are numerous factors associated with the rise in female-headed families. Certainly the increased ability of women to support themselves and their children (as opposed to either living with their parents or of not divorcing their husbands) is a major factor. The financial support available to female-headed families, either from their own earnings or government programs, has made it possible for women with children to live alone. To a lesser extent the reduced number of widowers who are heads of family are a factor.

The increase in the numbers of divorced and single women who head families means that there are more minor children being raised in families with only one parent. An analysis by M.J. Bane (1976) has shown that the total percentage of children living in families with at least one of their natural parents has been increasing also. This is explained by the significantly lowered mortality rates for the parents of minor children. Therefore, since recent increases in divorce have not been as large as the decline in deaths among parents of young children, while in 1940, 90.5 percent of the children in America were living with either or both of their parents, by 1977 this figure had increased to 94.5 percent. It is now less likely that the divorce of parents or the death of one parent would result in the placement of the children in a public institution, with foster parents, or other relatives.

Far fewer children are exposed to total familial disruption today than in the past (tables 2–6 and 2–7). The extent of this decline is illustrated in table 2–7 for successive cohorts of children born in this century. Well over one-quarter of all children born in the first decade of this century were likely to lose one or both parents prior to reaching the age of majority. The bulk of

Table 2-4
U.S. Families by Marital Status of Head, 1940–1977

	1940		1950		1960		1970		1977	
	Number	Percent	Number	Percent	Number	Percent	Number	Percent	Number	Percent
Total families	32,166	100.0	39,303	100.0	45,111	100.0	51,586	100.0	56,710	100.0
Husband-wife headed	26,971	83.8	34,440	87.6	39,329	87.1	44,755	86.8	47,497	83.8
Single head	5,195	16.2	4,863	12.3	5,782	12.8	6,830	13.2	9,213	16.2

Source: U.S.,¡Bureau of the Census, Series P-20, no. 313 (Washington, D.C.: Government Printing Office, 1977).

Table 2-5
Single Male and Single Female Heads of Families, 1940–1977

	1940		1950		1960		1970		1977	
	Number	Percent	Number	Percent	Number	Percent	Number	Percent	Number	Percent
Single-head families	5,195	100.0	4,863	100.0	5,782	100.0	6,830	100.0	9,213	100.0
Female head	3,616	69.6	3,679	75.7	4,507	77.9	5,591	81.9	7,713	83.7
Male head	1,579	30.4	1,184	24.3	1,275	22.1	1,239	18.1	1,500	16.3
Total families	32,166	100.0	39,303	100.0	45,111	100.0	51,886	100.0	56,710	100.0
Female-head only	3,616	11.2	3,679	9.4	4,507	10.0	5,591	16.8	7,713	13.6
Male head only	1,579	4.9	1,184	3.0	1,275	2.8	1,239	2.4	1,500	2.6

Source: U.S., Bureau of the Census, Series P-20, no. 313 (Washington, D.C.: Government Printing Office, 1977).

these children lost their parents through death (22.6 percent), and only 5.2 percent of all children lost a parent through divorce. For the children born between 1951 and 1960, not all of whom have reached the age of majority, the probability is that only about 19 percent of them will lose a parent through death or divorce. Therefore, though the number of children likely to experience the divorce of their parents is now double what it was at the turn of the century, increase in life expectancy has more than offset the loss to a family because of divorce. Of children born at the turn of the century, three out of four reached adulthood with both parents alive. Of children now reaching maturity more than four out of five still have both of their parents living with them.

Table 2–6
Living Arrangements of Children Under Age Fourteen, 1940–1970

	1940	1950	1960	1970
Population under fourteen (in thousands)	32,973	40,651	55,901	58,014
Percent residing with				
Parent(s)	90.5	90.2	93.6	94.5
Other relative	7.8	7.9	5.2	4.5
Nonrelative family	1.1	.7	.4	.5
Institutions	.6	1.0	.8	.5

Source: Mary Jo Bane, *Here to Stay: The American Family in the Twentieth Century* (New York: Basic Books, 1976). Reprinted with permission.

Table 2–7
Percent of Minor Children in Families Dissolved by Divorce or Death of Parent(s)

	Decade of Birth of Cohort					
	1901–1910	1911–1920	1921–1930	1931–1940	1941–1950	1951–1960
Parental death	22.6	22.2	16.6	14.5	10.2	8.6[a]
Parental divorce	5.2	4.9	7.0	9.8	9.2	10.5[a]
Total dissolutions	27.8	27.1	23.6	24.3	19.4	19.1[a]

Source: Mary Jo Bane, *Here to Stay: The American Family in the Twentieth Century* (New York: Basic Books, 1976). Reprinted with permission.

[a]Based on estimates since not all members of this cohort will be eighteen years old until the end of 1978.

Changing Structure of the Family

In addition to the restructuring of the proportion of male-headed to female-headed families, two other major changes are occurring in the structure of family life in America. These are the decline in family size and the greater life expectancy of the family.

The Shrinking Family

Since 1940 mean family size in America has declined from a high of 3.76 individuals to the 1977 level of 3.37. This means that the average family size four decades ago was approximately 12 percent larger than it is today. A significant reason for the decline in family size is the declining birthrate. However, only 28 percent of the decline in family size is due to fewer children being born (table 2-8). Almost three-fourths of the decline has been brought about by a reduction in the number of adults in the family. This aspect of the decline in family size has received almost no attention. Recently there has been an effort to debunk the whole notion that *extended family households*, a grouping of related individuals beyond the nucleus formed by parents and their offspring, ever existed (Bane, 1976; Laslett and Wall, 1972). "The extended family household, populated by a friendly assortment of related people of all ages and their equally cheerful animal friends, is a cornerstone of American mythology" (Bane, 1976, p. 27).

In essence this critique of the extended family myth is correct. The United States has never had a common pattern of all or parts of a number of related nuclear families residing together. In the effort to counter that mistaken perception (if it ever was a widely held perception), the pendulum has swung too far in the other direction. What such basically sound assessments miss is that the family of previous generations often consisted of one or two other adults in addition to the primary husband-wife pair. These other adults were often relatives who had not themselves formed families or had lost their family connection, or were unrelated individuals residing with the family for a variety of socioeconomic reasons. It is true that families were not composed of several couples each with their own children, but many families did include a widowed grandparent, the proverbial maiden aunt, or some of their own adult children who had not married.

Solely within the decade of the seventies there was a 43 percent increase in the number of people living alone (see table 2-2). As discussed in chapter 3, most of this increase is due to young adults who leave the home as soon as they are old enough to live alone. A large proportion of the increase is accounted for by the assorted relatives who would have been living within a family unit in 1940.

Table 2–8
Mean Family Size, 1940–1977

	1940		1950		1960		1970		1977	
	Number	*Percent*	*Number*	*Percent*	*Number*	*Percent*	*Number*	*Percent*	*Number*	*Percent*
Total family	3.76	100.0	3.54	100.0	3.67	100.0	3.58	100.0	3.37	100.0
18 and above	2.52	67.0	2.37	66.9	2.26	61.6	2.25	62.8	2.24	66.5
Below age 18	1.24	33.0	1.17	33.1	1.41	38.4	1.34	37.4	1.13	33.5

Source: U.S., Bureau of the Census, Series P-20, no. 313 (Washington, D.C.: Government Printing Office, 1977).

Note: Decline in mean: Family size .39; 28% decline due to children; 72% decline due to adults. Numbers may not total due to rounding.

Part of the exodus of adults is unquestionably attributable to the free choice of the departing adult. With increasing economic resources available to the individual (such as social security for the elderly, and greater employment opportunities for unmarried women) many people who were not able to live alone in 1940 are now capable of doing so. However, there is no conclusive research that adequately explains the decline of the mean number of adults per family. Where the question is considered at all, it is usually assumed that these individuals wanted to leave and were simply prevented from doing so by lack of economic and social resources in prior generations. What many analysts have not considered is the effect that numerous governmental policies may have had on this process. Many governmental programs geared toward aiding young families to become established have affected and changed family living patterns. For example, in the postwar period because of a housing crisis, government housing of types only suitable for small families was made available to young couples (Downs, 1977). Although the aim of these programs was to provide for the short term, it would be interesting to know what the impact has been of such programs on familial patterns. Also larger-scale and longer-term programs such as Federal Housing Authority (FHA) and Veterans Administration (VA) housing loans have been geared toward providing and encouraging the building of small houses for small families, usually in the suburbs. It is difficult for a family with four children and three bedrooms to have a resident grandmother, and there would be great pressure on a nineteen-year-old son or daughter to move away from a family in such a position. Other governmental programs have removed the benefits of large families living together. Under recent tax practices, for example, a husband-wife family were able to deduct expenses for the care of their children while they worked, but they were not able to make such deductions if the caretaker were a relative. Formerly relatives could have earned a part of their keep by residing with the family and helping with such family activities as taking care of the children. No attempt has been made to evaluate the number of families who might have preferred having their children cared for by a relative if they could have received the same tax incentive they received for employing nonrelatives. Recent attempts to correct the situation continue to impose restrictions on payments to relatives for childcare that are not applied to others. The rate of income tax is higher for a married couple than it would be for a couple living together without benefit of marriage, and there are similar inequities in the social-security system that penalize certain families. This same pattern runs throughout policies governing welfare, social security, foster care, and even local zoning ordinances. In all of these areas governmental agencies have taken it upon themselves to define "permissable" family groupings or offer incentives that encourage some family living patterns and discourage others.

The Greater Life Expectancy of the Family

Along with the phenomenon of shrinking family size, consideration must be given to the greater age span of the family, which is due to the higher life expectancy of the individual members. With the radical increases in life expectancy that have occurred in recent decades, more married couples are surviving longer as a family unit. In the past the problem of the aged involved individuals who were only remnants of a family. This applied in particular to widowed women and to a lesser extent to widowed men. While widowhood remains a threat to either member of any marriage, the age at which it occurs has been steadily climbing. The amount of time that couples live together beyond their child-rearing years has increased dramatically in this century.

Recently the elderly have become the focus of more attention because of their growing numbers. In terms of housing, increased employment opportunities, and improved medical services the past few decades have produced decided governmental sensitivity to the special problems of the aged, but the demands to be met are increasing even faster than the government's response. Everyone today is aware of the fact that the population includes more older people than ever before. What many people do not seem to be aware of is that the proportion of older people in society today is small compared to what can be expected within a few decades. In a little over a decade the cohort born in the 1920s will begin to retire. Proportionally and in absolute numbers they are much larger than the cohort preceding them. Just after the beginning of the next century, the post–World War II baby-boom cohort will begin reaching retirement age. It is quite possible that as much as a fifth of the American population will then be above the age of sixty-five, and many of these people will be part of families made up of an elderly husband and wife.

As the general population is slowly becoming aware, the problems of families with aged members is a double-edged one. On the one hand there are very real needs of these elderly in terms of care and basic services. As a higher proportion of the population grows older, the cost of these services increase. At the same time, however, there will be proportionally fewer people in the working force to finance these extended needs and services for the elderly. This very problem has been at the root of the recently emerging crisis within the Social Security administration. There is a limit to the taxation that the working population can bear to finance the pensions of the retired population. Part of the solution to this problem may be emerging in a greater willingness of the government (and to a lesser extent industry) to allow the elderly who wish to do so to continue working as long as they are capable. Through the removal or modification of mandatory retirement policies, a great part of the older population can continue to earn their own keep for a longer period of time. This solution is at most a partial one but at least it does have the support of many of the elderly themselves, who often receive emotional and psychological benefit from employment above and beyond the financial benefits. Not all of the problems inherent in a population with a higher proportion of elderly people are amenable to a single or simple solution. The complexities of the matter will multiply and become more apparent in the coming decades. Even the proposed abolition of mandatory retirement, while easing financial burdens for the elderly, may increase such burdens for younger members of the population in terms of employment opportunities. The full impact of such a change in governmental and business policy has not been analyzed yet for its impact on the entire population. But in spite of the complexities of the issue the question must be dealt with soon as there are indications that the American government is nearing the limit of the general social services that it can provide on the basis of the present system. Now is the time not only to rethink many of the priorities of already existing programs but, more important, to search for policy guidelines rather than just concentrating on the immediate economic solutions. While the abolition of mandatory retirement, for example, helps to solve a series of pressing problems without increasing government spending on costly programs, what the long-term ramifications will be, particularly in the economic sphere, needs further study in terms of all-around policy. Now that the population of this country is living increasingly full lifetimes and realizing a goal that mankind has sought for centuries, we have to cope with the question of how to finance this dream-come-true.

3   Family Life Cycle

Introduction

If the institution of the family is as strong and persuasive in America as indicated in the first chapter, one might wonder exactly why there is all the hue and cry about the plight of today's family. This chapter narrows the focus from the aggregate American family portrait to a series of cameos depicting the life cycle of the American family. By arranging the available data serially, an approximation of the flow of life events becomes apparent so that it is possible to isolate the specific problems of the family at particular phases of the family cycle. Thus it becomes clear that the relative strengths and weaknesses of a family with minor children are quite different from those of a completed family with nearly grown children or a family composed solely of an elderly husband and wife. The American family does not share one problem; it cannot be helped with one solution or with a national policy geared only to one segment of the family cycle. It is possible to lose sight of this truism when dealing with the family on the basis of collected data.

The recording of life events such as birth, marriage, death, and divorce are within the jurisdiction of the fifty individual states. Some states, however, still do not maintain statewide records of these events, and other states have only recently begun to do so. Because of this, the available national data used in this chapter are supplemented with illustrations based on the data compiled by the state of North Carolina. This state benefits from one of the most comprehensive vital statistics collection and processing centers in the nation. They provided us with provisional 1977 statistics prior to national availability. Whenever North Carolina is used as an example, past trends for the nation as a whole are also indicated so that the pattern of North Carolina's deviation, if any, can be properly assessed.

The utility of the domestic or family cycle has been developed in anthropology (Fortes, 1966; Goody, 1966) and demography (Glick, 1947) as an abstracted description of the course of events in family life. This perspective analyzes measures of central tendency and by so doing creates an idealized and primarily statistical portrait of the family. Through examination of the primary events in family life (birth, death, marriage, and departure of children), the course of the family's life is divided into phases of development. The three major phases are:

Establishment: time from the marriage of a couple until the birth of the first child.

Reproduction: time from the birth of the first child until the last child reaches the age of majority.

Completion: time from the achievement of majority by last child until the death of one of the two spouses.

The precise structuring of these phases may vary according to a number of factors such as ethnicity or region. Some of this variation is noted, but the major focus here is on general trends for the population as a whole. It is for this reason that the phases are so broad in scope and definition.

Contemporary Family Cycle

Establishment Phase

The family cycle begins anew with each marriage. Prior to that time the prospective bride and groom were a part of the family cycles of their parents. With the new marriage, however, these two individuals from two separate family units create a new nuclear family. The age at which this creation of another conjugal unit usually occurs varies from society to society as well as from generation to generation. During the twentieth century there has been a general worldwide conversion on the early twenties as the appropriate age for marriage. In the United States this has meant an overall and fairly consistent decline in the median age of marriage, with the sharpest declines occurring for the ages at which males marry. As depicted in table 3-1 and figure 3-1, the median age at marriage for males in 1890 was above age 26, and for females it was just below age 22. For a half a century the median age for females declined only slightly until the rash of marriages that followed World War II. Between 1940 and 1950 the median age at marriage for females dropped over a full year from age 21.5 to 20.3. This new low persisted throughout the 1950s and into the first half of the 1970s.

During the early 1970s the median age at first marriage for females began rising again as did that for males but at a more moderate rate. Why did the decade of the seventies begin to reverse the trend that began in and continued through the forties? To answer this question the change in age at marriage must be viewed from short-term and long-term perspectives.

Looking at the median age in the long-term, historical perspective, the age of marriage for females is finally returning to the pre–World War II levels. Apparently it is readjusting after a generation that married at an unusually low age in the wake of the Depression and Second World War. This would explain the rising age at marriage for contemporary females and

Table 3-1
Median Age at First Marriage, 1890–1976

	Males	*Females*
1976	23.8	21.3
1970	23.2	20.8
1960	22.8	20.3
1950	22.8	20.3
1940	24.3	21.5
1930	24.3	21.3
1920	24.6	21.2
1910	25.1	21.6
1900	25.9	21.9
1890	26.1	22.0

Source: U.S., Bureau of the Census, Series P-20, no. 306 (Washington, D.C.: Government Printing Office, 1977).

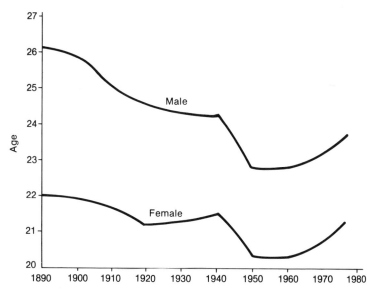

Figure 3-1. Median Age at First Marriage, 1890–1976

bring it more into accord with the traditional pattern of American history from the end of the nineteenth century until the 1940s. It also makes American ages at first marriage more consistent with the patterns in other industrialized societies.

In addition to positing the contention that the median age at marriage in America is returning to its historical patterns, there is a need to analyze this phenomenon with a short-term perspective in order to understand how and why it is doing so. To do this the mate-selection process needs to be considered. Women in American society tend to marry men who are slightly older than they are. This age differential has declined in the last century, but the normal pattern followed is that the male is two to three years older than the female. If the cohorts of males and females who came of marriageable age in the late 1960s are examined, it is obvious that these are the children of the baby boom. Just as in 1946 there was a dramatic increase in the number of infants in society, in 1966 there was a rapid increase in the number of twenty-year olds. This means that in 1966 there was suddenly a much larger than normal cohort of twenty-year-old males and females at the then normal preparatory age for marriage. For these females there was a relative scarcity of males two to three years older than they were. There were plenty of twenty-year-old men, but these are not the men that twenty-year-old females usually marry. This scarcity of appropriate partners for this cohort of women was worsened by the fact that large numbers of the eligible men were removed from civilian life by the war in Viet Nam. Such factors as these made for a very poor marriage market at the end of the 1960s and beginning of the 1970s.

In contrast the year 1977 was the year in which the last of the baby-boom children became twenty years old. For the females of this cohort there are now ample males two to three years older (older members of the baby-boom cohort) for marriage partners. For the males who turned twenty in 1977, however, there is a smaller cohort of females behind them, and this situation will prevail until the early 1980s when these males are in their mid-twenties. Therefore, in the late 1960s there was an excess of females in the prime marriage ages, and in the late 1970s there was an excess of males in the prime age. This temporary imbalance in the marriageable population brought about by the baby boom was diagnosed in the works of Carter and Glick (1976) and Parke and Glick (1967) who aptly termed it the "marriage squeeze."

The short-term view of marriageability in the 1970s sheds some light on the reasons for the recent decline in marriage rates. In addition to being influenced by a diversity of social and economic factors ranging from the Vietnamese war to the women's movement, at least part of the decline in marriage rates can be explained by the simple characteristics of the marriageable population. Some of the dynamics of this process are evident in the recent statistics for North Carolina.

In North Carolina, as in the rest of the nation, the median age for males at first marriage has remained relatively static while that for females has increased by an average of several weeks per year during the last decade

(Alston and Tessenear, 1976). The median age for first marriage for males in 1975 was 22.1 years (approximately the same as in 1965), but the age for females was 20.2 (a six-month increase in age since 1965). This means that there was a 2.4 year difference in the median age for males and females at first marriage in 1965, but this difference in the median ages declined to 1.9 years in 1975.

During the seventies there was substantial movement toward convergence of the age of marriage for males and females. In keeping with the marriage-squeeze hypothesis, the women coming of normal marriageable age in the late 1960s were forced to delay marriage until some of the younger men came of age. This meant that the age of marriage for the women was somewhat higher while for the men the age stayed the same. It also meant that women were marrying men closer to their own age. This created an inevitable drop in the overall marriage rates as more women were forced to postpone marriage. This drop, however, was only temporary since these same women would eventually marry. Had each cohort of women coming of age between 1965 and 1975 been the same size, then the delay of six months would have meant a drop in the marriage rate for six months. As it was, however, each year the number of women was larger than the year before because each year from 1946 to 1957 the birth rates had been higher. This meant that the drop in marriage rates was extended over several years. Since 1969 there has been a steady decrease in marriage rates for both the United States as a whole and for North Carolina in particular. With the last of the baby-boom children turning twenty in 1977, the drop in marriage rates should have ceased. Data for 1977 in North Carolina indicated that this was the case (table 3-2). Not only did the marriage rates stop declining, but there was an increase in the marriage rate for the first time in exactly a decade, and throughout 1978 this higher marriage rate for North Carolina remained steady.

Reproduction Phase

The second major phase in the domestic cycle is that of biological reproduction and socialization. This phase begins with the birth of the first child and ends when the last child reaches adulthood. The median age of married mothers at which this phase began in North Carolina in 1976 was twenty-one; that is, about one and a half years after the median age for marriage (figure 3-2). A total of 24,159 North Carolina families entered the reproductive phase in that year. The biological reproductive phase for an individual family covers the period from first gestation until the birth of the last child. In recent years the length of time devoted to producing children has steadily declined as women have had fewer children. Not only has the

Table 3–2
Marriage Rates: 1965–1977, United States and North Carolina
(*per 1000 population*)

	Marriage Rates	
	U.S.	*N.C.*
1978	—	7.9
1977	—	7.9
1976	—	7.8
1975	10.0	7.8
1974	10.5	8.4
1973	10.9	8.8
1972	11.0	9.3
1971	10.6	9.5
1970	10.6	9.5
1969	10.6	9.7
1968	10.4	9.6
1967	9.7	9.1
1966	9.5	8.9
1965	9.3	8.4

Sources: Cecile Alston, and Clara Tessenear, *Marriages and Dissolution of Marriages* (N.C. Public Health Statistics Branch, 1977, Department of Human Resources. North Carolina *Vital Statistics: 1978* (Raleigh, N.C.: 1979).

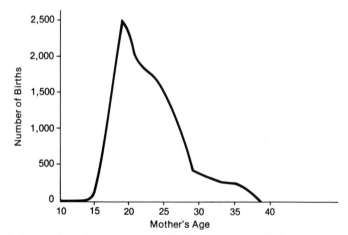

Source: Computed from *Basic Automated Birth Yearbook 1976*, Department of Human Resources, Raleigh, North Carolina.

Figure 3–2. First Births by Age of Mother, North Carolina, 1976

birthrate fallen, but the spacing of the children has become increasingly constricted to the younger years. In 1976 the median age of a mother in North Carolina at the time of her second birth was age twenty-three, which is only two years more than the median age for first births. If these women follow the pattern of their cohort and cease childbearing after the second child, they will be forty-one years old when their last child reaches the age of majority. So a representative female's personal reproductive stage would be confined to slightly over twenty years. The father in this case would have been twenty-three years old when the reproductive phase began and forty-three when it ended. This same family then would have had two preschool children in the home for a total of eight years, during which period they would have had full-time responsibility for the care and training of their own children. As for the mother in this family, after age twenty-nine she would have no preschool children in the home during the day.

For the United States as a whole approximately one-half of all families were in the reproductive phase in 1977; that is, one-half of all families had children under the age of eighteen. These children comprise approximately one-third of the total family members in the country, while two-thirds of all family members are adults.

It is during the reproductive phase of the family cycle that the greatest pressure is placed on the parents for the care and supervision of the family. This is the time when the family has minor children, the size of the family is at its greatest, and greatest parental or supervisory demands are placed squarely and often solely on the parents. Because this is the time when the family is at its maximum size, this is also the phase of the life cycle when per capita income for family members is normally at its minimum.

Completion Phase

By the time that the model couple is in their early forties with just over twenty years of marriage completed, they have finished the process of biological reproduction and the socialization of their offspring. The couple, however, is not yet halfway through their married life. If they stay together until death, they have another quarter of a century of married life ahead of them before one of the spouses (usually the husband) dies. Approximately half of the family's life is then spent without resident children in the home. For the woman this could mean twenty-five years of employment ahead of her prior to retirement. The man has another two decades of work life before he retires (figure 3-3).

The fact that more and more families are spending greater numbers of years in this completion phase of the family cycle is the most radical change experienced by the family in the twentieth century. Earlier in the century

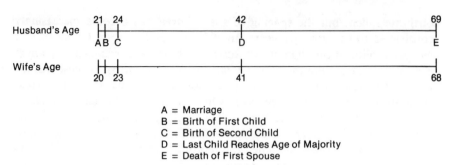

A = Marriage
B = Birth of First Child
C = Birth of Second Child
D = Last Child Reaches Age of Majority
E = Death of First Spouse

Figure 3–3. Family Life Cycle

less than three families in four survived as an intact unit to this phase of the family life cycle. Today the overwhelming proportion of parents survive to see not only their own children reach adulthood but in many cases their grandchildren. Heretofore the parents of the majority of families at any point in time were in the reproductive phase; however, it is quite possible that with the extended life expectancy of families and the low birthrate, the majority of families may be living in the completed phase by the end of this century. In other words, the model family will then consist of only a husband and a wife with no resident children. Already almost half of all families in America are of that type.

It is ironic that just when more and more people are surviving to be grandparents, the role of the grandparent in society is a largely symbolic one. Through a variety of causes, families in the reproductive phase of life have been largely isolated from members of their family only one generation removed. Part of the cause for this severing of ties must be attributed directly and indirectly to the impact on the family of various government policies. The tax structure has made it difficult for family members to rely on other family members for such services as childcare. This policy persists despite the large number of studies in anthropology and sociology that attest to the strong bonds of mutual assistance connecting relatives in very urban and seemingly anomic situtations (Adams, 1968; Bott, 1971; Stack, 1974). Certainly ties of kinship are strong, and if government interference were removed, they could reassert themselves, particularly where proximity makes it possible for families to bear the responsibilities that most people feel are rightfully their own. In other industrialized nations there is a tendency to rely far more on the family to solve social problems than in the United States. In West Germany there is a well-articulated concept of state support for attempts of family members to assist one another (Weatherford, 1977). The establishment of three-generational households are encouraged. Sometimes a grandmother who has completed her own child-rearing will assist in the rearing of the grandchildren so that both of the parents can work outside the home.

In general there is little awareness of the potential that senior members of completed families have for assistance of younger families in the reproductive phase. Either the people of the United States will be faced with the task of supporting ever-growing numbers of retired couples living in isolation from the younger generation or else society will have to find ways of encouraging and allowing these completed families to remain actively involved with the younger generation in a strong supportive role.

Variations in the Family Cycle

Historically the life cycle of families varies according to the social, economic, and political climate of the era. Cross-culturally the patterning of family life changes according to these same variables. How is the family cycle changing now? What new developments are underway in regard to how Americans establish families, socialize their children, and then terminate the family?

Establishment Phase

Currently the greatest amount of variation is in regard to how Americans establish their families. More variation in the accepted manner for starting families has developed and a whole new group of false starts have gained prominence, particularly among middle-class Americans. The most significant development in this area is the increasing occurrence and acceptability of short-term marriages that end in divorce. Most young people who marry and divorce will also remarry. The rising divorce rates, which are decried by many as evidence of the decline of familialism in the United States, may be representative of a new mode of starting the family cycle. All evidence overwhelmingly supports the idea that people who divorce do not do so from dissatisfaction with the institutions of marriage and family but because they feel that they have chosen the wrong partner. And because of many developments within society, choosing the wrong partner is no longer the burden it once was. Such a couple is free to divorce and remarry. That is exactly what they are doing.

Among a smaller portion of the youth, living together has become another type of family start (see table 2–3). Statistically the number of such unions is quite small, representing less than 1.5 percent of the total population. Generally these are couples who might not be able to afford the economic liabilities of setting up a family or who may not be mature enough to commit themselves to a long-term union but are ready to begin testing the commitments involved in marriage. In some societies this form of trial marriage has a long tradition. In parts of West Germany, for example, divorce rates are extremely low, partially accounted for by the fact that built into the family cycle is the phase of trial coupling. Americans who try this type of relationship still marry. Sometimes they marry the person with whom they have been living and sometimes they seek another partner. Living together is not so much an alternative to marriage as just a variation on the establishment of a marriage and an eventual family.

The rising rates of illegitimacy may be interpreted in a similar manner. The bearing of children prior to marriage is in some respects a variation on the traditional beginning of family life. Often these are not cases of women who have opted out of marriage. Numerous economic and social supports now exist for women who are pregnant and unmarried. With these supports a woman is able to live independently of the child's father until she decides to marry him or someone else. For poor women, in particular, in some respects this may be the more intelligent way to start a family in light of present government policy. The reason for this anomaly is that if the father of the child is unemployed or underemployed, the mother might be able to provide better care for herself and the child on the basis of governmental welfare by not marrying the child's father. Later as the father of the child grows older, his chances of employment increase. By that time he may be able to support the mother and child, or the mother may have found another man who is able to support them. In any event the mother is likely to marry and establish a family. In this way illegitimacy may be considered another variation on the traditional family life cycle. As a variant mode it poses real practical advantages to some segments of the population. Even though such families are initially living at variance with the family cycle, it does not mean that the entire cycle will be aberrant.

These variations on how a family is established are relevant for different segments of the population. In North Carolina, as in the nation as a whole, it is black women who are most apt to have illegitimate children prior to establising a two-parent family. Divorce rates, on the other hand, are highest in the United States for women with higher incomes (Carter and Glick, 1976, p. 437). Women with incomes over $15,000 per annum are almost three times as likely to be divorced as women with no income at all (divorce rates of 30.0 versus 10.5). Among couples experimenting with family living prior to marriage, there are likely to be included better-educated women of both races who are delaying marriage while they continue their education. Considered in this manner, living together, rising divorce rates, the bearing of illegitimate children, delaying marriage, and related old and new trends are all differential adaptations of the process of establishing a family. Depending on the social and economic conditions of the individuals involved, one variant pattern is more likely to be enacted than another, but the end result is normally marriage and family life. Making these choices does not indicate an overall dissatisfaction with marriage, but it is based on practical considerations of how to best cope with the modern situation.

The fact that phenomena such as living together outside of marriage and illegitimacy are not serious detriments to marriage in the long run is shown in table 3-3. Between 1960 and 1976, there was an increase in the never-married population for people under age thirty-five. For the population above age thirty-five, however, there was a noticeable decline in the percentage of those who have never married.

For example, in 1960 almost 8 percent of the males reaching age sixty-five had never been married. By 1976 the number of never-married men in this age category had dropped to 4.4 percent. Thus even though young people in their twenties were less likely to be married in 1976 in comparison with 1960, a person was more likely to be married by age thirty-five. There is no evidence that marriage and family as institutions are declining or that fewer people are participating in them. The real variation is that people seem to be delaying marriage, or they are starting marriages in less traditional ways. When viewed in the long-term perspective of the individual's entire life cycle, there is some evidence that people are more likely to establish a family albeit somewhat later in life than was true for the previous generation.

Table 3-3
Percent Single (Never Married), 1960 versus 1976

	Male		Female	
	1960	1976	1960	1976
20–24	53.1	62.1	28.4	42.6
25–29	20.8	24.9	10.5	14.8
30–34	11.9	12.3	6.9	7.0
35–39	8.8	7.9	6.1	5.2
40–44	7.3	6.6	6.1	4.2
45–54	7.4	5.6	7.0	4.4
55–64	8.0	5.6	8.0	4.9
65 and over	7.7	4.4	8.5	5.9

Source: Compiled from U.S., Bureau of the Census, Series P-20, no. 306, table C (Washington, D.C.: Government Printing Office, 1977).

Reproductive Phase

The changes in the reproductive phase of the American family are not as dramatic as those in the establishment phase, but from a policy perspective they are much more important. Fewer children are being born per family, and they are spaced closer together. This results in an overall shrinking of the reproductive phase of the cycle. Despite this shrinking, the needs of the family in this phase are increasing radically. The economic costs of having and rearing children are so high today that few families can afford it on the basis of one salary. Women have been forced into the labor market. This has produced a strain on the childcare capacity of the family. The problems associated with this phase of the family are examined in detail in chapters 4 and 5, since it is in this area that the greatest demands have been made for increased governmental assistance.

The Completed Family

The biggest change in the phase of completion is that it is lasting longer. At the terminal end of the phase (after retirement) the needs of the elderly family have always been great. Today these needs are more pressing for the society as a whole because more and more people are surviving longer. Today death rates in the younger years of life are declining, and the chances that a person will live for a decade or more past retirement are growing. For most people, however, the phase of family completion comes in their mid-forties, not in the age of retirement. At this time in life they are still highly productive and capable. It is quite possible that these people are America's greatest underutilized resource. The willingness of people of this age to help their children and grandchildren is not in doubt; however, numerous governmental restrictions make it difficult for them to do so. As already explained the mere removal of some of these barriers to intergenerational cooperation and assistance might go a long way in meeting some of the needs of the severely strapped young families in the reproductive phase.

4 Employed Wives and Mothers: Labor-Force Participation

The single largest focus of attention concerning American families in the decade of the seventies and beyond is the labor-force participation of wives and mothers. There is no doubt that the growing dependence of the American family on wages earned by the female head of family is changing, and will continue to change, what has come to be regarded as the traditional structure of family life.

According to the idea still held by many people, the basic family structural unit ought to consist of a wage-earning male head, a homebound female, and two children cared for within the family unit until early adulthood. Only 27 percent of American families in 1978 still filled the ideal image of father at work and mother at home. This figure dropped to 7 percent when limited to families with four persons, mainly families with two children. (U.S. Department of Labor, 1979) Thus a serious reevaluation of the images and ideals concerning the American family is decidedly called for. We can no longer afford to subjugate the facts to the ideal and ignore the new realities of American family life.

All Americans must become aware that the ideal family is becoming highly unrepresentative of reality and cannot continue as the most significant force in American life. For that reason what follows here is a statistical profile that concentrates on the millions of people in families who have learned to cope, or will have to learn to cope, with a female head, be she a wife or a single parent, who is away from home for a fixed number of hours and has to divide her energies between work and home. Exactly how employment as a wage earner will change the quality of her relationship to her family cannot be quantitatively determined. What can be accepted a priori is that it will have some impact on her role as homemaker and principle nurturer of the young children of the family. Furthermore it is likely to cause changes in the emotional relationships between husband and wife and mother and child. The data are presented in terms of the immediate past, the present, and projections for the future.

Statistics cannot personalize the problems faced by individual families. They can, however, draw attention to the commonality of these problems and thereby transfer some of the burden from the individual to the group, where it properly belongs. There the problem becomes a policy question demanding attention and treatment in the broader sense and, it is hoped, becomes more susceptible to resolution by force of concerted effort. As

Americans become aware of how widespread certain family concerns are, it is to be expected that greater attention will be given to these areas. Perhaps this attention will lead to policies specifically designed to help families that need help and give rise to attitudes that support rather than fault families in that situation.

The modern roots of the question of labor-force participation by wives and mothers dates to the Second World War.

> As a result of the manpower shortage and the aggressive campaign to recruit female workers, women's economic status changed significantly for the first time in thirty years. During the war, the proportion of women who were employed jumped from slightly over 25 percent to 36 percent—a rise greater than that of the preceding four decades. By V-E Day, the female labor force had increased by 6.5 million, or 57 percent. For the first time, more wives were employed than single women, more women over thirty-five than under thirty-five. Manufacturing took the largest number of new workers—2.5 million—but an additional 2 million entered the clerical field, and the only areas of female employment to suffer a relative decline were those of domestic servant and professional. At the close of hostilities, nearly 20 million women were in the labor force—35 percent of all workers in contrast to 25 percent in 1940. [Chafe, William H. *The American Woman: Her Changing Social, Economic, and Political Roles, 1920 to 1970.* London: Oxford University Press. p. 148. Reprinted with permission.]

Although the end of the war and the return of men to the labor force meant that many women workers were fired, the anticipated massive decline of female labor-force participation did not occur.

> The Bureau of Labor Statistics had predicted that 6 million people would lose their jobs in the year after the war, a substantial proportion of them women. In fact, only a small percentage of that number remained permanently out of work. A great many women left their former jobs, creating the impression of widespread unemployment, but a majority rejoined the labor force at a later date. Between September 1945 and November 1946, 2.25 million women left work, and another million were laid off. But in the same period, nearly 2.75 million were hired, causing a net decline in female employment of only 600,000. . . . Thus while women lost some of their better-paid war positions, they did not disappear from the labor market as some had anticipated. [Chafe, 1972, pp. 180–181. Reprinted with permission.]

As can be seen from table 4–1, the labor-force participation of wives and mothers during the twenty-five-year-period between 1951 to 1976 has shown a very substantial and steady rise reflecting the fact that once the barrier to female employment was broken by World War II it permanently remained breached. Particularly noteworthy is the fact that mothers of

Table 4-1
Labor-Force Status and Participation Rate of Wives and Married
Mothers, 1951–1976

| | Total Married Females | | Married Females with Children | | | |
| | | | Children Ages 6 to 17 Years | | Children under 6 Years | |
	Number (Thousands)	Partici-pation Rate	Number (Thousands)	Partici-pation Rate	Number (Thousands)	Partici-pation Rate
1951	9,086	25.2	2,400	30.3	1,670	14.0
1956	11,126	29.0	3,384	36.4	2,048	15.9
1961	13,266	32.7	4,419	41.7	2,661	20.0
1966	15,178	35.4	4,949	43.7	3,186	24.2
1971	18,530	40.8	6,424	49.4	3,674	30.0
1976	21,554	45.0	7,270	53,7	4,424	37.4

Annual Growth Rates

| | Total Married Females | Married Females with Children | |
		Ages 6 to 17	Age Under 6
1951–1956	4.1	7.1	4.2
1956–1961	3.6	5.5	5.4
1961–1966	2.3	2.3	3.7
1966–1971	4.1	5.4	2.9
1971–1976	3.1	2.5	3.8

Source: Computed from U.S. Department of Labor and Department of Health, Education, and Welfare, *Employment and Training Report of the President* (1977).

preschool-age children entered the labor force at a significantly higher rate than that for all married females during the period 1956 to 1966. Although their growth rate fell below that of the total group in the period 1966 to 1971, it climbed back up in the period 1971 to 1976. The total number of all married females in the U.S. labor force has more than doubled within the past twenty-five years and continues to grow at a 3 percent annual rate for the most recent period.

In 1978 the picture for the total female labor-force shows the preponderance of married women with husbands in the home (figure 4–1). Single women, the only group of female workers who are most likely to have little or no family responsibilities, represent only one-quarter of the total female workforce.

But not only do employed wives constitute 60 percent of all female

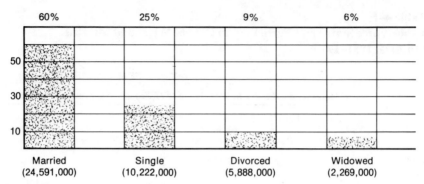

Source: U.S., Bureau of Labor Statistics, *Women in the Labor Force: Some New Data Series,*
Report 575 (October 1979).

Figure 4–1. Female Labor Force by Marital Status, March 1978

employees workers, their share of this workforce is continuing to increase at
a much more rapid rate of growth than any other group of women divided
according to marital status. Table 4-2 depicts their increase in absolute
numbers; their percentage increase, which can be accounted for by the
greater numbers of women who have entered the category during the five-
year period; and the percentage increase due to greater net participation in
the labor force.

The percentage increase shows that during the five-year period between
1970 and 1975 an additional 2.7 million women became employed wives
(table 4-2). When the 1 million women who would have entered the labor
force because of population increase is subtracted from this total, a net
increase of 1.7 million employed wives must be accounted for as new
recruits from the home. These are women who would have been classified as
homemakers a few years ago. Between 1970 to 1975 they voluntarily chose
to change their status and accounted for 79 percent of the increase in the
female labor-force participation rate.

The impact on the family of an employed wife is not nearly as significant as the way the family is changed when a mother, particularly a mother
of preschool-age children, chooses to or must find a job and contribute to
the support of her family. Table 4-3 summarizes the employment situation
of employed wives and children of employed mothers. An estimated 28.9
million children under the age of eighteen were living with an employed
mother in 1977. Furthermore, 6.4 million children under school age were
cared for by employed mothers and need additional care by a person other
than their mother for all or part of the day. The matter of childcare, particularly of day care, directly involves 11.4 million husbands living with their
families, 13.7 million working mothers, and 28.2 million children under the

Table 4–2
Increase in Female Labor-Force Participation by Marital Status,
1970–1975

	Total Increase in Female Labor Force 1970–1975	Percent Increase Due to Population Increase	Percent Increase Due to Change in Labor-Force Participation
Number (thousands)	5,274	3,111	2,163
Percent	100	100	100
Marital Status			
Married, husband present	52	33	79
Divorced	18	30	1
Separated	4	3	4
Widowed	−2	4	−10
Never Married	28	30	26

Source: U.S. Department of Labor, Bureau of Labor Statistics, *The Labor Force Patterns of Divorced and Separated Women* (1977).

age of eighteen. So 53.3 million persons, or one-quarter of the total U.S. population, must cope with the special problems that face families when both heads, or the sole head of the family, have work responsibilities outside the home and there are young children in the family in need of care or supervision.

Day care is an unsettled matter which engenders important questions with no fixed answers. How are these children to be cared for when their mothers are at work? Who is to share responsibility for providing this care? Who is to pay for it and who is to provide it? Table 4–4 records childcare arrangements that are estimated as having been made by mothers for the care of their children in 1975.

The ongoing debate over the problems of day care reveals that much more is involved than a mere dispute over social versus private spheres of responsibility in terms of the numbers of persons involved. The issue of what constitutes adequate care for children has never and cannot ever be solved on a formulaic basis. The family's right to set standards that conform with its own aspirations and desires for its children and with the wants and needs of its kin, race, and ethnic group are gradually being acknowledged. The question of what constitutes adequate day care must be given separate treatment in future research. However, it is apparent from the statistics that the need for resolution is pressing and growing more acute with each passing year.

Table 4–3
**Children Under Eighteen Years, by Age, Type of Family, and Employment
Status of Parents, March 1977**
(*numbers in thousands*)

Item	Total	Under 6 Years	6 to 17 Years Total	6 to 13 Years	14 to 17 Years
Total children[a]	60,584	17,117	43,467	27,810	15,657
Mother in labor force	28,892	6,431	22,462	13,811	8,651
Employed	26,398	5,569	20,829	12,741	8,088
Unemployed	2,494	861	1,633	1,069	563
Mother not in labor force	30,885	10,582	20,304	13,675	6,629
Husband-wife families	50,279	14,780	35,499	22,877	12,622
Mother in labor force	23,341	5,411	17,930	10,969	6,961
Employed	21,587	4,782	16,805	10,251	6,554
Unemployed	1,753	629	1,125	718	407
Mother not in labor force	26,938	9,369	17,559	11,908	5,661
Father employed	45,029	13,196	31,833	20,649	11,184
Mother in labor force	21,217	4,873	16,344	10,023	6,321
Employed	19,875	4,357	15,428	9,437	5,991
Unemployed	1,432	515	917	586	331
Mother not in labor force	23,812	8,324	15,488	10,626	4,863
Father in armed forces	1,091	550	541	380	161
Mother in labor force	376	141	235	163	73
Employed	314	114	200	137	63
Unemployed	62	27	35	26	9
Mother not in labor force	715	409	306	217	89
Father unemployed	2,056	696	1,360	904	455
Mother in labor force	915	268	647	394	253
Employed	731	195	535	326	209
Unemployed	185	73	112	67	45
Mother not in labor force	1,141	428	712	510	202
Father not in labor force	2,102	337	1,765	944	821
Mother in labor force	832	129	703	389	314
Employed	758	116	642	351	291
Unemployed	74	13	61	38	22
Mother not in labor force	1,270	208	1,062	555	507
Families headed by women[b]	9,499	2,233	7,266	4,608	2,658
Mother in labor force	5,551	1,020	4,532	2,841	1,690
Employed	4,811	787	4,024	2,490	1,534
Unemployed	740	233	508	352	156
Mother not in labor force	3,947	1,213	2,735	1,767	968
Families headed by men[b]	807	104	702	325	378

Source: U.S., Department of Labor, Bureau of Labor Statistics, *Children of Working Mothers: March 1977*, Special Labor Force Report 217 (January 1978).

Note: Because of rounding, sums of individual items may not equal totals.

[a] Children are defined as "own" children of the family head and include never-married sons, daughters, stepchildren, and adopted children. Excluded are other related children such as grandchildren, nieces, nephews, cousins, and unrelated children. Included is total number of children for widowed, divorced, separated, or single women.

[b] Widowed, divorced, separated, and never-married family heads.

Table 4-4
Childcare Arrangements, by Number and Age of Children of Employed Mothers, 1975
(*numbers in thousands*)

	Children		
Arrangement	3 to 13 Years	3 to 6 Years	7 to 13 Years
Total children	16,046	4,658	11,388
Care in own home	13,354	3,027	10,327
Child's parents	9,797	2,514	7,283
Child cares for self	1,595	20	1,575
Other relative	1,504	346	1,158
Nonrelative	458	147	311
Care in someone else's home	2,097	1,342	755
Relative	932	570	362
Nonrelative	1,165	772	393
Group care center	279	193	86
Other	72	——	72
Not reported	247	98	149

Source: U.S., Department of Labor, Women's Bureau, *Working Mothers and Their Children* (1977).

What does the future hold for wives and mothers in the American civilian labor force? Has the critical time passed and will things resolve themselves into manageable incremental units? Have we somehow managed to muddle through the crucial period and will the future be less of a problem as things finally settle down after a period of unprecedented change? A quick glance at table 4-5 indicates that this is not so. The rate of female participation in the labor force is projected to increase in every age category up to age fifty-four. In terms of family considerations, the all-important age groupings of females in their late teens to their early fifties are projected to have participation rates well over 50 percent.

The prime-age labor force, which is composed of the twenty-five-to-fifty-four age group, is projected by the Department of Labor to grow more rapidly than the sixteen-to-twenty-five and the fifty-five-and-over age groups. Their growth rate is projected at 2.4 percent for the early 1980s, then 2.1 percent until 1990. A contributing factor to this high-growth projection rate is the increased labor-force participation of women in that age category since 1970. The special significance of this age group is that these women are caring for a very large percentage of all children under eighteen. Therefore, even with a declining birthrate for the nation as a whole, the problem of care for children of working mothers will not be alleviated by the passage of time within the decade of the eighties.

Table 4-5
Female Participation in the Civilian Labor Force by Age, 1970 and 1975, and Projected for 1980, 1985, and 1900

	Civilian Labor Force Annual Averages					Participation Rates (Percent of Population in Labor Force)				
	1970	1975	1980	1985	1990	1970	1975	1980	1985	1990
Total, 16 years and older	31,520	36,998	41,673	45,699	48,619	43.0	46.3	48.4	50.3	51.4
16 to 19	3,241	4,038	4,226	3,76	3,649	43.3	49.1	51.8	53.6	55.2
20 to 24	4,874	6,069	7,066	7,329	6,656	57.4	64.0	68.4	72.5	75.2
25 to 34	5,698	8,546	10,394	12,210	13,077	44.8	54.5	57.4	61.2	63.5
35 to 44	5,967	6,493	7,633	9,723	11,678	50.7	55.9	58.3	61.1	63.0
45 to 54	6,531	6,665	6,609	6,761	7,795	54.4	54.6	57.1	59.1	60.3
55 to 64	4,153	4,244	4,628	4,740	4,514	42.5	41.0	41.9	42.2	42.3
65 and over	1,056	1,033	1,117	1,174	1,250	9.6	8.2	8.1	7.8	7.6

Source: U.S., Department of Labor, Bureau of Labor Statistics, *New Labor Force Projections to 1990* (1977).

Table 4–6
Corrections to 1973 Projections for Female Labor-Force Participation

| | *Percent Change* | | |
Women	*1980*	*1985*	*1990*
Total	+6	+10	+11
16 to 24	+10	+14	+15
25 to 54	+9	+13	+15
55 and over	−9	−9	−10

Source: U.S., Department of Labor, Bureau of Labor Statistics, *New Labor Force Projections to 1990* (Washington, D.C.: Government Printing Office, 1977).

The question of projecting female labor participation is still a thorny one for the Department of Labor. The upward correction that has had to be applied to the 1973 projection figures for females is very high (table 4–6). The fact that the Department of Labor has had to revise their projection figures so substantially in only a few years time indicates that the dramatic entry of females into the labor force has not been fully analyzed and accounted for. There is therefore a strong possibility that the revised projections may be too low and inadequately detail the present and future problem of how many families will have to be taken into account when programs and special considerations are devised for them by agencies at the local, state, and federal levels.

Beyond governmental remedies to aid the families of working women, the potentially most exciting arena for action is the business world. If the sole or both heads of a family are being employed by business concerns, family well-being then becomes the concern of business. This aspect of policy research has barely been touched and is a very convoluted matter. According to Rosabeth Moss Kanter:

A needed next step, then, in research and policy on personal well-being, is to consider the *joint* effects of work and family system memberships. To ask what kinds of work situations maximize and minimize the prospects for family well-being and what kinds of personal-familial arrangements maximize and minimize the prospects for well-being are only first questions. We must go further and consider the likely interaction of work situation and family dynamics. Some things that are fine in themselves are lethal in combination. What kinds of families are most vulnerable to stresses introduced by the nature of the occupational worlds with which members interact? How does personal stress-producing work affect the lives of other people close to the worker, and how is this mediated by those others' own work situations? How do strained family processes affect the prospects for satisfying work life, for people in different kinds of occupational situations, for women as well as men? [Kanter, 1977, pp. 88–89]

The little research that has been done on ways in which business policy can become more responsive toward the family needs of its employees has produced some interesting data. For example, a vice president of a corporation, when asked about the firm's flextime program, responded, "Flexible hours make better mothers and fathers of our employees" (Keniston, 1977, p. 125). In contrast, a California corporation which on its own initiative introduced a modified four-day-week plan was asked by the employees to discontinue it. "Some of the complaints make clear how much the *timing* of free time may have been at fault: e.g., the time was used for home chores that could as easily have been done on Saturdays, it was lonely on Mondays with everyone else at work or at school, and daytime television was designed for women and children" (Kanter, 1977, p. 34). Obviously the answers to the question of how business can best respond to the family needs of its employees cannot be arrived at simply by deduction or in the laboratory. The entire realm of social-science research techniques must be employed to try to determine how business and governmental policies can work best to promote the social well-being of American families while not undermining their economic well-being. Creative approaches to more flexible work arrangements for mothers and fathers, such as maternity leaves for either parent, childcare leave, flextime, work-sharing arrangements, the 9-to-3 day, and the interrupted career must be examined carefully to determine the situations where they work best for all parties concerned. These options will become one of the most significant areas of concentration in the field of public policy and the family.

5 Employed Wives and Mothers: Women as Wage Earners

Why have married women and mothers moved away from their traditionally assigned place and joined the workforce in such numbers? The answer in one word is "money." Women are supporting or helping to support their families by wage earning because their families need the money in order to function at what they consider a necessary level. As in the case of standards of childcare, individual families must be given the privilege of setting their own standards of what they consider necessary for the maintenance of their well-being. Value judgments and value-laden words such as "frivolous" and "unnecessary" only cloud the issue.

Aside from a small minority of doom sayers, few Americans would claim that great numbers of families are living too luxuriously in comparison with the standards of the community. Working American families are well off in comparison to third-world families but are not nearly as well off as families living in other industrialized nations. While it might be possible to arrive at rock-bottom monetary needs for families living in any particular area, very few people are philosophically committed to asking themselves and others to live at this level. A good case can be made for a more equitable distribution of resources among the families of the world, however, the average working mother is not striving to put her family into the plutocrat class. According to her lights and the view of her family, her salary is necessary to maintain the family's basic standard of living.

In recent years the problem of maintaining families' standards of living has become an increasingly worrisome one. Inflation began making inroads into family earnings in the early 1960s (table 5–1).

According to Douty, "In 8 of the 15 years between 1947 and 1962, real rates of pay increased by 2.5 percent or more. During [the period 1962-1976] this rate of increase occurred only in the two years which coincided with the first two phases of the wage-price control program beginning in August 1971. Real rates actually declined over two years, and the increase was negligible in a third."

The impact of this decline in real earnings, which produced a resultant loss of buying power, is directly reflected in the entry or reentry of millions of wives and mothers into the labor force. Table 4–1 shows that mothers of preschool-age children began entering the labor force at a higher rate than that for all married females during the period 1951 to 1976. The only periods when their entrance into the labor force was at a higher rate than

Table 5-1
Year-to-Year Percent Changes in Money and Real Earnings, Production and Related Workers, Private Nonfarm Economy, and Consumer Price Index 1961–1976

Year	Percent Change in Real Earnings	Percent Change in Consumer Price Index
1961–1962	2.2	1.1
1962–1963	1.7	1.2
1963–1964	1.5	1.3
1964–1965	2.0	1.7
1965–1966	1.3	2.8
1966–1967	1.9	2.9
1967–1968	2.1	4.2
1968–1969	1.3	5.3
1969–1970	0.7	5.9
1970–1971	2.8	4.3
1971–1972	3.2	3.3
1972–1973	0.1	6.2
1973–1974	−2.1	11.0
1974–1975	−0.3	9.1
1975–1976	1.3	5.7

Source: H.M. Douty, "The Slowdown in Real Wages: A Postwar Perspective, *Monthly Labor Review,* Department of Labor, (August 1977), p. 9.

that of both total married females and of females with school-age children was during 1961 to 1966 and 1971 to 1976. This is the result of economic strains that were being felt strongly by young families at a particularly vulnerable time in their life cycles.

Although it is apparent from the data that American mothers are working to maintain the material well-being of their families, psychological factors cannot be totally ignored. Although no U.S. government figures are available for citation, it is apparent that many women derive satisfactions from their jobs beyond the pay check, just as do men. The need for status, variety, opportunities to meet different people, to get away from the routine of housework, and so forth all contribute to the desire of women to work.

Therefore, even if an economic miracle were to occur and present trends were reversed so that families could maintain their standard of living on one salary, it is unlikely that great numbers of mothers, particularly those of school-age children, would leave the workforce and remain at home. However, as many signs point to a worsening of the economic pic-

Table 5-2
Income by Family Type, 1976 versus 1975

	1976		1975	
	Number (thousands)	*Median Income (dollars)*	*Median Income (dollars)*	*Percent Increase Income*
All families	56,710	14,958	13,719	9.0
Male head	48,997	16,095	14,816	8.6
Wife in labor force	21,554	18,731	17,239	8.7
Wife not in labor force	25,943	13,931	12,759	9.2
Female head	7,713	7,211	6,844	5.4

Source: U.S., Bureau of the Census, Current Population Reports, *Money Income and Poverty Status of Families and Persons in the United States: 1976* (*Advance Report*) (1977).

ture, it is likely that more women, whether they want to or not, will feel impelled to become employed. For that reason, the data presented in this chapter are important for depicting the present and future situations.

In table 5-2 the median family incomes for all families, male-headed families, and female-headed families during the period 1975 to 1976 are presented in dollars. It is immediately apparent that the families that are best off in terms of income are two-wage families with a wife in the labor force. Families in which the wife did not participate in the labor force had a median income 7 percent below total family income in both 1975 and in 1976. Where wives contributed to the families' financial support, however, the families had a median income 26 percent above that for families in which the wife did not work in 1975 and a 34 percent higher income in 1976. Female-sole-headed families, on the other hand, had to survive on an income 54 percent below that of male-headed sole-supported families in 1975 and 52 percent lower in 1976. Furthermore, their condition is worsening in relation to other families since they had the lowest percentage increase in income of all groups. Their increase in earnings was only 40 percent of the rise experienced by all families from 1975 to 1976.

The problems that females experience in terms of lower income extend across the board. Their income is lower than that of males and tends to remain lower in most marital categories, even when the female is the sole support of her family. Table 5-3 demonstrates how universal this discrepancy is.

Divorced women earn higher wages than single and widowed men but do not come close to matching salaries of any group of men with family responsibilities. Since divorced females have a significantly higher median age as a group than single males, it is no surprise that their median wage is higher. In fact, a comparison of the wages of these two groups ought to be considered specious in any context.

Seventy-three percent of all female-headed households are clustered in the lowest three income categories (table 5–4). Only 27 percent of male-headed families are similarly grouped. This can be partially explained by comparing the occupations held by women with those held by men. The

Table 5-3
Median Individual Income by Sex and Marital Status, 1976
(*dollars*)

	Total	Single	Spouse Present	Spouse Absent	Widowed	Divorced
Male	10,051	4,540	12,151	7,245	4,613	9,234
Female	3,882	3,599	3,845	4,147	3,442	6,233

Source: U.S., Bureau of the Census, Current Population Reports, *Money Income and Poverty Status of Families and Persons in the United States: 1976 (Advance Report)* (1977).

Table 5-4
Income of Families by Sex of Head of Household, 1976
(*percentages*)

	Male Head	Female Head
Total number	55,903	18,238
Under $4,000	6	35
3,000–6,999	10	23
7,000–9,999	11	15
10,000–11,000	8	7
12,000–14,000	12	8
15,000–17,499	11	4
17,500–19,000	9	2
20,000–24,000	13	3
25,000–29,000	8	1
30,000–49,000	9	1
50,000 and over	2	a

Source: U.S., Bureau of the Census, Current Population Reports, *Money Income and Poverty Status of Families and Persons in the United States: 1976 (Advance Report)* (1977).
Note: Figures do not add to 100% due to rounding.
a negligible.

placement of women in the lower paying jobs within each occupational division becomes apparent with a cursory examination of table 5–5. According to the occupational breakdown:

1. The majority of female white-collar workers hold clerical positions which provide the lowest full-time salaries of all white-collar work.
2. Among blue-collar workers females tend to be operatives and receive the lowest wages for skilled workers.
3. Almost one-quarter of the female workforce is employed in service work. This work offers only the lowest paying jobs available.

But obviously this is not the whole picture. Rank discrimination in terms of wage earnings is apparent at every occupational level. Therefore, even where females work in the higher paying jobs, such as at the professional, technical level for white-collar work, their median wage is only 55 percent of that received by male employees. This imbalance is true for every occupation with the exception of private household workers (table 5–6).

Table 5–5
Occupations by Sex and Median Earnings, 1976

	Male		Female	
Occupational Category	*Percent*	*Median Income*	*Percent*	*Median Income*
White-collar workers	39	13,751	60	5,811
Professional, Technical	35	15,272	25	8,362
Salaried	90	15,105	—	—
Self-employed	10	20,373	—	—
Managers and Administrators	34	15,584	9	7,511
Salaried	82	16,457	—	—
Self-employed	18	10,201	—	—
Sales workers	16	10,446	11	2,285
Clerical	16	10,343	55	5,683
Blue-collar workers	46	9,482	15	4,618
Craft	42	11,836	11	5,323
Operatives	39	9,102	81	4,689
Laborers	13	3,940	8	2,791
Service workers	10	4,931	24	1,854
Private household	1	574	18	699
Other	99	5,042	82	2,327
Farm workers	5	2,626	—	—
Farmers and managers	49	4,836	—	—
Farm laborers and supervisors	51	1,531	—	—
Totals	60,450	10,301	44,545	4,296

Source: U.S., Bureau of the Census, Current Population Reports, *Money Income and Poverty Status of Families and Persons in the United States: 1976* (*Advance Report*) (1977).

Table 5-6
Comparisons of Earnings of Females versus Males by Occupational Categories, 1976

Occupational Category	Female Income as a Percentage of Male Income
White-collar workers	42
Professional, technical	55
Managers, administrators	48
Sales	22
Clerical	55
Blue-collar workers	49
Craft	45
Operatives	52
Laborers	71
Service workers	38
Private household	122
Other	46

Source: Computed from data in table 5-5.

With this exception, where the sample is very small and unrepresentative, the median female income tends to be much less than that paid to males in the same occupational category. When those occupations that are full-time for both male and female employees are considered (excluding sales, unskilled labor, and service work), the wages of females average about 60 percent of the males' wages.

Justification for this glaring inequity might still be found in the late entrance of females into the labor force, although it is problematical as to how much of the difference could be actually accounted for in this way. However, education or lack thereof no longer offers an explanation for the basic fiscal inequity that exists between men and women in our society.

It is a startling fact that a male with a high-school education earns a higher median wage than a female with postgraduate work (table 5-7). Since the figures in this table only include full-time wage earners, it cannot be denied that female wage earners were still receiving grossly prejudicial treatment in terms of salary fourteen years after the passage of the Equal Pay Act of 1963. And in 1980 this pattern persists.

It is now obvious that the Equal Pay Act of 1963 has only provided a limited remedy for discriminatory wage practices. The reason is that the act is limited to dealing with pay differentials based on sex in "substantially equal" job categories. Employers have now become aware that they cannot pay their female accountant less than their male accountants, all other factors being equal. They have even become aware that they cannot pay their

Table 5-7
Education by Sex and Median Earnings of Full-Time Employees, 1976

	Male		Female	
	Percent	Median Income	Percent	Median Income
Elementary	12	10,173	8	5,993
High School (1 to 4 years)	48	13,703	58	8,069
College (1 to 4 years)	29	16,875	26	10,243
Postgraduate (5 years or none)	11	20,597	8	13,569

Source: U.S., Bureau of the Census, Current Population Reports, *Money Income and Poverty Status of Families and Persons in the United States: 1976* (*Advance Report*) (1977).

male flight attendants more than their female flight attendants even if they call them stewards and stewardesses, although this awareness took longer to achieve. And still the pay differential has not budged during the period 1967 to 1978 when the Equal Pay Act was in full operation (table 5-8).

Pay inequities in the American society are based on deep-rooted patterns that have kept women clustered in the lower-paying occupations and echelons and have paid lower wages to those areas. Those occupations that have traditionally been considered female occupations traditionally have been low paying. In addition, occupations that become female dominated have become devalued in the process. This is true the world over in spite of the fact that a female occupation may be considered a male occupation in another country. A case in point is the fact that the practice of medicine is a low-status, poorly rewarded one in the USSR where it is a female occupation, and just the opposite attitude is prevalent in the United States where it is a traditional male occupation.

Some attempts to explain this phenomenon have been based on theories such as the "taste for discrimination," which holds that employers are willing to pay a higher wage differential to the category of employees they prefer or that those groups for which they have no taste must be willing to work for less pay in order to be hired. The "dual labor market theory" divides employment into the primary sector offering good paying jobs with security, advancement, and equity, and the secondary sector with low wages, poor working conditions, low job security, and few opportunities for advancement. Minorities, and to a lesser extent women, dominate the secondary sector and face the almost insurmountable task of breaking into a primary sector controlled by white males. Studies that have attempted to measure the gap in terms of differences among firms within the same industries or the location of various firms have accounted for some of the differ-

Table 5-8
Median Usual Weekly Earnings of Full-Time Wage and Salary Workers by Sex, 1967–1978

	Usual Weekly Earnings		Women's Earnings as
Year	Women	Men	Percent of Men's
May of:			
1967	$ 78	$125	62
1969	86	142	61
1970	94	151	62
1971	100	162	62
1972	106	168	63
1973	116	188	62
1974	124	204	61
1975	137	221	62
1976	145	234	62
1977	156	253	62
1978	166	272	61

Source: U.S., Bureau of Labor Statistics, *Women in the Labor Force: Some New Data Series,* Report 575 (October 1979).

ential and indicate that certain market factors are operative in terms of explaining part of the gap. But, as shown in a paper presented by Isabel Sawhill in 1974, after male-female differences in terms of age, education, race, residence, experience, unionization, turnover, absenteeism, and hours worked were accounted for in the equation, a residual gap equal to a 33 percent differential in pay between males and females remained. The major culprit is occupational segregation by sex that treats equals differently simply based on which sex dominates their chosen occupation. (A good summary of further theories and studies that attempt to explain the reasons for the existence of the earnings gap between males and females can be found in the U.S. Department of Labor publication *Women and Work*, Employment and Training Administration, R & D Monograph 46, 1977). That is why Eleanor Holmes Norton, chairperson of the Equal Employment Opportunity Commission, has called equal pay for jobs of comparable value the issue of the eighties. In setting the agenda for public informational hearings into the matter of job segregation and wage discrimination under Title VII and the Equal Pay Act to be held in 1980, Norton stated: "The hearings will examine whether the wage rates assigned to traditionally segregated jobs are depressed because those jobs are viewed as 'less valuable' or because their occupants are minorities and women."

If inroads are made into eliminating pay differentials caused by occupation segregation, dramatic changes in the composition and structure of the labor force would be expected to occur. Presumably more freedom of occupational choice would come about and males, who in the past may have shunned certain attractive occupations because of the low pay, may be motivated to go into new fields; females may feel that certain occupations are finally truly open to them; parents presumably would change old habits of socialization and show more flexible attitudes to their child's choice of occupation. The dreary pattern of figures shown in table 5-3, whereby female employees are very poorly compensated in comparison with male employees, should begin to break up. And the deprivation of female-headed households depicted in table 5-2 should lessen, to the overall benefit of society.

But the question of equal pay for jobs of comparable value is a thorny one. How does one determine what jobs are truly comparable and have the same value to the employer? Can bias-free job evaluation systems perform this task and, if so, can employers be forced to use them? What impact will such changes have on the economy? Questions like these will be some of the major issues of the 1980s and beyond. Public attitudes will shape a public policy that will demand equity for all employees regardless of sex, race, national origin, age, or handicap. Such a social revolution is likely to be beneficial to all families because it engenders more equality of opportunity for everybody's children.

Summary

The growth of female labor-force participation historically has been tied to woman's position in the family life cycle and economic circumstances. Therefore, while the tendency has been to expect married women to work only within the confines of their homes, the poor, the temporarily displaced, and groups suffering economic discrimination, such as racial minorities and recent immigrants, have all relied heavily at one time or another on the earnings of wives and mothers. Within the United States after the turn of the century, unmarried women were allowed but not encouraged by accepted social attitudes to work outside of the home. When they married it was expected that employment would give way to homemaking. Following World War II, it became more common for young brides to work for a few years after marriage, particularly for brides of returning servicemen, who had suspended their educations and were now flocking back to college campuses to pick up where they had left off. But even under these circumstances, employment for young married women was expected to cease with pregnancy.

In spite of these expectations, the traditional pattern had been broken and, like Humpty-Dumpty, could not be put back together again. Wives began returning to the labor market in the late 1950s and 1960s as jobs became available and they no longer had the pressing burdens of infant care to tie them to their homes. At the same time women also began to remain in the workforce for longer periods of time both before and after marriage, many postponing pregnancy in order to do so. Furthermore, those women who did leave the labor force in order to rear children began returning to the labor force at an earlier age. They were able to do this in part because of a trend toward shortening of the number of years given to child-bearing and infant care. In this manner the labor-force participation of women has grown to include significant percentages of married women without children, married women with older children, and married women with preschool-age children. The most resistant stage of the cycle has been women with preschool-age children, but almost four out of ten married females in the labor force fit into this category (see table 4-1).

The reasons why some phases of the life cycle are more resistant to female employment outside of the home are obviously tied to the types of family responsibilities that women incur at the various stages. Even today it is extremely difficult on women with children to maintain full-time jobs outside of the home. Over three-quarters of the children of mothers working full- and part-time were being cared for within their own homes (see table 4-4). Ten million of these children were being cared for solely by their parents. Then the question is: Why should these women increase their work burdens by adding employment to the already demanding tasks of child care? A large part of the answer is clearly one of economic necessity. The financial need to work is greatest for families with the most dependents; that is, during the reproductive cycle. During this phase, therefore, the financial strain on the family is very high and can often only be relieved when both parents work outside of the home. Yet it is also during this same reproductive phase, between the birth of the first child and the departure of the last child from the home, that the needs within the family for care and nurturing are greatest. Because of these contradictory demands and women's response to them, the American family has been increasingly viewed as an endangered species. Beside alarm over increasing divorce rates, it is the realization that fewer and fewer mothers are working full-time at motherhood that has created so much pessimism over the state of the family in the modern world.

Aside from the obvious loss of what has come to be accepted as the traditional family pattern, the full impact of dual careers on families has yet to be adequately assessed. Much attention by social scientists in the 1950s and early 1960s was devoted to condemning female employment because it was seen as having a negative impact on the family, particularly in terms of childcare. There has been a noticeable shift in recent years brought about by fuller data, and the positive aspects of the situation have begun to be recognized. In a recent publication reference is made to studies showing that little difference actually exists in the number of hours given to childcare by mothers in the workforce and full-time homemakers (Bane, 1976). Another study has found that having an employed mother was not necessarily a disadvantage from the point-of-view of the children in the family (Clarke-Stewart, 1977). In addition, full cognizance has not yet been given to the impact of the shrinking number of functions allotted to individual families within an urbanized, industrialized society. Society has tended to assume responsibilities, such as providing auxiliary care for the aged, the mentally ill, and the disabled, which at one time were considered solely familial responsibilities. Since the burden, in terms of expenditures of time allocated to care, tended to fall on the homemaker, this development has freed a certain amount of the homemaker's time, in addition to other considerations. Labor-saving devices and new technology have been acknowledged and credited with substantially reducing the responsibilities and work load of the homemaker, thereby allowing even more time to be devoted to other pursuits without causing physical deprivation to members of the family. These and many other factors have brought about a change in the role of the homemaker. Perhaps now that some of the more emotional debate has subsided and actual data exists for testing, less biased assessments can be made determining what these more recent developments presage for the American family. It cannot be overstressed that employed wives and mothers are here to stay, and it is a fact that must be dealt with. It must also be stressed that this phenomenon may be the most revolutionary development to affect the modern American family. No attempt to understand the modern family will succeed while so little is understood about its consequences and the new needs that it raises for families and for the greater society.

Beside concern over the institution of the family, one might question the affect this situation is having on individuals within the family. This question has never adequately been answered in terms of the employed father, who has worked away from the home for some centuries now, much less for the employed mother. What is needed is a thorough understanding of the interrelationships between work and the family. For so long now it has been possible to consider work and family as totally separate domains simply because the nuturant role of the father was subjugated to that of the provider. This total subordination of men (and thereby of their families) to the demands of the workplace was at least feasible when each family normally had an adult female to oversee the home. But when the family, through economic necessity and the development of new concepts of gender roles, becomes subordinated to the demands of maintaining two jobs, the strain on individual families cannot be ignored by any society concerned for its basic values and institutions.

The growing conflict between the demands of home and the demands of employment may become the major factor dominating government policy toward the family in the future. Prior to that development, however, there is an urgent need to document the precise nature of this work-family dichotomy so that recommendations can be based on fact, not fiction. The whole realm of family policy involving work and family considerations includes numerous policies and programs such as flexible hours, at-work childcare, maternal and paternal leaves of absence, and flexible career scheduling. Innovative approaches to these areas are being tried in many parts of the world including the United States but little exists in the way of general assessments of their impact on the family. Social scientists and policy analysts now need to focus some attention on those problems which have already been so clearly recognized by millions of individual working men and women themselves and have already affected the lives of millions of children.

Finally, when referring to government policy considerations, it is clear that inequities based on past realities continue to subvert policy stances that have been taken by federal, state, and local authorities concerning equality between the sexes. The ring of the slogan "equal pay for equal work" suits the modern ear. Unfortunately, as the data show, this laudable sentiment still lacks implementation. Beyond considerations of its impact on individuals, this lack of implementation has a direct impact on the American family (see table 5-4). The most apparent effect is the gross economic inequity that continues to exist between male-headed and female-headed families. Statistical data can show this clearly. What is less obvious is the psychological effect on women and their families of the fact that women remain, in general, unequal partners within the labor force. It is clear that no government policy or law will completely eliminate these inequities until Americans accept the new role of women in family life and the labor force. Perhaps the acceptance or realization that they are not punishing the family when they reward the employed wife and mother will help create attitudinal changes requisite for full implementation of existing government policy and will promote equality in opportunity and wages for all males and females.

References for Part I

Adams, Bert N. *Kinship in an Urban Setting*. Chicago: Markham, 1968.

Alston, Cecile S., and Clara Tessenear. *Marriages and Dissolution of Marriages, 1965-1975*. Raleigh, N.C.: Human Resources, 1976.

Bane, Mary Jo. *Here to Stay: The American Family in the Twentieth Century*. New York: Basic Books, 1976.

Blaydon, Colin C., and Carol Stack. "Income Support Policies and the Family." *Daedalus* 106 (1977): 2

Bott, Elizabeth. *Family and Social Network*. 2nd ed. New York: The Free Press, 1971.

Carter, Hugn, and Paul C. Glick. *Marriage and Divorce: A Social and Economic Study*. rev. ed. Cambridge, Mass.: Harvard University Press, 1976.

Chafe, William H. *The American Woman: Her Changing Social, Economic, and Political Roles, 1920-1970*. London: Oxford University Press, 1972.

Clarke-Stewart, Alison. *Child Care in the Family: A Review of Research and Some Propositions for Policy*. New York: Academic Press, 1977.

Douty, H.M. "The Slowdown in Real Wages: A Postwar Perspective." *Monthly Labor Review*. U.S. Department of Labor, 1977.

Downs, Anthony. "The Impact of Housing Policies on Family Life in the United States Since World War II." *Daedalus* 106 (1977): 2.

Fortes, Meyer. "Introduction." In *The Development Cycle in Domestic Groups*. Edited by Jack Goody. London: Cambridge University Press, 1966.

Giraldo, Z.I., and J.M. Weatherford. "Life Cycle and the American Family: Current Trends and Policy Implications." Duke University Institute of Policy Sciences and Public Affairs Working Paper Series, no. 378, March 1978.

Glick, Paul. "The Family Cycle." *American Sociological Review* 12 (1947).

Glick, Paul, and Arthur J. Norton. "Perspectives in the Recent Upturn in Divorce and Remarriage." Demography 10 (1973): 3.

Goody, Jack, ed. *The Developmental Cycle in Domestic Groups*. London: Cambridge University Press, 1966.

Hirschhorn, Larry. Social Policy and the Life Cycle: A Developmental Perspective. *Social Science Review* (September 1977): 434-450.

Kamerman, Shelia B. "Public Policy and the Family." In *Women into Wives: The Legal and Economic Impact of Marriage*. Edited by Jane P. Chapman and Margaret Gates. New York: Russell Sage Foundation, 1977.

Kanter, Rosabeth Moss. *Work and Family in the United States: A Critical Review and Agenda for Research and Policy.* New York: Russell Sage Foundation, 1977.

Keniston, Kenneth, and the Carnegie Council on Children. *All Our Children: The American Family Under Pressure.* New York: Harcourt Brace Jovanovich, 1977.

Laslett, Peter, and Richard Wall, eds. *Household and Family in Past Time.* Cambridge, England: Cambridge University Press, 1972.

National Center for Social Statistics. *AFDC: Standards for Needs by States,* 1977.

National Research Council, Advisory Committee on Child Development. *Toward a National Policy for Children and Families.* Washington, D.C.: National Academy of Sciences, 1976.

North Carolina, Department of Human Resources. *Basic Automated Birth Yearbook.* Raleigh, North Carolina, 1976.

———. *North Carolina Vital Statistics: Quarterly Provisional Reports.* Raleigh, North Carolina, 1977.

———. *PHSB Studies,* numbers 1–7. Raleigh, North Carolina, 1977.

Oberken, Howard. "Studies of the Characteristics of AFDC Recipients." *Social Security Bulletin,* September 1977.

Parke, Robert Jr., and Paul C. Glick. "Prospective Changes in Marriage and the Family." *Journal of Marriage and the Family* 29 (1967): 2.

Rein, Martin, and Lee Rainwater. "How Large is the Welfare Class." *Challenge: The Magazine of Economic Affairs* (September-October 1977).

Ross, Heather L., and Isabel V. Sawhill. *Time of Transition: The Growth of Families Headed by Women.* Washington, D.C.: Urban Institute, 1975.

Sawhill, Isabel V. "The Earnings Gap: Research Needs and Issues." Paper presented at a Workshop on Research Needed to Improve the Employment and Employability of Women. Convened by the U.S. Department of Labor, Women's Bureau, June 7, 1974.

Stack, Carol B. *All Our Kin: Strategies for Survival in an Urban Black Community.* New York: Harper and Row, 1974.

Stack, Carol B., and Herbert Semmel. "The Concept of Family in the Poor Black Community." *Studies in Public Welfare* 12 (1973).

U.S., Bureau of the Census. "Marital Status and Living Arrangements." *Population Characteristics,* Series P-20 no. 306 (1976).

———. "Money Income and Poverty Status of Families and Persons in the United States: 1977 (Advance Report)." *Current Population Reports,* Series P-60, no. 119 (1979).

———. "Characteristics of Households Purchasing Food Stamps." *Current Population Reports* (1977).

———. "Households and Families by Types." *Population Characteristics,* Series P-20, no. 313 (1977).

———. "Money Income in 1975 of Families and Persons in the U.S." *Current Population Reports* (1977).

———. *Statistical Abstract 1976,* 1977.

U.S., Department of Health, Education and Welfare. *Food Plans for Poverty Measurement,* 1976.

———. *The Measure of Poverty.* Technical Paper XII (1976).

———. *Medicaid Statistics: Fiscal Year 1976,* 1977.

U.S., Department of Housing and Urban Development. *Statistical Yearbook,* 1975.

U.S., Department of Labor. *Marital and Family Characteristics of the Labor Force.* Special Labor Force Report, 183 (1975).

———. Bureau of Labor Statistics. *New Labor Force Projections to 1990,* 1977.

———. Bureau of Labor Statistics. *The Labor Force Participation Pattern of Divorced and Separated Women,* 1977.

———. *Women and Work. Employment and Training Administration.* R & D Monograph 46, 1977.

———. Bureau of Labor Statistics. *Children of Working Mothers: March 1977.* Special Labor Force Report 217, 1978.

———. Bureau of Labor Statistics. *Women in the Labor Force: Some New Data Series.* Report 575, October 1979.

U.S., Department of Labor and U.S., Department of Health, Education and Welfare. *Employment and Training Report of the President.* 1977.

U.S., Department of Labor, Women's Bureau. *Working Mothers and Their Children.* Washington, D.C.: Government Printing Office, 1977.

U.S., Congress. Senate. *Who Gets Food Stamps? Hearings of Select Committee on Nutrition and Human Needs.* 1975.

Weatherford, J.M. "Family Culture, Behavior, and Emotion in a Working-Class German Town." Ph.D. dissertation, University of California, San Diego, 1977.

**Part II
Tax Policy and the
Dual-Income Family:
The Marriage Tax and
Other Inequities**

. . . the marriage penalty wasn't even noticed when it went into effect. The effort of the [House Ways and Means] committee was to help out single people. I had gone home, and there was nobody on the conference committee that had a working wife.—Statement of Congresswoman Martha Griffiths before the hearings on the Economic Problems of Women, Joint Economic Committee, 93rd Congress, first session, 1973

The present tax law encourages . . . . I started to say extracurricular activities . . . that's a fact. I don't want to publicize it.—President Jimmy Carter, in a speech delivered 16 February 1977 before the Department of Agriculture

6

The Historical Development of the Marriage Tax

The genesis of differential tax liability based on marital status can be traced to a legal anomaly arising from the early European settlement of North America. Two legal systems, one based on English common law and the other on Spanish and French codes, became established within the territories that eventually formed the continental United States. By virtue of these systems married couples were viewed either as one legal person represented by the male partner (in common-law states) or as two legal entities with the male as controller and manager of the marriage community (in community-property states). These definitional differences did not have a significant impact on taxation until the introduction of the federal Income Tax Laws (1913) and even then did not cause much concern until World War I. Prior to the war the taxation rate was low. During and immediately after the war large sums of money had to be raised via taxation, and Americans began to feel the pinch. The discomfort was relieved considerably in the community-property states of Arizona, California, Idaho, Louisiana, Nevada, New Mexico, Texas, and Washington by the simple expedient of dividing the taxable income in half on the basis that a couple's income, no matter who earned it, legally belonged to two distinct individuals. Since the United States had enacted progressive tax rates, income splitting had the effect of lowering the applicable tax rate and allowing certain couples to pay less in taxes, or even no taxes, in comparison with other couples with the same income but without the benefit of community-property laws (table 6–1).

Responding to a situation whereby citizens were taxed differently on the basis of geography, in 1921 the House of Representatives passed a bill (House Report 8245) that included a provision for taxing the gross income of the spouse having "management and control over such income." The provision was eliminated by the Senate, and a further attempt to bring it into law in 1924 by the Secretary of the Treasury also failed. This approach to bringing the income tax in community-property states up to the level in common-law states was made untenable by the 1930 Supreme Court decision in *Poe* v. *Seaborn*. According to the interpretation of the court, couples residing in the eight community-property states were entitled to this income-tax relief because the income in question was the property of two people and could not be taxed as if it belonged to one person. For the next decade and a half attempts were made to get around the Supreme Court

Table 6-1

Example of How Income Splitting Affected Taxes of Couples Living in Community-Property States versus Couples with the Same Taxable Income in Common-Law States, 1919

Jurisdiction and Net Income Group	Tax Liability
Common-law state $20,000	$2,070[a]
Community-property state $20,000	$1,340
$10,000 @ $670	
$10,000 @ $670	

Source: U.S., Bureau of the Census, *Historical Statistics of the United States: Colonial Times to 1970* (1976) part 2, p. 1111.

[a] Tax liability somewhat overstated as 1919 tax rate schedule for two exemptions is unpublished. Therefore, this tax liability is based on rate schedule for one exemption.

ruling by making joint returns mandatory. This form of tax return would make a married couple subject to taxation for the total earned income of the two individuals who made up the couple. Each of these attempts at closing what was perceived by some as a loophole in the tax structure failed, largely due to the zeal of the representatives of community-property states. The situation became more and more inequitable as taxation rates climbed during the period encompassing World War II. By 1948 the dollar differential for a couple reporting income in the $5,000 to $25,000 brackets ranged from $38.00 to $2,622 (table 6-2).

Between 1945 and 1947, Oklahoma, Oregon, Michigan, Nebraska, and Pennsylvania turned themselves into instant community-property states to achieve income-tax equity with the original community-property states. At the federal level there was consternation over what were considered hasty and ill-advised tamperings with fundamental legal institutions. The Supreme Court agreed with this assessment in the case of Pennsylvania and voided that state's attempt to define itself as a community-property state. But even so the specter of states successfully circumventing federal legislation in this manner was brought up frequently in the tax-reform hearings of 1948. The total amount of money involved was a substantial $744 million tax differential chiefly borne by married couples in common-law states. Therefore much sentiment was being expressed in the nation about the obligation of a state to protect its married citizens from what was now seen as an unfair tax burden. According to the House Report accompanying the tax-reform bill, "a number of States have shifted from the common law to the community property system. In these cases benefits under the Federal income tax which residents of the State would obtain . . . were largely responsible. . . . Many responsible State officials have reached the conclusion that the difference between the impact of the Federal income tax as it

Table 6–2

**Difference in Amounts and Percentages of Income Tax for Selected
Incomes in Community-Property States versus Common-Law States, 1948**

Income	Dollar Difference	Percentage Difference
$ 5,000	$ 38.00	5
10,000	342.00	18.56
15,000	893.00	28.31
25,000	2,622.00	40.59

Source: U.S., Congress, House, 80th Cong., 2d sess., 1948, H. Rept. 1274, vol. 11209, p. 22.

applies in the common property and common law jurisdictions is so great that the use of community property cannot be avoided'' (House Report 1274, 1948, p. 23). This report goes on to warn: "If the necessary action is not taken, there will be a flood of ill-advised state legislation intended to produce the same results, but doing so in a manner which has most unfortunate consequences, not only for the taxpayer involved, but also for all the persons who must use or administer the property laws of the States which rush into the community-property system.'' It would be interesting to speculate what would have evolved in this country if income splitting had not been introduced on a national basis and the community-property movement had continued to evolve according to the manner predicted by the report.

The dilemma of unequal taxation was finally resolved with the adoption of the so-called Surrey Plan. The plan, presented in a speech made in 1947 by tax specialist and economist Stanley S. Surrey, called for granting the benefits of income-splitting to married citizens everywhere in the United States. This represented a complete turnabout from previous strategies of bringing all taxation up to the level achieved in common-law states. Instead, tax rates were brought down to the level then existing in community-property states (table 6–3).

In a postwar tax-cutting mood Congress approved this measure and overrode President Truman's veto. Although testimony by individuals at later tax hearings pointed to Truman's veto as being directed against income-splitting, according to Truman's own words the major target was the national debt. In his prescient message to Congress, Truman referred to the $253 billion debt and stated that "if we do not reduce the public debt by substantial amounts during a prosperous period such as the present, there is little prospect that it will ever be materially reduced'' (House Document 589, 1948). After solidly overriding these objections, many members of Congress probably believed that equity had finally been incorporated into this part of the tax system. However, at least the members of the House

Ways and Means Committee probably were aware of a Treasury Department report entitled "The Tax Treatment of Family Income." It pointed out that "allowing married couples in all states the option of equal division of income for income-tax purposes would not change the tax liabilities of single persons; it would increase their relative tax load since they would not share in the tax reductions which would accrue to married couples under the plan. . . ." (Treasury Department, 1947). This report, prepared as a press release by the Treasury Department, was inserted into the record of the House hearings on House Report 4790 by Wilbur Mills, not yet chairman of the Ways and Means Committee (House Hearings, 1948, p. 844). But in 1948 this new group of aggrieved citizens who had become disadvantaged from a relative point of view, the singles who could now claim unfair treatment by the U.S. government, were a distinct minority. By and large, many of them considered themselves only temporarily resident in this single-tax-payer category and showed no interest in forming a lobby group to push for tax reform. So temporarily things became quiet on the tax front.

In many ways Congress had every reason to feel self-congratulatory. The Revenue Act of 1948 had effectively sliced apart a twenty-five-year-old Gordian Knot that had defeated many previous attempts to unravel it. Not only had Congress resolved a long-festering problem that had recently become acute, but they had done so in a singularly appropriate manner. Logically, income splitting made sense since the two adult individuals in a family shared the income earned by one or both of them. Therefore, when two people shared one income it would seem reasonable to tax each on the basis of their individual income benefit. Allowances for dependents had already been incorporated into the system in 1917, and income splitting appeared to be the final fine-tuning the system needed to make it apply equitably to married couples everywhere.

Three years later the military action in Korea made necessary the Tax Reform Act of 1951. The major purpose of the act was to "provide extraordinary increases in revenues to meet essential national defense expenditures" (House Report 586, 1951, p. 1). Congress also devised a new taxpayer category, that of head-of-household, to equalize another inequity that had been brought to their attention. The rationale for establishing this new category was that it "is believed that taxpayers, not having spouses but nevertheless required to maintain a household for the benefit of other individuals, are in a somewhat similar position to married couples who, because they may share their income, are treated under present law substantially as if they were a single individual each with half of the total income of the couple" (House Report 586, 1951, p. 11). To a certain extent this stipulation might be termed the "war-widows" tax provision. Sentiment for the plight of a single person raising or supporting a dependent on her (or his)

Table 6–3
A Comparison of the Effective Individual Income-Tax Rates before and after the Tax Reform Act of 1948

Income	Single Persons, No Dependents		No Dependents		Married Persons					
					2 Dependents, Undivided Income		2 Dependents, Income Split 50/50			
	Before (%)	After (%)	Before (%)	After (%)	Before (%)	After (%)	Before (%)	After (%)		
$ 5,000	18.43	14.54	15.96	11.55	11.78	7.72	11.40	7.72		
$10,000	23.47	20.03	21.85	14.55	18.62	12.10	16.15	12.10		
$15,000	28.47	24.82	26.98	17.52	24.26	15.47	19.13	15.47		
$20,000	33.23	29.28	31.97	20.03	29.45	18.29	21.85	18.29		

Source: U.S., Congress, House, 80th Cong., 2d sess., 1948, H. Rpt. 1274, vol. 11209, p. 2.

own blurred the strict logic of income splitting. The question then became: "If a tax benefit could be granted a married couple why not half a tax benefit to a deserving war widow?" The fact that this head-of-household was already achieving an income tax savings compared to a single person without dependents because of the dependency allowance did not deter the Congress from its attempt to benefit a specific, deserving, portion of the population. Therefore, a new compromise category halfway between the rate applied to single taxpayers and the rate granted to the married taxpayer via income splitting was enacted.

The logic of income splitting was further blurred in the Tax Reform Act of 1951 by a procedural adjustment made with regard to joint returns filed by married couples. The Revenue Act of 1948 had provided that after a couple had split their income, they would use this figure to compute the dollar amount of their tax payment, applying the same-tax rate schedule used by everyone else. The rationale for this method of computation was immediately apparent to even the most casual observer. When preparing their own returns, all taxpayers could understand why a couple was paying lower taxes than a single person earning the same income by realizing that it came about because of income splitting. But to a bureaucrat the system was unnecessarily circuitous. The same effect could be produced mechanically by setting up a separate tax table for the benefit of married couples. And, therefore, in the Tax Reform Act of 1951 "the brackets and rates are adjusted so that it is unnecessary for persons using this table to divide their income by two and then multiply the tax by two as is presently required of married persons filing joint returns, who receive the full benefit of income splitting" (House Report 586, 1951, p. 8). Unfortunately, this bit of bureaucratic tidying-up had the effect of appearing to set up a special tax rate for married couples. Every year after 1951 every American taxpayer could note that there were three categories of taxpayers in the United States and that the single person was the most heavily taxed (table 6–4).

It was inevitable that these tax-rate differentials would be challenged, and in 1958 it reached the Court of Appeals in *Faraco* v. *Commissioner of Internal Revenue*. The claim of Antoinette M. Faraco was that upon the death of her husband she was moved into the single person category and, as a result, was being taxed at a 40 percent higher rate than previously. Judge Clement Haynsworth, who ruled in favor of the Internal Revenue Department position, stated: "Classification of taxpayers according to marital status is not unreasonable, however, and there was much reason behind the purpose to equalize the tax burden as it falls upon married couples. . . . The fact that the change gave a proportionately greater tax reduction to married couples with large incomes is wholly irrelevant; if the rapid acceleration of the progressive tax rates ran afoul of no constitutional guarantee, a slight withdrawal may not be said to have done so. . . ." This terse, unsympa-

Table 6–4
Examples of Marginal Tax Rates Established by the Tax Reform Act of 1951

Income Bracket	Married Couple (%)	Head-of-Household (%)	Single Person (%)
$0–2,000	22.5	22.5	22.5
$2,000–4,000	22.5	23.6	24.8
$4,000–6,000	22.5	27.0	29.3
$6,000–8,000	29.3	33.8	38.3
$14,000–16,000	33.8	43.9	52.9
$18,000–20,000	38.3	48.4	59.6
$24,000–26,000	48.4	57.4	66.4

Source: U.S., Congress, House, 82d Cong., 1st sess., 1951, H. Rpt. 586, p. 9.

thetic, and narrow presentation of the issues, combined with the Supreme Court's refusal to grant *certiorari* left a growing class of single taxpayers feeling slighted and abused. A new constituency sprang up seemingly overnight. Groups with names like War Singles (Not War Widows), Single Persons Tax Reform, Single People United, Single Persons for Tax Equality Association, and Committee for Single Taxpayers, began lobbying for relief from the singles penalty. In 1962 Senator Eugene McCarthy introduced the first bill (S. 35) to give tax relief to certain categories of single people, the so-called "working-girls bill," which would have extended the head-of-household category to all persons thirty-five years of age, or over, apparently for no logical reason other than the fact that these people felt aggrieved and had mounted a successful campaign to attract a champion. To a certain amount of ridicule on the floor, he reintroduced the same bill in each succeeding Congress, that is, the eighty-eighth, eighty-ninth, and ninetieth. By the Ninety-first Congress the issue had become an important one, and the House Committee on Ways and Means took action on it in the Tax Reform Act of 1969 (House Report 13270, 1969).

The sections of the House bill dealing with issues of concern to single taxpayers attempted to (1) extend the head-of-household tax rate to all single persons thirty-five years and older and to widows and widowers regardless of age, and (2) extend for an unlimited period the joint-return privilege (which had already been granted for a two-year period) to a surviving spouse maintaining a home for a dependent child. It was the Treasury Department's recommendation to the Senate Committee on Finance that called for the elimination of the second proposal and substitution of a different tax schedule applicable to singles that was eventually enacted. The new rate schedule, which applied to all single taxpayers regardless of age, was structured so that no one paid over 20 percent more than the amount of tax due from a married couple with the same taxable income (Senate Prints, 1969, pp. 126–127). The technique for implementing this change produced the tax-rate schedule shown in table 6–5. According to the Treasury Department the new rates would be applicable as follows:

> Married persons would use the regular rate schedule by determining the tax on one-half the income in the joint return and then doubling the amount of the tax so determined, as under existing law. Single persons would use the intermediate rate schedule. It is not appropriate to eliminate the regular rate schedule and construct a new rate schedule for joint returns because married persons filing separately are not to be eligible for the intermediate rate schedule. This treatment is necessary to prevent married persons from arranging their affairs so as to have amounts of income on which, if they could separately use the intermediate rate schedule, the combined tax would be less than the amount payable on a joint return. [Senate Prints, 1969, p. 129]

Although the Tax Reform Act of 1969 was hailed as a "milestone in tax legislation" by Treasury Secretary David M. Kennedy, it has demonstrated a singular ability to please none of the people, none of the time. To many of the single taxpayers whom it set out to mollify, the act is still inequitable because it continues the so-called singles' tax. To them an injustice is still an injustice even when cut by 50 percent. Even more annoying to a much larger segment of the population is the fact that the act introduced the marriage tax into the income-tax system. Table 6–6 shows the numbers of individuals involved in each category. The marriage tax can affect all two-wage-earner families depending on the total family income and the proportions of it earned by the husband and wife. The marriage tax (also called marriage penalty or sin subsidy) is effective when two salary earners marry and lose the privilege of using the intermediate tax-rate schedule. Even though they are now entitled to income splitting, in a large number of cases their combined tax as a married couple exceeds their combined tax as a singles couple. And although the term "singles couple" sounds like a self-contradiction, it attempts to describe a social development which has had an enormous impact on American attitudes. The *singles couple*, that is, the relationship of two wage-earning, independent, self-sufficient individuals, has achieved widespread acceptance in contemporary American society. Most people have learned or are learning to cope with the problem of identifying or describing the situation of friends and relatives maintaining a conjugal relationship outside of marriage. However, many people, along with the laws of certain states, also regard the relationship as a lesser one than the legally married state. An example is Virginia which in 1978 attempted to stop a female lawyer from taking its bar exam. As she had stated in her ap-

Table 6–5

Examples of Marginal Tax Rates Established by the Tax Reform Act of 1969

Income Bracket	Regular Rate (%)	Head-of-Household Rate (%)	Intermediate Rate (%)
$1,000–1,500	15	15	15
$3,000–4,000	18	17	18
$4,000–6,000	21	19	20
$8,000–10,000	27	22	24
$14,000–16,000	37	27	30
$20,000–22,000	44	32	35
$24,000–26,000	47	36	37

Source: Technical Memorandum of Treasury Position on the Tax Reform Act of 1969 (HR 13270) presented to the Senate Committee on Finance, 91st Cong. 1st sess., p. 129.

Table 6–6

U.S. Adult Population by Marital and Labor-Force Status, 1977

	Total Millions of Individuals	Percent of Total Population
One-wage-earning couples (25.4 million couples)	50.8	45
Dual-wage-earning couples (21.9 million couples)	43.8	39
One person householders	15.5	14
One person with nonrelative(s) present	2.1	02
Total	112.2	100

Sources: U.S., Bureau of the Census, Series P-60, no. 116 (July 1978) and Series P-20, no. 324 (April 1978).

plication form that she was living with a man, she was accused of violating Virginia laws against "fornication" and "lewd and lascivious cohabitation" and, claimed Virginia's assistant attorney general, she had no right to the "certificate of good moral character" necessary to qualify her for the bar. Since cohabitation is not completely accepted by society and is illegal in states such as Virginia and North Carolina, the fact that a couple would have to pay higher taxes after marriage must be condemned not only as a disincentive to marriage but also as an incentive to commit a criminal act. This policy is an acknowledged embarrassment to the federal government.

Table 6–7 illustrates the impact of the marriage tax on families in accord with what proportion of total family income is earned by each of two wage earners within those families. One example of how the marriage tax affects different couples in different circumstances and even treats married couples differently according to how and by whom that couple's income is earned is in the case of a married couple where one spouse earns $16,000 per year and the other earns $4,000. They pay $79 more per year in taxes than two single persons each earning these amounts. Another example is a married couple where the husband and wife each earn $10,000 a year. They pay $227 more than two singles with the same income and $148 more than the couple in the previous example. The hierarchy of income tax payments for the year 1977 with respect to a taxable income of $30,000 per year is as follows:

$7,883 paid by a single person who earns $30,000;

$5,957 paid by a married couple with only one wage earner;

The same $5,957 paid by a married couple each earning $15,000; and $4,944 paid by two single individuals each earning $15,000 (Gray, 1978).

If the two singles in the last example decide to marry, they ought to be aware that it will cost them an additional $1,013 per year in taxes. This is not an insignificant yearly penalty to pay, and presumably couples earning this amount of income are tax conscious. Therefore, the fact that cohabitation has risen by 80 percent since 1970 (just prior to the first year that these new rates went into effect) would lead one to believe that tax policy may have had something to do with the fact that almost 2 million persons are now living with an unrelated person of the opposite sex. Even if tax reasons are behind the decision not to marry of only a small number of these couples, the inadvertent impact of tax policy on marriage is another example of government legislation going awry and having an unwanted, deleterious effect on benign groups of citizens.

There is also evidence that tax policy is affecting decisions concerning divorce. A case in point was described by Christine Beshar, representing the Bar Association of the City of New York, at the House Hearings of 1972: "The problem came to my attention when at a time last December a client ran into my office and said, "'I need a divorce, quick.' I said, 'I'm sorry to hear you are having problems,' She said 'Just more tax. I have been living with this man three years and then we decided to jump over the broom. We are each making $18,000 and now it is costing us $1,800 more in tax to be married'" (House Report 781-12, 1972, p. 41). More recently a couple in Endicott City, Maryland, Angela and David Boyter, admitted to obtaining three quickie divorces for the sole purpose of avoiding the marriage tax. They were involved in a court case with the Internal Revenue Service (IRS) and, if they lost, planned to remain divorced (*New York Times,* 16

Table 6–7
1976 Marriage Tax According to Selected Income Combinations

Adjusted Gross Income of Other Spouse	Adjusted Gross Income of One Spouse									
	2,000	4,000	6,000	8,000	10,000	12,000	14,000	16,000	18,000	20,000
Zero	Zero	-177[a]	-248	-319	-405	-458	-486	-625	-787	-932
2,000	54	121	91	61	-13	-40	-123	-190	-287	-328
4,000	121	229	240	222	174	92	81	79	32	-53
6,000	91	240	253	271	168	158	212	250	213	213
8,000	61	222	271	224	193	248	352	410	448	443
10,000	-13	174	168	193	227	332	446	579	622	685
12,000	-40	92	158	248	332	447	636	774	885	960
14,000	-123	81	212	352	446	636	830	1,036	1,159	1,235
16,000	-190	79	260	410	579	774	1,036	1,254	1,428	1,563
18,000	-287	32	223	448	622	885	1,159	1,428	1,611	1,797
20,000	-382	-53	213	443	685	960	1,285	1,563	1,797	1,992

Source: *Mapes and Bryson* v. *The United States*, U.S. Court of Claims, no. 403–77, Decided 17 May 1978.

Note: All calculations assume that each taxpayer elects the standard deduction. Computations do not include the 1976 General Tax Credit.

[a] A minus sign indicates a tax reduction in that particular instance.

October 1979). Such extreme behavior attests to the significance that public policy can have when it affects individuals' pocketbooks.

The Treasury Department in the Nixon administration regarded the marriage tax with equanimity as exemplified in the statement made before the House Committee on Ways and Means by Edwin S. Cohen: "Both ends of a seesaw cannot be up at the same time. Any rule that is selected will, in some cases, seem to penalize single persons. All we can hope for is a reasonable compromise. . . . If there is a 'penalty' on marriage, it occurs when two people having substantial separate income marry to maintain a single household, thus reducing their total living expenses and increasing their total ability to pay taxes" (House Report 781-12, 1972, pp. 79-80). Mr. Cohen did not deal with the situation of the singles couple who has already reduced living expenses prior to marriage and to whom the full burden of this tax actually applies if the couple is considering marriage. While Mr. Cohen can stoically accept this situation, the estimated 20 to 28 percent of married couples, that is, 6 to 9 million couples, who might have been affected by the penalty in 1969 (a number which has grown each year as the labor-force participation of married women has gone up), are not that keen about being singled out to permanently ride the down side of the seesaw. Although the tax-rate difference has received the most attention, other inequities in regard to the application of allowable deductions have also been noted. Mr. Cohen also did not seem perturbed by other inequities in the tax structure that he himself brought out in his testimony. He referred to the fact that the $2,000 maximum standard deduction could be used by a married couple up to the $13,333 income level, but an unmarried couple could apply two standard deductions of $4,000 up to the $26,000 income level (House Report 781-12, 1972, p. 89). This inequity has been reduced somewhat by the zero bracket amounts, which replace the standard deduction and presently allow $3,200 on a joint return and $2,200 on a single or unmarried head-of-household, with $1,600 for a married person filing separately. (See chapter 7 for further treatment of this point.)

Britten D. Richards, exdirector of the National Association of Married Working Couples, claims that there were at least thirty-three sections of the Internal Revenue Code of 1969 in which the maximum allowable deduction for a married couple is one-half that allowed a singles couple. Listed among the categories are capital gains and losses, moving expenses, investments credits, and depreciation (Richards, 1971).

Therefore, in addition to paying a specific annual sum of money to the government over and above what they had been previously paying, the couple who has decided to legalize a relationship, which has been accepted to a large extent by their community, may also lose the benefits of deductions protecting other parts of their income or estate. As in the case of income splitting, the benefits or penalties vary in accord with the amounts of income involved and with the earnings ratio maintained between the spouses. But as women achieve wage parity in the labor force, it will cost them more under the present tax system to maintain a marriage with a male wage-earning peer than to live with him in single-couplehood. And as a substantial and growing number of the 47 million husband-wife headed families in the United States fit this description, it is a very significant number of people who are involved in a socially significant relationship.

7 Tax Policy and the Working Woman

In the twenty-year period from 1956 to 1976, the labor-force participation of married women doubled, rising from 11 million to 22 million. Yet this dramatic development has not caused great outcries from society's traditional monitors nor has it greatly puzzled society's social scientists. The general acceptance of a quiet revolution in terms of women's traditional role as homemaker has been brought about by the widely accepted fact that wives are working at paid jobs out of economic necessity. The sizable participation of wives and mothers on the labor force can be accounted for to a large extent by looking at the economic picture. In a recent publication of the labor department the years 1961 to 1976 have been singled out as a period of postwar slowdown in real wages as depicted in table 5-1. Beginning in this same period women's labor-force participation rates began to climb significantly in all categories (see table 4-1). The five-year period from 1966 to 1971 yielded a doubling in the growth rate measuring the entrance of married females to the labor force. The rate of entry rose from an average 2 percent per year to 4 percent per year during those five years. During the entire ten-year period from 1966 to 1976, the total number of married women wage earners rose by 7 million.

Put simply in terms of income figures, the reason why so many married females are working becomes even more clear-cut. In 1976 the median family income for a two-wage-earner family was $18,731. This dropped to $13,931 in families where the wife was not on the labor force (U.S., Bureau of the Census, 1977). According to the Department of Labor it cost $16,236 a year to maintain a family of four at the middle standard of living in 1976 (U.S., Department of Labor, News Bureau, 1977). This figure rose to $17,106 for 1977. What these figures indicate is that the participation of wives and mothers on the labor force is keeping a large portion of Americans in the middle class. The American standard of living would be significantly reduced if every wife decided to leave the workforce and every family had to depend on the wages of only one provider. The American economy would also be completely disrupted inasmuch as the 6 million unemployed males age sixteen and over who were available in 1979 could not begin to make up for the loss of close to 25 million employed wives.

Although the significance of the contribution to a family's material well-being of a working wife is gradually being recognized by a society, many of the laws have not caught up with the actual situation. To a certain extent the reason for this is that the federal tax system has undergone little revision since the Tax Reform Act of 1969. "Payroll taxes have been increased, income taxes have been reduced, and the investment tax credit has been suspended, reinstated, and then increased. But the basic structure of the income and payroll taxes, which now account for over 90 percent of federal tax revenue, has not been altered" (Break and Pechman, 1975, p. vii). Therefore, the present tax system at the beginning of the 1980s is attempting to deal equitably with the major tax-paying groups of the mid- to late 1960s. During this period employed wives were just beginning to increase their labor-force participation rate from approximately 35 percent in 1966 to 45 percent in 1978. In 1969, when Congress completed its last general tax overhaul, the special tax problems of employed wives were ignored in favor of relieving the problems of more vocal groups with long-standing grievances against the tax system. Because of this, there is a gap in the present tax laws that is penalizing women and their families in a variety of ways.

The most obvious tax inequity striking working wives is that the federal government demands a higher income-tax payment from a dual-income married couple than it does from two single persons earning the same combined income. The term *dual-income* family or married couple is an attempt to define families described as those "where both spouses have 'significant' income (significant is generally 20 percent or more of the couple's total income) . . ." (see *Johnson* v. *U.S.* for examples of the awkwardness caused to the courts because no adequate term exists that describes these particular couples).

The marriage tax paid by Americans ranges from a few dollars to thousands of dollars per year, every year. These penalties are paid by employed persons who choose marriage. Furthermore, the highest penalties in each income range are paid when the salary of the two individuals is almost equal. So as women's wages rise it will cost them more to maintain a marriage with a man earning an equivalent salary than simply to cohabit with him. Their other option would be to marry men with insignificant earnings and take advantage of the fact that the system was structured with only one wage earner in a family in mind. So instead of viewing the marriage tax as a sin subsidy it could also be termed a "househusband subsidy" for career women who are so minded. It is apparent that in 1969 the men who drafted the tax laws had not grasped, or were not in a position to determine, the full significance of the large-scale entrance of wives into the labor force. When they assumed that they were providing supports for families, the only families that they had in mind were those that fit the idealized view of the American Family or families like their own. No attention was given to the fact that the group whose interests were being ignored would eventually constitute almost half of all intact American families. Although most of these families are presently only minimally affected by the marriage tax because of the disparity that exists between incomes earned by husbands as opposed to that earned by wives, as this disparity narrows this ignored constituency will grow and feel even more put upon.

It has been estimated that in 1974 about 13 million couples, 24 percent of all American families, paid the marriage tax to the tune of an additional $1.9 billion (*Mapes and Bryson* v. *U.S.,* September 1978, p. 6). The Joint Tax Committee estimated that ending the marriage tax would cost $4.8 billion in 1979, indicating how rapidly this problem has grown in scope. The prime age labor force (the twenty-five to fifty-four age group) of women is projected to grow at over 2 percent per year until 1990 (U.S., Department of Labor, New Labor Force Projections, 1977). If the marriage tax is not eliminated from the tax code these women and their families will feel unjustly penalized because, in effect, the IRS is saying that women have to pay extra taxes for the right to work while maintaining a marriage. The sheer ridiculousness of this fact is only topped by the realization that this situation has been allowed to prevail for over a decade.

Working wives are being penalized in other ways by the tax structure. The progressive tax rate, combined with women's present secondary status in terms of dollar earnings, has had a dampening effect on women earners and their families. This dampening effect is produced by the fact that all of the income reported on a joint return is combined for purposes of taxation rather than taxed according to the individual rates that apply to the earner. Therefore, each dollar earned by secondary workers in the family is taxed at that family's marginal or highest tax rate. As males still tend to be the primary earners in the majority of families, their income sets the family's marginal tax rate. So long as women continue to work part-time or remain grouped in low paying job categories, their income will normally be the secondary one. If the wife of a man earning $20,000 earned $7,000 on her own, the couple would have to pay about 30 percent of her income in federal income taxes. This rate would be close to double the one she would be liable for if she were taxed as an individual. The rate would rise to about 40 percent if her husband earned $30,000 a year. The net impact of these tax realities is very discouraging for the individual wage earner and her family regardless of the total family income (table 7-1). Every family in these categories is forced to ponder seriously what it means for them to have the female of the household, or rather the second earner in the household, have a career outside of the home. Again, this appears to be an inadvertent intrusion by the federal government into the right of a family to choose its own life style and the right of women to be wage earners and combine careers with family life. Furthermore after paying such high rates for this additional income, this same family is not allowed to deduct the costs of maintaining a second job. Under present tax law, if a taxpayer holds two jobs,

Table 7-1

1977 Income-Tax Rates for Incomes up to \$52,200 (Married Individuals Filing Joint Returns)

If the taxable income is:	The tax is:
Not over \$3,200	No tax
Over \$3,200 but not over \$4,200	14% of the excess over \$3,200
Over \$4,200 but not over \$5,200	\$140 plus 15% of excess over \$4,200
Over \$5,200 but not over \$6,200	\$290 plus 16% of excess over \$5,200
Over \$6,200 but not over \$7,200	\$450 plus 17% of excess over \$6,200
Over \$7,200 but not over \$11,200	\$620 plus 19% of excess over \$7,200
Over \$11,200 but not over \$15,200	\$1,380 plus 22% of excess over \$11,200
Over \$15,200 but not over \$19,200	\$2,260 plus 25% of excess over \$15,200
Over \$19,200 but not over \$23,200	\$3,260 plus 28% of excess over \$19,200
Over \$23,200 but not over \$27,200	\$4,380 plus 32% of excess over \$23,200
Over \$27,200 but not over \$31,200	\$5,660 plus 36% of excess over \$27,200
Over \$31,200 but not over \$35,200	\$7,100 plus 39% of excess over \$31,200
Over \$35,200 but not over \$39,200	\$8,660 plus 42% of excess over \$35,200
Over \$39,200 but not over \$43,200	\$10,340 plus 45% of excess over \$39,200
Over \$43,200 but not over \$47,200	\$12,140 plus 48% of excess over \$43,200
Over \$47,200 but not over \$55,200	\$14,060 plus 50% of excess over \$47,200

Source: Internal Revenue Service, P.L. 95-30, The Tax Reduction and Simplification Act of 1977.

the costs of traveling to and from that second job and all meals eaten away from home in the performance of that job would normally be tax deductible. But if it is the spouse in the family who is holding down that second job, these expenses are not tax deductible. Then the question is: "What difference does it make who holds the second job in the family as long as expenses are incurred to maintain it and that family is paying the marginal tax rate for that wage?" All this regulation accomplishes is to make it more economical for males to work two jobs and for females to stay home.

But even more inequitable is the fact that families in which both parents work have to bear the additional strain of having no one home to provide the care and upkeep that these families need. Therefore, two-wage-earner families are paying an extra penalty in that their taxes are as high as the one-wage-earner family's taxes and they do not have the services of an adult to tend to their homelife. While this situation seems to be more a matter of choice in families where a husband earns \$15,000 or \$20,000 per year, what about the families where the husband's income is \$10,000 or less. These families account for almost half the total number of employed wives. How much choice do they actually have? In their cases, when they attempt to achieve a decent living standard for themselves and their families they find the value of their income eroded by a succession of small burdens imposed on them by the federal government. And since the U.S. government has taken no overt position in opposition to their employment, these impositions seem thoughtless and cruel.

In terms of household responsibilities, the options normally open to families with employed wives are (1) to share out the domestic and childcare duties between the couple (even though they may already feel overworked), (2) to pay for domestic service, or (3) to have the secondary earner drop out of the labor force and thereby lower the family's standard of living. The choice most often opted for is that of combining housework with wage earning, and all studies show that it is the employed wife who shoulders the larger share of these responsibilities even when she works as many hours as the male of the household. A 1967–1968 study of employed wives in Syracuse, New York, found that they spent thirty-four hours per week on household chores. This represents 60 percent of the time spent on these tasks by nonemployed wives and represents almost five hours a day of household work (Chapman, 1976, p. 45). (Chapter 15 has details of a survey conducted in Mecklenburg County, North Carolina.) Women who work too hard while trying to combine wage earning and homemaking are commonly acknowledged American phenomena. Unfortunately little thought has been given to finding ways of alleviating this problem, and the tax system seems to encourage overwork by limiting deductions available to families with two wage earners. While recent liberalizations in the law allow most parents to claim deductions for the amount they spend on childcare, a step in the right direction, no such option is available for paid household help.

Working wives are also penalized in terms of their contributions and benefits from the social-security system. The discriminatory practices built into the payroll tax take many forms and affect many women differently according to circumstances. All payments into the system are based on individual earnings, although benefits are predicated on a per-family basis. This means that in one-earner families once the taxable base has been passed, that family pays nothing further into the system. In 1978 the salary subject to tax was $17,700, and the maximum tax was $1,071 for a wage-earner and $1,434 for a self-employed person. But two-earner families continue to pay, and pay, to a maximum of double these amounts when each earner reaches the maximum taxable base. Although the two-earner family may acquire some additional disability and survivors' benefits from the second wage contributions, these benefits are normally not prorated to the value of the additional contributions and often are never forthcoming. In fact, it is single men and women, unmarried heads-of-households, and employed wives and their families who are all working to subsidize the one-wage-earner family. It is these families alone who are entitled to draw benefits for two people while only paying for one person.

In addition, wives who choose part-time employment may find themselves out in the cold if they are divorced before the marriage has lasted for ten years. (Up until December of 1978, only twenty-year marriages qualified.) These divorced women have no claim on the benefits the couple accrued during the course of their marriage and are only entitled to their own personal benefits. Her contributions to the maintenance of a home count for nothing.

She is still better off than a homemaker who loses all of her coverage when divorced. And it is the divorced homemaker who best exemplifies the tragic inequities built into the social-security system. It is presumably a family-oriented, humanitarian system, but it only works properly when families conform to the old pattern; it only protects wives lucky enough to maintain a marriage until they have reached the age of sixty-two. Young widows, single people, divorced women, and employed wives all have much to complain about. That these complaints are not falling on deaf ears is attested by a statement made on 15 February 1979 from the office of Joseph A. Califano, then secretary of Health, Education, and Welfare. Califano takes issue with many of the inequities in a report entitled "Social Security and the Changing Roles of Men and Women" prepared by the Social Security Administration. The text of Califano's statement is appendix 9D and it contains information on present problems inherent in the Social Security system and presents two proposed plans for reform. The two plans that have been sent to Congress are entitled the Earnings Sharing plan and the Two-Tier Benefit Structure. The Earnings Sharing plan sets up a structure in which couples would share Social Security credits for their earnings, thereby granting credit for the contribution of an employed wife and sharing out the loss that would normally be borne solely by a divorced female by entitling her to one-half the credits accumulated by the couple during the marriage. The major feminist organizations have come out in favor of this plan. The Two-Tier Benefit Structure is a more far-ranging program that would incorporate concepts of minimal benefits due to all citizens depending on need into the overall structure of the Social Security administration. These concepts have been acknowledged in Western European nations but have yet to gain wide support in the United States. The debate on this issue bears close watching as it is likely to result in policy decisions that will have an impact on every American.

8 Challenging the System: Legislative Approaches to Tax Reform

The Tax Reform Act of 1969 left so many issues unresolved and so many groups of taxpayers dissatisfied that the need for tax reform quickly resurfaced as a vital and pressing concern. During the General Tax Reform Hearings before the House Ways and Means Committee that began in 1973, those testifying on the issue of tax equity regardless of marital status were mainly concerned with single Americans. Representatives of groups who had worked for the singles' cause in the sixties appeared at the hearings to indicate that they continued to regard the tax structure as inequitable. Miss Vivian Kellems of East Haddam, Connecticut, who testified at length in the tax hearings of 1969, reappeared to assure the Congress that she was not getting "discouraged" and that having "spent four years" of her life on the quest for equity for singles she planned to continue her activities for a good long time as she was "only seventy-seven years old" (House Document 781-3, 1973, pp. 2946–2949). One group, however, did appear to give testimony specifically on the impact of the marriage tax. Married Americans for Tax Equity, represented by its president, Anita Murray, delivered testimony that pointed out that when a similar tax structure "was tried in Sweden, tax divorces became so popular, and so respectable, that the law was finally changed to eliminate tax penalties for marriage" (House Document 781-3, 1973, pp. 2981–2982).

The outcomes of these hearings and the hearings that followed in reference to the specific needs of dual-income couples were the implementation of more liberalized policies in regard to deductions for childcare expenditures and a more equitable standard allowable deduction. The liberalized childcare deduction provided that "[u]nder the present provision, married couples with both working full-time and single persons may deduct up to $200 a month for the care of one child, $300 a month for two children, and $400 a month for three or more children. The deduction is reduced by fifty cents for each dollar of adjusted gross income above $35,000 a year. The deduction, which was used on 1,569,000 returns in 1972, amounted to only $1.1 billion and probably had a tax value of $275 million" (Break and Pechman, 1975, p. 35). Therefore, in 1972, taxpayers spent $1.1 billion on childcare and saved $275 million in taxes they would have been liable for if they had spent that money in other ways. Currently, the childcare tax credit is equal to 20 percent of the first $2,000 of childcare costs to a maximum of $400 for the first child under age fifteen. For two or more children under that age the allowable credit is 20 percent of the earned income of the spouse with the smaller earned income to a maximum of $800. There are additional allocations made for nonworking spouses who are full-time students and handicapped persons who cannot meet the work-eligibility requirement. The change in the maximum standard allowable deduction, section 141 of the Internal Revenue Code, had the effect of reducing the dollar difference between the deduction allowed to a singles couple and that granted to a married couple by $800. The difference went from $2,000 in 1976 to $1,200 in 1977 (table 8-1).

Offsetting the impact of the change in the maximum allowable standard deduction were the general tax credits allowed in 1975, 1976, and 1977, section 42 of the Internal Revenue Code. These credits had the effect of adding another inequity to the tax system because of the way they affected the difference in the amount of taxes paid by dual-income couples and singles couples. The reason is that the tax credit is structured so that a married couple with an income of $9,000 or more can only claim a maximum $180 credit on their taxes. The singles couple in the same financial situation can claim two such deductions for a total credit of $360. In the example given in table 8-2 the net result of the tax credit on these particular couples is a difference of an additional $180 per year marriage tax paid by the married couple. (The current tax bill has eliminated this credit and in its stead has raised the exemption per dependent from $750 to $1,000. While this will have the effect of eliminating this aspect of the marriage tax, any bill drafted with the intention of completely removing the marriage tax ought to cover any possible future reinstitution of a tax credit that would affect married couples unequitably.)

In the Ninety-fourth Congress (1975 and 1976) and again in the Ninety-fifth Congress (1977 and 1978), Congresswoman Millicent Fenwick of New Jersey introduced bills with the intention of correcting the inequities of the marriage tax. House Report 11270, introduced 3 March 1977, sought to amend the Internal Revenue Code of 1954 by giving married couples the options of computing their taxes on the basis of either the married (joint) rate or the single rate (see appendix 9C for the full text of this bill). By the provisions of this bill, those couples who are presently subject to the marriage tax would be allowed to file as single individuals and, by doing so, eliminate the marriage tax. It would not be in the interest of one-wage couples or couples whose second income is insignificant to choose this option since community-property laws are specifically overridden in this act. The broad impact of the Fenwick Bill would be the establishment of two classes of married persons; that is, married persons would henceforth be subjected to two different tax-rate tables. Up until 1977 the position of the IRS was that for purposes of taxation all married individuals belonged together as a class. According to the Office of Tax Analysis, one of the four

Table 8-1

Standard Allowable Deduction for Single and Married Persons before and after the Tax Reduction and Simplification Act of 1977

	Maximum Deduction for Single Person	Maximum Deduction Married (Joint Return)	
Before			
Taxpayer 1	$2,400	$2,800	
Taxpayer 2	$2,400		
Total	$4,800	$2,800	
Difference in standard deduction between singles couple and married couple			$2,000
After			
Taxpayer 1	$2,200	$3,200	
Taxpayer 2	$2,200		
Total	$4,400	$3,200	
Difference in standard deduction between singles couple and married couple			$1,200

Source: Computed from *IRS 1977 Instructions for Form 1040.*

Table 8-2

A Comparison of Marriage Tax Paid by a Dual-Income Family Earning $10,000 with That Paid by a Singles Couple, Each Earning $5,000, before and after the Application of Income-Tax Credit (1977 Taxable Year)

	Dual-Income Couple	Singles Couple		Marriage Tax
Taxable income	$10,000	$5,000 +	$5,000	
Tax liability	$765	$288	$288	
Total tax liability	$765	$566		
Marriage tax—pre-tax credit				$199
Less maximum allowable tax credit − $180	−$180	−$180	−$180	
Total tax liability	$585	$206		
Marriage tax—post-tax credit				$379

Source: Computed from *IRS 1977 Instructions for Form 1040.*

principles of taxation presently accepted in the United States is that there should be no distinction among married couples (see appendix 9A). But in attempting to discern a "direction for the future" for tax policy the Office of Tax Analysis points out:

> The marriage penalty is one of the most widely discussed weaknesses in our income tax. Nobody defends it on its merits. Those few who can defend it at all, do so by emphasizing the three principles . . . that must compete with the marriage penalty principle. But opposition to the marriage penalty is now so widespread that one of the competing principles must be overturned, and it seems clear that it must be the second principle: that is, there must be some distinction between one-earner and two-earner married couples.

> This is the intent of every bill introduced in Congress recently to reduce or eliminate the marriage penalty and it is the course taken by almost every other major democratic nation that has an income tax [see appendix 9A].

Therefore, in terms of the IRS, it is likely that the way has been cleared for passage of House Report 11270 or some bill embodying its provisions, if Congress so chooses. However, there are certain problems inherent in House Report 11270 that cannot be overlooked in spite of the fact that the bill is well intended and attempts to address a pressing social need—that of finally eliminating the marriage tax.

The basic problem with the Fenwick Bill is that for tax purposes it would divide those married couples who would be eligible to file under it into two single individuals. These individuals would then have to maintain separate records or two sets of records to support their claims for deductions. And while there are existing IRS guidelines for married couples filing singly to help these individuals work out the resultant tax complications, it is not likely that this extra burden would be greeted with pleasure by the couples to whom it would apply. Even less enthusiastic would be the IRS, which would have to process perhaps as many as 20 million doubled tax returns every year. Some of these returns, particularly those that itemize deductions and deduct childcare expenses, would be likely to face extra audits. This would be a prospect neither the IRS nor the American taxpayer would relish.

Aside from the doubled labor that would be required of millions of persons, an additional problem introduced by the Fenwick Bill is the specter of reviving the whole issue of income splitting, presumably laid to rest in 1948. The bill, as presently worded, gives all married couples the option of choosing to file as individuals but prohibits those couples who do so from splitting their income. The law achieves this by disregarding community-property laws and in effect disallowing income splitting. This prohibition is necessary because a one-income couple could achieve the tax advantage meant only for dual-income couples and restore the wide (pre-1969) tax liability gap between married persons and single persons simply by applying the single rate to an income split in half. Then almost all married citizens would pay lower taxes. Unfortunately, this could lead us back full circle to pre-1948. Little noted has been the fact that income splitting was abrogated de facto but not de jure by the Tax Reform Act of 1969. As the singles rate was lowered so that no single person paid more than 20 percent higher taxes than a married couple with the same income, married couples could make the claim that they have been denied the right granted them in 1948 of splitting their income in half for purposes of taxation. While it is true that the Fenwick Bill may attempt to prohibit income splitting by legislative fiat abrogating community-property laws for purposes of taxation, it is also equally true that there are no guarantees that this ban would not be overturned in the courts. A substantial body of precedent has been set establishing the rights of income splitting in community-property states, and these precedents could be dragged out of the judicial storage bin once again. There is no doubt that if the bill passes, one-income families will begin decrying a new marriage tax, and new challengers will emerge attempting to topple a new tax inequity. Their claim would point to the fact that some married couples have access to lower rates while their access to such rates is blocked. They would not only be able to bring up all of the community-property aspects of the matter but all of the arguments that once upheld the right of married couples to a lower tax rate than single persons.

The fundamental reason House Report 11270 is so vulnerable to challenge by one-income married couples is that it sets up two classes of married persons while attempting to sidestep the basic issue of why it is necessary to divide married taxpayers into two groups. By avoiding this issue and yet using this tactic the bill leaves itself open to a series of strong challenges. It is therefore apparent that any attempt to alleviate the problem of the marriage tax by dividing married persons into two categories ought to be grounded in the larger realities of balancing the tax burdens of all classifications of taxpayers, not just those of a particular class. When a rational basis is established for determining how taxpayers ought to be grouped for tax purposes, the differences between one-income couples and dual-income couples could then be analyzed and established. It is true that dual-income families are different in many ways from one-wage-earner families, however, this difference is predicated on more than just the payment of a marriage tax. Therefore, if married taxpayers are to be separated into two classes, the boundaries ought to be drawn according to the specifics that differentiate them. It is these differences that ought to form the basis on which the tax liabilities of distinct groups of taxpayers must be predicated. In this particular case it would require the computation of allowable deductions to offset the additional work-related expenses demanded of a family maintaining two jobs plus the granting of deductions for the calculated dollar values equivalent to additional expenses incurred to maintain this status, such as the costs of hiring household help; higher clothing bills necessitated by the maintenance of a suitable wardrobe for the second earner; and the higher costs of family meals because of greater reliance on convenience foods and restaurant meals. All of these categories of expenses ought to be examined before any determinations are made concerning the differing tax liabilities of these two groups of taxpayers.

According to tax specialists at the Brookings Institute: "It is obviously impossible to calculate the exact amount by which the tax income of the two-earner couple is overstated as compared with that of the one-earner couple" (Break and Pechman, 1975, p. 35). Even so, this limitation need not be viewed as an impossible obstacle to overcome but merely another constraint on the exactitude that would be expected or required of such calculations. The Internal Revenue Code includes a number of such calculated approximations (the standard allowable deduction is the most obvious) which are arrived at by using averaging techniques. A similar method could be used to arrive at a standard deduction allowable for families maintaining two heads-of-household on the workforce. This would be the positive approach to correct an inequity described by Break and Pechman from the negative point of view that the one-income couple is getting more than it should. "Two-earner couples are treated unfairly under income splitting, not because a system based on the combined income of married couples is unfair, but because the taxable income of the one-earner couple is understated in that it does not include the value of services provided by the spouse who stays at home" (Break and Pechman, 1975, p. 35). It is also a matter of reducing taxes on the dual-income couple rather than raising the tax base of the one-income couple. Given these limitations, even if an attempt were made to approximate the most important differences between these two classes of married couples, it is apparent that any such determination and any changes that implement such a basic change in the tax structure ought to be analyzed minutely not only in terms of married taxpayers but of the entire system. It has long been acknowledged by tax experts that the system is in need of basic reform, a complete rethinking, and possibly a completely new foundation.

> Inequities in Federal income taxation have been the center of controversy and the subject of public concern for nearly six decades.
>
> Dissatisfaction with our Federal tax structure has continued in spite of periodic episodes of tax reform legislation. The public questions the soundness and fairness of our revenue system. While such doubts are directed primarily at the individual income tax because of its direct and almost daily impingement upon the livelihood and financial planning of the great majority of Americans, they have been extended to the corporation income tax and the estate and gift taxes. [Fund for Public Policy Research, 1973, p. 3]

Although the mood favoring reform or restructuring is general, a cautious, careful approach to the entire question of tax reform is called for.

What changes, if any, will be made in the U.S. tax system will depend largely on the persuasiveness of those presenting the case for the reform. For if it does not serve the general welfare, tax reform is a costly kind of zero-sum game. It is zero-sum because pure tax reform, by definition, generates monetary gains to some taxpayers by imposing monetary losses of equal size on others. It is costly because no tax reform plan can be developed without much time and effort; moreover, discussion of who should gain and who should lose often creates divisive ill-will that any society would be better off without. If tax reform is no more than a blatant power struggle of conflicting special interests, in other words, it will not rate high on the agenda of urgent public policy issues. That tax reform will produce larger gains than losses and is therefore a positive-sum game well worth playing is the firm belief of most fiscal economists. Past failures in the tax reform movement may well be due mainly to the experts' lack of success in conveying this message to the general public.

The key to action on tax reform, then, is both a broader public agreement on the proper distributional, or equity, goals of society and a deeper public understanding of the contributions that a better tax system can make to the achievement of the best and most efficient use of the society's available resources. Bad taxes may counteract many of the intended good effects of government economic policies. Good taxes, in contrast, provide the lubrication essential to the smooth pursuance of the society's economic priorities. [Break and Pechman, 1975, pp. 15–16]

But does all of this mean that partial reforms are out of the question, that the marriage tax per se cannot be eliminated until the entire tax structure has been overhauled? Absolutely not. However, it is clear that any attempt to perform this as minor surgery ought to be strictly local and as painless as possible. There are a number of approaches that could accomplish this by using the standard tax reform methods of allowable deductions and tax credits. The solution I propose is that of using a unique form of tax credit. This credit, which I call a "variable tax credit," would try to correct the imbalance that presently exists between the dual-income married couple and the singles couple while leaving the present tax system intact until large-scale reform can be attempted. The implementation of such an allowance would be computed on the basis of the present marriage tax plus any other inequities caused by tax credits and deductions existing in the system. All dual-income families would be entitled to a variable tax credit sufficient to bring their taxes down to the level they would normally be liable for if they were a singles couple. The variable tax credit would also be identified for what it is, namely an attempt to alleviate a tax imbalance solely affecting dual-income couples. The method of computation would differ from the normally accepted method used by the IRS of determining the size of a lump-sum tax credit by fixing a dollar amount to be returned to the taxpayer and multiplying that amount by the lowest tax rate, namely 14 percent. The usual method would not work in eliminating the marriage tax since the amount of the penalty varies in accord with the income split of each particular couple. Therefore, a variable of individualized tax credit is made necessary. A sample table has been computed (table 8-3). It is based on adding $180 (the maximum tax credit presently not granted to married couples) to the marriage penalty as computed in table 8-2. This amount constitutes the full marriage penalty paid by dual-income families prior to 1979, with the exception of the inequity caused by differential application of the standard allowable deduction.

All families entitled to use the variable tax credit would do so after they have computed their gross taxable incomes for the year, subtracted their deductions and exemptions, arrived at their net taxable incomes, and used the married (joint) tax rate to determine their taxes. The variable tax credit would be the next to the last computation which, while nominally leaving dual-income families in the class with their fellow married taxpayers, would completely eliminate the extra amount they pay in taxes over and above that paid by similarly situated singles couples.

As is apparent from table 8-3, no correction has been attempted for the present $1,200 inequity resulting from the difference in the maximum standard allowable deduction. The reason for this omission is that not all couples will elect to use the standard deduction. Therefore, rather than compute separate variable tax credit tables allowing for these variations, I have opted to use table 8-3 as an illustrative but inexact example of how a variable-tax-credit table might be devised. It would be up to the IRS to compute the differences that would occur among a variety of cases and arrive at a percentage figure or figures that would represent an acceptable compromise between the extremes.

A further compromise made necessary by using a variable tax credit concerns allowable deductions, such as, employee business expenses, charitable contributions, and depreciation. While individuals using the single taxpayers rate would deduct these costs and expenses from the appropriate income, that is, from the income of the individual bearing the expense or loss, married couples filing jointly must subtract these deductions from their joint earnings. Therefore, in order to compute the exact marriage tax each couple would be paying over and above the tax they would be paying as a singles couple, it would be necessary to know which deduction is being applied to which income. The only way this could be achieved is to have the married couple each subtract their individually allowable tax deductions from their individual incomes to arrive at their individual net taxable income. This would be sheer nonsense since it would require that dual-income couples first fill out two individual returns and then a third, joint return. It is obvious that a workable compromise is called for in order to avoid this problem. The premise for such a compromise would be to take it as a given that half of all deductions claimed by the couple be applied to the

Table 8–3
Hypothetical Tax Credit Table (Variable Tax Credit) Computed for a Selected Number of Dual-Income Families

Adjusted Gross Income of Other Spouse	Adjusted Gross Income of One Spouse				
	6,000	8,000	10,000	12,000	14,000
6,000	443	451	348	338	392
8,000	451	404	373	428	532
10,000	348	373	407	512	626
12,000	338	428	512	627	816
14,000	392	532	626	816	1010

Source: Computation based on table 6–7 (1976 Marriage Tax According to Selected Income Combinations) plus addition of $180 to each figure equaling the tax credit that singles couples receive and to which dual-income couples are not presently entitled.

income of one spouse, and the other half to the income of the other spouse. Thus before referring to the variable-tax-credit table, the couple would subtract one-half of their total allowable deductions from each of their two incomes. Then they would use these income figures to find the dollar amount of the variable tax credit to which they would be entitled according to the tax-credit table.

Considering the inexactitudes of these compromises and the fact that use of the variable tax credit would result in a more complicated tax form directly counter to the current trend for simpler, more comprehensive tax forms, what rationale can be offered to support this method of eliminating the marriage tax over the apparently simpler, more direct one employed in the Fenwick Bill? I am convinced that implementation of House Report 11270 would reopen legal issues vis-à-vis income splitting that are better left closed. The thought of asking the courts to reexamine the whole question of property and income in terms of common law and community-property law is a worrisome one. Secondly, the burden of filing a more complicated tax form is certainly preferable to the burden of filing two tax forms or a doubled tax form. Finally, it appears to be time to return to a serious attempt to devise an equitable tax system. Recent attempts at tax reform reflect the weakness that has developed in the political process, making it vulnerable to pressure from single-issue lobbying groups. The Fenwick approach is an example of this kind of reflex-response syndrome that has taken over the political process and toppled the recognition that the overall aim of tax policy should be to achieve as much equity as possible. The bill thwarts this aim by tampering with the underlying structure of the system without thinking through what its impact will be on taxpayers in general. No balance is possible as long as pressure groups are allowed to eliminate their problems by shifting them to someone else. A large share of the blame for what has happened to tax policy must be placed on the shoulders of the House Ways and Means Committee. Its hearings have degenerated into horse-trading sessions with no one taking the responsibilities for monitoring the whole system and maintaining proper balance. We cannot horse trade our way to equitable tax policy. Until vision returns to the process, all attempts to relieve pressure on one group or another should be based on a fix-it approach. It is long past the time for fumbling corrections but any fumbling correction proposed should be open about what it is and should shun any attempt to tamper with tax theory in a superficial way.

The mood of the country since 1978 has been pro tax reform. The passage of Proposition 13 in California has been heralded everywhere as a tax revolt. Beyond sweeping tax cuts, public sentiment has also begun to focus on a tax-remedy approach to the economic malaise presently afflicting the nation. The tax system, and particularly the heavy capital gains tax (also approved in the Tax Reform Act of 1969) have come under fire for discouraging business investment and the flight of venture capital. The anemic productivity gains made in this country in recent years, the frightening growth of inflation, and the downturn in the growth of real and discretionary income have all been labeled symptoms of the present tax system. All of the current gloom about taxation certainly indicates a growing awareness and concern about the tax structure on the part of the American public. Jimmy Carter's "disgrace to the human race" is due for an upheaval and will no doubt be subjected to some rude shocks in the coming years. But where does the marriage tax fit into the picture? When the general outlook for the future is so foreboding, refined questions of equity and fairness seem almost fussy and overwrought. When the entire nation stands poised, awaiting the great reform that will save the economic system, the small voice in the rear crying out "fair play for me" is not bound to attract much interest.

Furthermore, considering the millions of taxpayers currently being penalized by the marriage tax, and the numbers of news stories that have featured it, that voice is surprisingly small, timid, and weak. Perhaps it is because it is so tired from overwork, from putting in a full day at the office or plant and rushing home to cook, clean, help the children with their homework, do the shopping, and get all of the other chores done that have been postponed from that day and from previous, overcrowded days. It would not be too exaggerated to say that the couples paying the marriage tax are the hardest working segment of the population. They are the least privileged in terms of having caretakers and assistance from others. Also, they are the most afflicted by guilt pangs, particularly those who are raising children. They feel guilty because they do not have the time to give their children the complete attention that twentieth century parents have been told is necessary for the well-being and proper development of each child. They also feel guilty because they do not have the time to participate in the community, join civic organizations, help with volunteer activities, in short, to join networks that serve to bind people to each other and causes. Perhaps these reasons explain why no organizations geared specifically to combat the marriage tax have emerged, nor are they likely to emerge given the time constraints of the people involved. The singles had it relatively easy. They had the time, energy, and interest. Even a cursory scanning of their activities on behalf of tax reform indicates that the mid- to late-sixties must have been heady times for the people involved. Anyone who today chooses to become a champion for the interests of the dual-income families is probably heading down a lonely road. But given the fact that we are talking about millions of people, no one who takes up their cause is likely to feel unsupported. These people represent millions of votes and are likely to cast them in favor of candidates pledged to tax reform on their behalf. Let us hope, however, that any attempt to help them will not set off a new round of conflict pitting one taxpaying group against another.

9

Challenging the System: Using the Courts to Achieve Tax Reform

In the last few years the courts have become a forum for dual-income families that have the time, interest, money, and forebearance to challenge public policy via the channels of judicial review. A summary of the conduct of these cases is presented here in order to estimate how the courts have viewed their role in the issue.

In November 1976, Judge Eschback, of the U.S. District Court, Northern District, Indiana, found against two couples who were the first to challenge the marriage tax on constitutional grounds (*Johnson* v. *U.S.*, 1976). (The court refrained from deciding the case of a third petitioner, Sarah Johnson, who claimed that she paid an additional $2,816.82 in taxes in 1971 because she was not allowed to use the unmarried head-of-household tax rate because of a technical ineligibility.) In this case William and Wanda Barter claimed that they had paid $160.50 more in taxes during 1971 than they should have because they were not allowed to use the rate schedule for single persons, and Ralph and Pauline Blair claimed to have paid an additional $479.58 in taxes for the same reason. They argued that they were denied due process under the Fifth Amendment by: (1) having one spouse taxed for the income of the other spouse, (2) being subjected to gender-based differentiation which placed a greater burden on married female workers than that imposed on married male workers, and (3) suffering differentiation on the basis of marital status. In addition, they claimed abridgment of their First Amendment rights because of their religious beliefs in marriage, and, lastly, abridgment of their "fundamental right to marry" as guaranteed by the First, Fourth, Fifth, Ninth, and Tenth Amendments.

Eschback's opinion, later described by the appellate court as "thoughtful and workmanlike," was very narrowly drawn and, while generally based on a thorough investigation of the background of the marriage tax, appears almost obtuse in regard to the first argument presented by the plaintiffs concerning the charge that one spouse was being taxed for the income of the other spouse. The argument used to challenge this policy was based on a judgment delivered in 1931 in *Hoeper* v. *Tax Commission.* In that case the Supreme Court upheld the claim that one spouse's income could not be taxed on the basis of the other spouse's income. Eschback held that the precedents set in the *Hoeper* case did not

apply because while it "is true that in most instances it is more advantage-
ous for the couple to file a joint return because the rates . . . applicable to
separate return income are generally higher, and at least always equal, to
those provided in [the tax rate applicable to joint returns] . . . the fact
remains that each married taxpayer may make the individual choice to file a
separate return and thus avoid 'attribution' of his income, if that it be, to
the income of his spouse" (*Johnson* v. *U.S.*, 1976, p. 968). The fact that
this regulation, as was acknowledged by the judge, was specifically drawn
up to provide married taxpayers with a choice in name only and, in fact,
represented no choice at all was not taken into consideration in the
judgment. By not delving below the surface of the argument, the court
avoided deciding on the fundamental argument of income "attribution."
This legal question still remains open and was later used in another case. In
general, however, Eschbach treats the other constitutional issues carefully
and overrules each of the other arguments presented by the plaintiffs with
pertinent citations and solid, conservative reasoning.

Citing an article by the tax specialist Boris Bittker, Judge Eschbach
accepts the government's contention that the marriage tax is inevitable. In
the judge's words: "[A]t least one scholar has noted . . . the inevitable result
of simultaneously reducing the differential between single and married
couples, maintaining the progressive rate structures, and adhering to the
policy of equal taxes for all equal income married couples was the imposition of a 'marriage penalty' on some two-job married couples" (*Johnson* v.
U.S., 1976, p. 973). And it is primarily the acceptance to this line of reasoning that governs the judgment delivered in this case. As Eschbach points
out: "Absent the complexities of the Internal Revenue Code, the Government would normally bear the burden of demonstrating that no less burden-
some means exist which would satisfy its interests" (*Johnson* v. *U.S.*, 1976,
p. 974). But since all of these complexities are not absent and, in fact, do
exist within the tax structure, the court's opinion was that to require the
government to demonstrate that they could not provide more equitable
alternatives to those regulations being challenged by the plaintiffs would
effectively "abrogate the constitutional taxing power of Congress"
(*Johnson* v. *U.S.*, 1976, p. 974). In simple terms, the court felt incapable of
dealing with complexities of the tax system and of interposing its own determination governing equity among individuals and classes. Carried to its
logical extreme, this argument would imply that more and more government agencies could exempt themselves from judicial oversight by the
expedient of building up such a complicated system of regulations that the
courts would feel stymied and incapable of arbitrating contested issues.

Nonetheless, Eschbach's opinion was upheld on appeal. "We agree
with the district court that the inequities asserted to inhere in the 'marriage
penalty,' whatever may be their persuasiveness as arguments for legislative

change, do not rise to the level of constitutional violations of appellant's rights" (*Barter* v. *U.S.*, 1977, p. 1240). And when the Supreme Court refused to review the case in January 1978, all hope for challenging the marriage tax via the courts seemed doomed. The decision by the court against granting a writ of *certiorari* was interpreted by the press to be an affirmation of the marriage tax. For example the *Chicago Tribune* headline: "The 'Marriage Tax' Is Upheld" appeared on 11 January 1978.

But the *Barter* case was only the opening shot in a judicial battle with the marriage tax. Americans have a long history of challenging the legislative process through the courts and are not likely to be deterred by one setback. There was at least one other attempt made by a dual-income couple to have the courts overturn the marriage tax on constitutional grounds. Paul Mapes and Jane Bryson sued the United States in the U.S. Court of Claims for $1,220.10. This is the amount they paid in additional income tax for 1976 over the amount they would have paid if they had each remained single. The constitutional arguments they present are based on the Fifth Amendment's Due Process and Equal Protection clauses. Citing the *Hoeper* case, they claimed that the marriage tax is arbitrary and capricious because it taxes one person's income on the basis of another's. They also pointed out that the stated purpose of the Tax Reform Act of 1969 was to alleviate the tax burden according to the ability to pay. As this has not been the case, they claimed violation of due process. Furthermore, since Congress never intended to establish a subclass of married individuals paying higher taxes than they normally would simply for the privilege of maintaining marriage, this lack of rational purpose to the effect of the law violates the guarantees granted by the Equal Protection clause. They also pointed out that while the reform that generated the marriage tax was partly justified by the reasoning that a married couple could be presumed to have lower total living expenses than two single taxpayers with an identical income aggregate (presuming they maintain separate residences), according to the Due Process clause, this justification would have to apply to all married couples as a class, which it does not. They also indicated that there exist even further differences among dual-income couples that have no relationship to earnings. "Some couples with relatively low incomes pay a comparatively large marriage penalty while others with higher incomes pay a lesser penalty. For instance, a couple with an evenly divided total income of $12,000 pays a $263 marriage penalty, while another couple with an evenly divided total income of $20,000 pays only $227" (*Mapes and Bryson* v. *U.S.*, October, 1977, p. 22). Therefore, the marriage tax, in addition to being unintended, is capricious in its application.

In the decision delivered by the court of Claims on 17 May 1978, the plaintiffs were "congratulated for the able way in which they have put a serious and important issue before this court" (*Mapes and Bryson* v. *U.S.*,

1978, p. 2). However, this did not deter the court from making the following statement:

> While the Code provisions involved are loosely called a "marriage penalty," their effects are thus more complex in reality. We expect all persons to make all important decisions in life in light of their tax effect. For the tax-minded young man or woman, with a substantial income, the Code adds to the attractiveness of a prospective spouse without taxable income, and detracts from one with it. Thus the provisions may have an income-levelling effect. But we have no data showing that as yet they operate in that manner. Love and marriage defy economic analysis. As one of Gilbert and Sullivan's heroines sang many years ago:
>
> True love must single-hearted be
>   Chorus: Exactly so!
> From every selfish fancy, free
>   Chorus: Exactly so!
> The maiden who, divinely true
> Devotes herself to loving you
> Is prompted by no selfish view
> Is prompted by no selfish view
>   Chorus: Exactly so!
>
> The humor of this was in the unattractiveness of the love object. But our Internal Revenue Code provides an opportunity to the young to demonstrate the depth of their unselfishness, however kind and beautiful the beloved may be. [*Mapes and Bryson* v. *U.S.*, 1978, pp. 2–3]

The court did not stop at this point, as extraordinary as it is, but continued to make an even more astonishing declaration:

> Formerly society frowned upon cohabitation without marriage, assessing various punitive sanctions by law and custom against the partners themselves, and their innocent offspring. Most of these have now been eliminated in our more "enlightened" society. Cohabitation without marriage, and illegitimacy, or whatever it is now called, are said to be rapidly increasing. Certainly the tax-minded young man and woman, whose relative incomes place them in the disfavored group, will seriously consider cohabitation without marriage. Thereby they can enjoy the blessings of love while minimizing their forced contribution to the federal fisc. They can synthesize the forces of love and selfishness. [*Mapes and Bryson* v. *U.S.*, 1978, p. 3]

The fact that a U.S. court would promote the blessings of cohabitation which, as has already been pointed out, is still illegal in certain states and would cynically refer to a "synthesis of the forces of love and selfishness" as the premise for a relationship is an astoundingly Old World interpretation of the facts of life. In a presumably more serious vein the court explained this reasoning further:

... the elevated tax burden might in fact dissuade some couples from entering into matrimony, but does not present an insuperable barrier to marriage. More often it changes the relative attraction of different prospective spouses for the tax-minded individual wishing to marry. For many it provides an incentive to marry. The additional tax liability suffered by two-income couples who cannot avail themselves of the rates for single persons is an indirect burden on the exercise of the right to marry. It is suffered not for marrying but for marrying one in a particular income group. This does not rise to the level of an "impermissible" interference with the enjoyment of a fundamental right. [*Mapes and Bryson* v. *U.S.*, 1978, pp. 8–9]

Therefore, while the court acknowledged the existence of all types of complicated patterns of interference with the institution of marriage as a result of the marriage tax, it was willing to accept them as a modern fact of life. Minor inconveniences, such as paying more to be married to the person you love, do not require court remedy or at least not according to the U.S. Court of Claims.

Finally the court threw up its hands in surrender, just as the court did in the *Barter* case, when confronted with tax policy decisions.

... tax disparities will exist no matter how the rates are structured. This is simply the nature of the beast. The tax law is complicated enough already without the added complexity a full solution to this problem would apparently require. We in the judiciary, are neither equipped nor inclined to second guess the legislature in its determination of appropriate tax policies.... Like the court in Johnson, we are satisfied that the present provisions pass a minimum rationality test, and should be upheld as constitutional. [*Mapes and Bryson* v. *U.S.*, 1978, p. 14]

Mapes and Bryson, with a great deal of justification, petitioned the Supreme Court for a writ of *certiorari* to have this case given a proper and more respectful hearing. The court declined to hear the case, however, and appears to have decided not to venture into the morass of tax equity. Although the Burger court is justly famed for having a more centrist orientation than the Warren court, the marriage tax is not a question of left, right, or center. But as the court has shown itself increasingly reluctant to get into the realm of legislating the legislature, the question of arbitrating an equity dispute within the tax system may have easily slid into this gray area. But when the Supreme Court refused to call up this case, the holding delivered by the Court of Claims was allowed to stand.

One recent development holds some hope that the last word on attacking the marriage tax via the courts has not been uttered. When an earlier version of this chapter was published as a Working Paper (Giraldo, 1978), a number of lawyers wrote expressing their interest in the marriage tax as a legal problem. In addition, Professor Duncan MacRae, director of the Public Policy Analysis Program at the University of North Carolina at Chapel Hill, discerned an entire aspect of the question that has not been debated or touched on by the courts. When Judge Eschback threw up his hands at dealing with the complexities of the tax system, he specifically noted that tax theory would not allow all married couples and single individuals to be treated alike with a progressive tax structure. This argument was based on tax theory that has been accepted by the IRS. The argument was further accepted by the Maryland Court of Claims in the *Mapes-Bryson* case. What has tied the justices' hands in the issue is the acceptance of the so-called Four Principles of Taxation analysis issued by the Office of Tax Analysis (see appendix 9-A). No court is in a position to challenge tax theory as it emanated from the tax specialists within the Department of the Treasury. MacRae's analysis, however, does exactly that and from an entirely different perspective than has been brought up by other analysts. While others have attempted to justify differential treatment to married couples on the basis of differences between one-wage-earner couples and dual-income couples, MacRae has discerned a fundamental flaw in the Four Principles of Taxation theory itself (appendix 9-B). According to this theory three principles of taxation, namely, no distinctions among married couples, no penalty for marriage, and no penalty for remaining single, cannot all be operative at the same time within a progressive tax structure. Therefore, at least one of the three groups has to be sacrificed in order to keep the system operational. Although tax theorists indicate a distaste for sacrificing one of the two married couple groups, on a theoretical basis all three groups are held equal in terms of the equation. MacRae's analysis indicates that the concept of "no penalty for remaining single" in itself violated the principle of progressivity in taxation and, therefore, does not belong among the four principles. The reason tax theory has not been able to lick the problem of marriage tax is that it has been working all along with an incorrect formula. It would appear to be impossible to have progressive tax rates and no singles penalty. It is possible to have progressive tax rates and no marriage penalty. Therefore, if a readjustment is made in tax theory, it is likely that the marriage tax would be one of the first things to go. It would be interesting to see how the courts would react if they were asked to ponder this question now.

Appendix 9A:
Federal Income Tax
Treatment of Married
and Single Taxpayers

*Office of the Secretary of
the Treasury, Office of Tax
Analysis*

The problem of determining the relative tax burdens of married couples and single individuals has been a subject of debate in the United States since the income tax was established in 1913. There has been controversy over what is the proper unit of taxation, individuals of families; and over how (or whether) to recognize the different situations or large and small families.

The controversy revolves around four principles of taxation, each of which is widely accepted in the United States:

1. *Progressivity.* The average rate of tax should be higher, the higher the income. For example, more tax should be collected from a single person earning $20,000 than would be collected from two single persons earning $10,000 each.

2. *No distinctions among married couples.* Married couples should be treated as economic units; therefore, no distinctions should be made according to which spouse earns their income or which spouse spends it. For example, a married couple earning $20,000 should pay the same tax, whether the husband earns all the income or the husband and wife each earn half of it. In the United States this principle is recognized by allowing married couples to file combined tax returns, or joint returns, showing all the income of either spouse.

3. *No penalty for marriage.* Two people who marry should not pay a higher tax as a result. For example, a man and woman earning $10,000 each should pay the same tax whether they are married or single.

4. *No penalty for remaining single.* According to this principle, a single person with $20,000 income should not pay less tax as a result of marrying a person with no income.

Each of these principles may seem sound at first. The problem for tax policy is that they are in conflict. The conflict is illustrated by [figure 9A-1.] Therefore, *every system of taxation must violate one or more of the principles.*

This paper includes a brief history of the Federal income tax, as it relates to these four principles. Then there is a discussion of the present

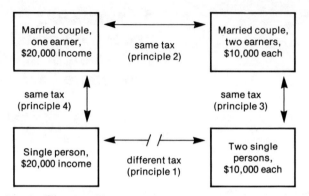

Figure 9A-1. The Conflict among the Four Principles of Tax Policy

state of the law (in 1977), followed by a suggestion as to the most likely direction for reform.

Development of the United States Income Tax

Each of the principles listed on page 95, except the first, has been violated at one time or another in the history of the Federal income tax.

Prior to 1948, the Federal income tax conformed to all of the principles except the second. People were taxed as individuals, and there was only one rate schedule applying to both married and single persons. A married couple could file a joint return if they wished, but they would pay the same tax as a single person with the same total income. Because of progressivity, a couple in which both spouses had income could save tax by filing separate returns; but a one-earner family with the same total income could not save tax in this way.

The result was discrimination among couples with the same total income, not only according to the way their incomes were divided, but also according to the state in which they live. This curious result was caused by the community property laws of some states. In 1930 the Supreme Court ruled that in states with community property laws, a husband and wife could file separate returns, each with half of the combined income, regardless of which spouse had earned the income. This automatic "income splitting" was unavailable in other states.

1948: Income Splitting

In 1948, the law was revised to embrace the "income splitting" principle for all taxpayers. Married couples were encouraged to file joint returns, and a separate rate schedule (the "joint schedule") was designed for these returns. Under the new schedule, a couple paid the same tax as two single people each with half of the combined income.

This represented no change for spouses who lived in community-property states or whose incomes actually were evenly divided; they simply received the same benefit on their joint returns as was already theirs if they filed separately. But for other couples, the automatic income splitting resulted in substantial savings. For example, consider a couple in which the husband's taxable income was $32,000 and the wife had no income. Using the rate schedule in force from 1965 to 1970, their tax if they filed a joint return was $8,660. But if the husband were taxed as a single person, his tax would have been $12,210. In this case income splitting saved $3,550.

This was the state of the income tax for the period 1948–1970. The second principle was completely satisfied, since a couple paid the same tax whether the spouses both had income or only one. Of course, in order to make the tax law conform to our second principle, one of the other principles had to be sacrificed, and in 1948, it was the fourth. A single taxpayer generally paid substantially more tax than a married couple with the same income. In the example just discussed, the single person paid 41 percent more tax than the married couple.

1951: Heads of Households

This differential is especially pronounced in the case of single taxpayers with children. Typically, these are widowed or divorced parents. Such taxpayers are hard to classify as single individuals or as married couples. Congress recognized the special status of this group in 1951 by classifying them as "unmarried heads of households" and allowing them half of the benefits of income splitting. A special rate schedule is provided—Schedule Z, the "head-of-household" schedule—which puts the tax for a qualifying taxpayer halfway between the amounts paid by a single person and a married couple with the same taxable income.

1954: "Certain Surviving Spouses"

Another special problem is the case of a parent made single by the death of a spouse. Even if the widow (or widower) was able to maintain the income previously received by the couple, she lost the benefit of income splitting and thus paid a higher tax.

To ease this burden, Congress provided in 1954 that a surviving spouse who maintains a household for a dependent child may continue to use the joint rate schedule for two full years after the death of her spouse. This

provision is still in effect, it is the only circumstance in which a single taxpayer may use the joint rates.

There are many more "heads of households" than "certain surviving
spouses." In 1975, the former group filed 5 million tax returns; the latter,
only 156 thousand. Both groups were small compared to the total of 82
million returns filed.

1971: New Single Rates

In spite of the special provisions for these small groups, most single taxpayers still faced a large tax "penalty." For a single taxpayer without
dependents, the tax burden remained much higher than a couple with the
same income. Because Congress considered the differential to be too large,
a new, lower single schedule was introduced in the 1969 Tax Reform Act,
becoming effective in 1971. The joint schedule was not changed. Under the
new single schedule, the single person's tax on a particular taxable income is
at most 20 percent higher than a married couple's tax (compared to over 40
percent under the old schedule). For example, a single person with taxable
income of $32,000 paid $10,290 in tax, which was 18.8 percent more than a
couple with the same income.

To prevent couples from saving tax by filing separately, the pre–1971
single schedule was preserved for use only on separate returns of married
persons.

The revised tax law still violated the fourth principle but not as severely.
This improvement was not obtained without a price. It was the 1969 Act
that first introduced a substantial violation of the third principle; that is, a
"marriage penalty." This condition remains part of the tax law in 1977.

The Standard Deduction

For low- and middle-income taxpayers, the marriage penalty was increased
by another provision of the tax law, the standard deduction. Any taxpayer
could elect to give up most of his personal deductions (such as medical
expenses or charitable contributions) and claim the standard deduction
instead. The amount of the standard deduction depended on income, but it
was limited to a fairly narrow range by minimum and maximum amounts.
In 1976, for example, the standard deduction for single returns (and heads
of households) could range from $1,700 to $2,400. For joint returns, the
range was from $2,100 to $2,800.

The minimum standard deduction was introduced at its present scale as part of the Tax Reform Act of 1969. At that time, the minimum and maximum amounts were the same for all tax returns, single or joint. Increases since 1974, however, have been twice as large for joint returns as for single returns.

The standard deduction presents the same conflict among the four principles as do the rate schedules. The present treatment is a compromise between the "marriage penalty" principle and the "single penalty principle. It causes a single penalty because a single person's standard deduction is subject to lower limits than that of a married couple. But there is a marriage penalty as well, since a married couple's standard deduction is smaller than they could receive if they filed two single returns, with two single standard deductions.

In 1977 the standard deduction was formally repealed. More accurately, it was made independent of income and built into the rate schedules themselves, so that it no longer requires a separate calculation. Each rate schedule now includes a *"zero bracket,"* which is an amount of taxable income on which the tax rate is zero. The zero-bracket amount is $2,200 for single returns and heads of households, and $3,200 for joint returns.

1975: The General Tax Credit

The tax reductions in 1975 and 1976 have introduced a general tax credit, which also complicates the problem. The credit is initially $35 for each taxpayer and dependent. But the taxpayer may claim, instead, a credit equal to two percent of taxable income (with an adjustment for the zero bracket in 1977. If the taxpayer chooses this second option, the credit is limited to $180. The upper limit is the same for single and joint returns. This creates an additional marriage penalty, since a married couple can usually receive only one $180 credit, while if they were single, they might qualify for two credits of up to $180 each.

1977: The Floor on Itemized Deductions

When the standard deduction was built into the rate schedules in 1977, it was also necessary to impose a floor on itemized deductions. The floor is the same as the zero-bracket amount. This means that a single taxpayer can only use his itemized deductions to the extent they exceed $2,200; and a married couple can only claim their itemized deductions to the extent they exceed $3,200. The difference in the floors represents the same compromise between the third and fourth principles as was made in the case of the standard deduction.

Summary of the Present Tax Law (1977)

In 1977, the income tax continues to reflect the compromise among the principles that was struck in 1971. The tax is progressive, and no distinction is made among married couples based on whether they include one earner or two. The last two principles are violated, however. A single person generally pays more tax than a married couple with the same income, and a married couple often pays more tax than they would if they were single.

The Internal Revenue Code contains four rate schedules that can apply to individuals. One is for single taxpayers, one for married couples filing joint returns, and one for married couples filing separate returns. A fourth is for single taxpayers with dependents, if they qualify as heads of households.

Married persons may file separately if they wish, but special provisions occur throughout the tax law to prevent couples from saving tax in this way. (Allowing such savings would violate the second principle, since it would offer an advantage to spouses whose income is evenly divided.) Separate returns are subject to a special rate schedule, with rates higher than any of the other schedules. (A separate return is sometimes necessary if one spouse is neither a citizen nor a resident of the United States, or if one spouse does not want to reveal his income to the other.)

A summary of the four rate schedules appears in table 9A-1, and the rate schedules themselves appear as an attachment at the end of the [original] paper. Note that the rate schedules are based on taxable income, which means that exemptions and itemized deductions (to the extent they exceed the floor) must be subtracted before applying the rates. Also, the tax determined from the rate schedules must be reduced by tax credits, including the general tax credit.

Examples of the Marriage Penalty in 1977 Law

If two persons, each with independent incomes marry, they may have to pay a higher tax.

For example, assume two persons each have taxable incomes of $15,000 (after subtracting their exemptions) and assume they do not itemize their deductions. If they file single returns, they each must pay $2,682 in tax ($2,862 from the rate schedule, minus $180 general tax credit). Their

Table 9A-1
Summary of the Rate Schedules

Name of Schedule in Form 1040 Instructions	Taxpayers Covered	Number of Returns Using Schedule in 1975	Amount of Zero Bracket[a]
Schedule X	Single persons other than heads of households	31 million	$2,200
Scheduly Y (part 1)	Joint returns of married couples, and certain surviving spouses	44 million	$3,200
Schedule Y (part 2)	Separate returns of married persons	2 million	$1,600
Schedule Z	Unmarried heads of households	5 million	$2,200
Total Individual Returns		82 million	

[a] The same amounts are used as the floor for itemized deductions. In effect, these amounts represent the standard deduction.

combined tax is therefore $5,364. If they marry and file a joint return, their taxable income is $30,000, and their tax is $6,488 ($6,668 from the schedule, minus $180). In this case, their "marriage penalty" is $1,124.

It is not necessary that the two incomes be equal in order for this problem to arise. Suppose that the two persons have taxable incomes of $24,000 and $6,000, for a combined taxable income of $30,000. Filing as single persons, their respective taxes are $5,734 and $576, for a total of $6,310. If they marry and file jointly, their tax is still $6,488, or $178 more.

If their income is divided even more unevenly, the couple may save tax by marriage. Note that a couple may not avoid a marriage penalty by filing separately because they would not be eligibile for the single rate schedule.

Direction for the Future

The marriage penalty is one of the most widely discussed weaknesses in [United States] income tax. Nobody defends it on its merits. Those few who can defend it at all, do so by emphasizing the three principles that must compete with the marriage penalty principle. But opposition to the marriage penalty is now so widespread that one of the competing principles must be overturned, and it seems clear that it must be the second principle; that is, there must be some distinction between one-earner and two-earner married couples.

This is the intent of every bill introduced in Congress recently to reduce or eliminate the marriage penalty, and it is the course taken by almost every other major democratic nation that has an income tax.

Many married couples, the reasoning goes, have the services of a full-time housewife. Since the housewife does not receive a salary, her services do not produce taxable income. But they do result in substantial benefits and increase the couple's ability to pay tax. (Of course, the same reasoning applies to a couple in which the wife is the only wage earner.) A two-earner couple, however, has no corresponding benefits. It is realistic to compare a two-earner couple to two single persons, but it is unrealistic to make the same comparison in the case of a one-earner couple.

Many proposals have been made to implement this distinction. They include mandatory or optional individual filing, deductions and credits based on the second earner's wages, and special deductions for the expenses of two-earner couples. Selecting the best of these proposals will require much public discussion. Then if a reform is enacted, it remains to be seen whether it will provide any more lasting satisfaction than did the reforms of earlier eras.

Appendix 9B:
Progressive Taxation,
the Marriage Tax, and
Ethical Consistency

Duncan MacRae, Jr.

The *marriage tax,* involving a higher income-tax payment from a dual-income married couple than from two single persons earning the same combined income, arose from an effort to lower the tax differential between married and single persons.[1] This effort resulted, in turn, from a principle of taxation that there should be "no penalty for remaining single"; that is, that when a higher-income earner marries a lower earner, the total tax paid by the two should not decrease. This principle leads to an inconsistency, however, when combined with other principles of taxation. Such an inconsistency, undesirable in an ethical system (MacRae, 1976, pp. 90–92), can be removed if we examine more closely the principle that there should be no penalty for remaining single. This principle proves to be inconsistent with the principle of progressivity and under certain plausible assumptions may have to yield to the principle of progressivity.

The Basis of Progressivity

To demonstrate this, the principle of progressivity must be examined; applied to individuals, while keeping in mind the same set of individuals with the same total earnings in the situations being compared; and it must be assumed that in marriage income is shared.

The justifications customarily given for taxing those with higher incomes more than those with lower (a more general category than progressivity) include the notions of ability to pay, equality of sacrifice, and marginal utility of income.

Those economists who admit the meaningfulness of a *notion of utility*—the value realized from income—often postulate in tax analysis that the marginal utility realized from an additional dollar declines as income increases. If this is so, an equal sacrifice of utility by high- and low-income taxpayers would require a greater amount of tax for the high-income taxpayer, corresponding to the greater number of dollars that would be required to deprive him or her of an equal amount of utility. Musgrave and Musgrave (1976, pp. 217–218), following this line of reasoning, point out that "it does not follow that a progressive tax will be called for. As may be shown mathematically, the required tax distribution will be progressive, proportional, or regressive, depending on whether the elasticity of the marginal income utility with respect to income is greater than, equal to, or less than unity." If this line of reasoning is followed and a progressive tax is chosen, the first of these three conditions is assumed implicitly.

Goode (1976, pp. 17–18) expresses the assumptions differently but arrives at a similar conclusion. Cautioning his readers about the nonscientific (ethical) basis of hedonistic interpretations of ability to pay, he nevertheless observes that "If A has more income than B, it seems reasonable to say that A has greater ability to pay taxes in the sense that the payment of a given amount will hurt A less and will be less likely to force a cut in socially desirable consumption. . . . The ability-to-pay principle supports progressive taxation only if taxpaying capacity increases faster than income, which is a stronger assertion. . . ."

The Tax Treatment of Married Couples

To arrive at a consistent basis for taxing couples, the husband and wife may be treated as individuals both before and after marriage. One way to do this is simply to consider their earned income, and tax them after marriage on the same basis as before (Hart et al., 1979). This procedure would clearly give rise to neither a "marriage tax" nor a penalty on marriage.

The actual benefit from income enjoyed by husband and wife, however, is affected by the way in which they use their income. There may be direct transfers of income from the higher earner to the lower, such as a periodic allowance or transfers for expenses from time to time when needed. The higher earner is also likely to make larger contributions to the purchase or rental of facilities used in household production (Becker, 1976, ch. 7) such as the home, furniture, kitchen equipment, or automobiles. Such transfers of money or of access to goods tend to equalize the benefits from income to husband and wife. Even though their earned incomes may differ, their levels of utility or welfare based on their consumption are likely to be similar.[2] There may also be economics of scale in consumption (Goode, 1976, p. 230) or utility effects that render the couple collectively better off than before such transfers.[3]

At the same time there may be a reallocation of the time that husband and wife spend in household production. The lower earner may devote more time to household production after marriage than before, and the higher earner less (Lemennicier, 1979). This assumption of a homemaker role may contribute both to efficiency and inequality in the family, depending on the extent to which the spouse in this role is compensated for it by the other spouse.

In order for the law to take account of these complex transactions some simplification is necessary, and the conventional simplification of income-splitting is most convenient (Goode, 1976, p. 227).[4] In the remainder of my argument, I shall assume that when a couple marry the effective income of each spouse becomes equal to half the sum of their individual incomes. The appropriate tax for the couple is then twice the tax on their average income. Thus if two persons with incomes of $20,000 and $4,000 married and shared equally, their total tax after marriage would properly be twice the tax on an income of $12,000.[5]

Now if the principle of progressivity leads (by definition) to a tax rate that increases with income, the rate for an income of $12,000 will be between that for $4,000 and that for $20,000. Under most actual progressive tax systems, this will lead to a marriage premium rather than a marriage tax, as is illustrated algebraically.

Let r_4 = the tax rate on an individual income of $4,000;

r_{12} = the tax rate on an individual income of $12,000;

r_{20} = the tax rate on an individual income of $20,000;

T_u = the total tax paid by two unmarried persons earning $20,000 and $4,000;

T_{m} = the tax paid by two persons, each with an income of $12,000 (which would be paid, according to the principle proposed here, by the married couple).

The principle of progressivity implies that

$$r_4 < r_{12} < r_{20};$$

we therefore write

$$r_4 = r_{12} - \Delta_4, \tag{9B.1}$$

$$r_{20} = r_{12} + \Delta_{20}, \tag{9B.2}$$

where Δ_4 and Δ_{20} are positive numbers. The total taxes to be paid are then

$$T_u = r_4 \times 4,000 + r_{20} \times 20,000, \text{ and}$$

$$T_m = 2 \times r_{12} \times 12,000 = r_{12} \times 24,000.$$

Under what conditions will there be a marriage premium? In other words, when is $T_m < T_n$? This is equivalent to

$$r_{12} \times 24{,}000 < r_4 \times 4{,}000 + r_{20} \times 20{,}000.$$

Substituting (9B.1) and (9B.2), we obtain

$$r_{12} \times 24{,}000 < (r_{12} - \Delta_4) \times 4{,}000 + (r_{12} + \Delta_{20}) \times 20{,}000.$$

Simplifying, this is equivalent to

$$0 < \Delta_{20} \times 20{,}000 - \Delta_4 \times 4{,}000 \text{ or}$$

$$\Delta_{20} > 0.2\Delta_4.$$

In other words, there will a marriage premium as long as the rate increase from \$12,000 to \$20,000 is at least one-fifth the increase from \$4,000 to \$12,000. For most actual progressive systems, rates increase more rapidly than this with income (Musgrave, 1969, pp. 182–183); a system that failed to lead to a marriage premium in this case would therefore be an oddity, even though technically progressive.

Thus the principle of progressivity as ordinarily applied will run counter to the principle of no penalty for remaining single, and if it is regarded as fundamental, it should take precedence over the latter principle. In the approach proposed here there will probably be a penalty for remaining single, because the higher earner who marries the lower earner lowers his consumption level by sharing income with his spouse, and lowers his appropriate amount of tax more than his spouse's appropriate tax increases.

Notes

1. I am indebted to James A. Wilde for helpful suggestions.

2. Consumption has been proposed as a basis for taxation (Musgrave and Musgrave, 1976, pp. 220–221). Kaldor (1955, p. 208) proposed dividing family expenditure into parts, with children counting as one-half unit each, and taxing on that basis.

3. If we consider utility or welfare to be a function that increases at a decreasing rate as income increases, a transfer from a higher earner to a lower will increase total utility. Moreover, economic analyses of this sort neglect the benefits from marrying a person one loves.

4. Some couples may share unequally; this would justify a tax rate higher than for equal sharing but lower than for nonsharing, according to the principle of individual progressivity. Such fine distinctions, however, cannot easily be incorporated in the law. The same administrative difficulty

arises for informal living and sharing arrangements that do not have the legal status of marriage.

5.   An example of two independent earners was chosen in order to be able to compare consumption in a simple closed system before and after marriage. The example presented in appendix 9A is not well chosen to illustrate the principles involved, as one of its situations is that of a single person with $20,000   income. To compare this situation with that of a married couple with one $20,000 earner implies that the spouse had zero income before marriage. A person could survive with zero income only as a dependent, such as a dependent family member. The marriage of such a person would reallocate consumption, and thus change the appropriate taxes in the family that had provided support—an unnecessary complication for this analysis.

References

Becker, Gary S. *The Economic Approach to Human Behavior,* Chicago, Ill.: University of Chicago Press, 1976.

Goode, Richard. *The Individual Income Tax.* rev: ed. Washington, D.C.: The Brookings Institution, 1976.

Hart, Janet; Judith Bartnoff, Sydney Key, and Sam Sanchez. "Report of the Action Group on the Marriage Tax Penalty to the Tax Subcommittee of the Interdepartmental Task Force on Women," Washington, D.C., 1979.

Kaldor, Nicholas. *An Expenditure Tax.* London: George Allen & Unwin, 1955.

Lemennicier, Bertrand. "The Economics of Conjugal Roles." In *Sociological Economics,* edited by Louis Levy-Garboua. Beverly Hills, Calif.: Sage Publications, 1979.

MacRae, Duncan, Jr. *The Social Function of Social Science.* New Haven, Conn.: Yale University Press, 1976.

Musgrave, Richard A. *Fiscal Systems.* New Haven, Conn.: Yale University Press, 1969.

Musgrave, Richard A., and Peggy B. Musgrave. *Public Finance in Theory and Practice.* 2nd ed. New York: McGraw-Hill, 1976.

Appendix 9C:
Full Text of House
Report 3609

*Provided by the Office of
Congresswoman
Millicent Fenwick*

96TH CONGRESS
2D SESSION

H. R. 3609

To amend the Internal Revenue Code of 1954 to allow certain married individuals
who file separate returns to be taxed as unmarried individuals.

IN THE HOUSE OF REPRESENTATIVES

APRIL 10, 1979

Mrs. FENWICK (for herself, Mr. MOLLOHAN, Mrs. SCHROEDER, Mr. GOLD-
WATER, Mr. ERDAHL, Mr. PRITCHARD, Mr. FITHIAN, Mr. CLEVELAND, Mr.
BEREUTER, Mr. GINN, Mr. BUCHANAN, Mr. LEWIS, and Mr. WOLPE)
introduced the following bill; which was referred to the Committee on Ways
and Means

MARCH 11, 1980

Additional sponsors: Mr. ADDABBO, Mr. BALDUS, Mr. BARNES, Mr. BAUMAN,
Mr. BEDELL, Mr. BENJAMIN, Mr. BETHUNE, Mr. BOLAND, Mrs. BOU-
QUARD, Mr. BOWEN, Mr. BROWN of Ohio, Mr. BURGENER, Mr. CARTER,
Mrs. CHISHOLM, Mr. CLINGER, Mr. COLLINS of Texas, Mr. CORCORAN, Mr.
COUGHLIN, Mr. COURTER, Mr. D'AMOURS, Mr. DAN DANIEL, Mr. DANNE-
MEYER, Mr. DASCHLE, Mr. DE LA GARZA, Mr. DELLUMS, Mr. DERWINSKI,
Mr. DEVINE, Mr. DIGGS, Mr. DONNELLY, Mr. DORNAN, Mr. DOWNEY, Mr.
DUNCAN of Tennessee, Mr. EDGAR, Mr. EDWARDS of California, Mr. ED-
WARDS of Alabama, Mr. EDWARDS of Oklahoma, Mr. EMERY, Mr. ERTEL,
Mr. EVANS of Delaware, Ms. FERRARO, Mr. FORSYTHE, Mr. FROST, Mr.
GIAIMO, Mr. GILMAN, Mr. GLICKMAN, Mr. GRAY, Mr. GREEN, Mr. GUAR-
INI, Mr. GUYER, Mrs. HECKLER, Mr. HOPKINS, Mr. HORTON, Mr. KEMP,
Mr. KINDNESS, Mr. KOGOVSEK, Mr. LAGOMARSINO, Mr. LEACH of Iowa,
Mr. LEE, Mr. LEHMAN, Mr. LELAND, Mr. LENT, Mr. LUKEN, Mr. MADI-
GAN, Mr. MARTIN, Mr. MATHIS, Mr. MAZZOLI, Mr. McCLOSKEY, Mr.
MIKVA, Mr. MITCHELL of Maryland, Mr. MOTTL, Mr. MURPHY of New
York, Mr. MURPHY of Illinois, Mr. NEAL, Mr. PANETTA, Mr. PATTEN, Mr.
PEPPER, Mr. PETRI, Mr. PRICE, Mr. PURSELL, Mr. RICHMOND, Mr. ROB-
INSON, Mr. ROE, Mr. ROSENTHAL, Mr. SAWYER, Mr. SCHEUER, Mr.
SLACK, Mr. SOLOMON, Mr. STOCKMAN, Mr. STOKES, Mr. TRAXLER, Mr.
TRIBLE, Mr. VAN DEERLIN, Mr. VANDER JAGT, Mr. WHITEHURST, Mr.
WINN, Mr. WYLIE, Mr. YATRON, Mr. YOUNG of Alaska, Mr. ZEFERETTI,

Originally introduced as H.R. 11270 in the 95th Congress, 2d session.

Mr. ANDERSON of Illinois, Mr. BARNARD, Mr. BINGHAM, Mr. CLAUSEN, Mr. COELHO, Mr. CONTE, Mr. CORRADA, Mr. DAVIS of Michigan, Mr. FASCELL, Mr. GINGRICH, Mr. HINSON, Ms. HOLTZMAN, Mr. JEFFORDS, Mr. McKAY, Mr. MARKS, Mr. MARRIOTT, Mr. McCLORY, Ms. MIKULSKI, Mr. PATTERSON, Mr. PAUL, Mr. PREYER, Mr. RITTER, Mr. ROUSSELOT, Mr. ROYER, Mr. SHUMWAY, Mrs. SNOWE, Mr. SPENCE, Mr. STANTON, Mr. WALGREN, Mr. WILLIAMS of Montana, Mr. BOB WILSON, Mr. WOLFF, Mr. WYDLER, Mrs. BOGGS, Mr. CLAY, Mr. COLEMAN, Mr. PHILIP M. CRANE, Mr. DIXON, Mr. FAZIO, Mr. FOUNTAIN, Mr. FRENZEL, Mr. GRAMM, Mr. GRASSLEY, Mr. GUDGER, Mrs. HOLT, Mr. JENRETTE, Mr. KASTENMEIER, Mr. LaFALCE, Mr. LIVINGSTON, Mr. LOTT, Mr. MITCHELL of New York, Mr. PASHAYAN, Mr. QUAYLE, Mr. SANTINI, Mr. SEIBERLING, Mr. STUDDS, Mr. TAUKE, Mr. ABDNOR, Mr. BADHAM, Mr. BLANCHARD, Mrs. BYRON, Mr. CAMPBELL, Mr. CHAPPELL, Mr. FISH, Mr. FLORIO, Mr. HOWARD, Mr. MARKEY, Mr. MATSUI, Mr. OTTINGER, Mr. RAILSBACK, Mr. THOMAS, Mr. APPLEGATE, Mr. BEARD of Rhode Island, Mr. DUNCAN of Oregon, Mr. EVANS of Georgia, Mr. FORD of Tennessee, Mr. HUBBARD, Mr. LONG of Maryland, Mr. LUNGREN, Mr. MATTOX, Mr. MONTGOMERY, Mr. PORTER, Mr. WAXMAN, Mr. WILLIAMS of Ohio, Mr. CHARLES H. WILSON of California, Mr. BROYHILL, Mr. CARNEY, Mr. EVANS of the Virgin Islands, Mr. FINDLEY, Mr. LEACH of Louisiana, Mr. MINISH, Mr. OBERSTAR, Mr. SEBELIUS, Mr. STANGELAND, Mr. SWIFT, Mr. WRIGHT, Mr. YOUNG of Missouri, and Mr. O'BRIEN

A BILL

To amend the Internal Revenue Code of 1954 to allow certain married individuals who file separate returns to be taxed as unmarried individuals.

1   *Be it enacted by the Senate and House of Representa-*

2   *tives of the United States of America in Congress assembled,*

3   That (a) part I of subchapter A of chapter 1 of the Internal

4   Revenue Code of 1954 (relating to tax on individuals) is

5   amended by redesignating section 5 as section 6 and by in-

6   serting before section 6 (as so redesignated) the following

7   new section:

8   "SEC. 5. ELECTION BY MARRIED INDIVIDUALS TO BE TAXED

9   AS UNMARRIED INDIVIDUALS.

10   "(a) ALLOWANCE OF ELECTION.—

1   "(1) IN GENERAL.—Every married individual (as

2   defined in section 143) who does not under section

3   6013 make a single return jointly with the spouse of

4   such individual shall, at the election of such individual,

5   be treated as an unmarried individual for purposes of

6   this chapter.

7   "(2) ELECTION.—

8   "(A) IN GENERAL.—The election under

9   paragraph (1) shall be made at such time and in

10   such manner as the Secretary may by regulations

11   prescribe.

12   "(B) BOTH SPOUSES TREATED AS MAKING

13   ELECTION.—In a case of a married individual (as

14   defined in section 143) who makes the election

15   under paragraph (1) for any taxable year, the

16   spouse of such individual shall be treated as

17   having made such election for the taxable year of

18   such spouse ending in the calendar year in which

19   ends the taxable year of such individual.

20   "(b) COMMUNITY PROPERTY LAWS DISREGARDED.—

21 For purposes of this chapter, in the case of any individual for

22 whom the election under subsection (a) is in effect for the

23 taxable year, the taxable income of such individual for such

24 year shall be computed without regard to community proper-

25 ty laws."

1   (b) The table of sections for such part I is amended by

2 striking out the item relating to section 5 and inserting in lieu

3 thereof the following:

> "Sec. 5. Election by married individuals to be taxed as unmarried individuals.
> "Sec. 6. Cross references relating to tax on individuals."

4   (c) The amendments made by this Act shall apply to

5 taxable years ending after the date of the enactment of this

6 Act.

Appendix 9D: Statement on Proposed Social Security Program Reforms

Joseph A. Califano, Jr.,
Secretary of Health,
Education, and Welfare,
February 15, 1979

I am today sending to the Congress a report that constitutes a vital step in our efforts to address the important issues that have been raised in the Social Security program by the changing roles of men and women in our society. As mandated by the Congress in the 1977 Social Security Amendments, this report takes into account the practical effect of "changes in the nature and extent of women's participation in the labor force, the increasing divorce rate, and the economic value of women's work in the home."

The report endorses no specific changes. Instead, it offers for debate two alternative models—and a number of more limited changes—that begin to take into account the realities of life in the 1970s.

The report, entitled "Social Security and the Changing Roles of Men and Women" was prepared by the Social Security Administration in consultation with the Department of Justice Task Force on Sex Discrimination, the staff of the Congresswomen's Caucus, and interested congressional committee staffs.

This report represents an in-depth study of a program, started in the mid-1930s, that has reached middle age with few adjustments for the new patterns of work and marriage in our society.

It is time for the Social Security program to begin to face the profound changes needed to assure that both men and women have the same opportunity for fair and adequate Social Security benefits.

The Social Security program has important strengths that we all recognize. But, as this report demonstrates, the Social Security program discriminates against women.

Let me list a few examples of ways in which the present benefit structure treats women unfairly.

1. Women unfairly lose protection against disability if they take time out from paid work to bear and raise children. For example, consider a woman who works for fifteen years in jobs that are covered by Social Security, and then takes five years out of the workforce and has two children. Then she becomes permanently and totally disabled. She cannot claim dis-

ability benefits because she has not worked "recently." In addition, although unable to work because of a disability, she must pay for medical care for herself and care for her children—all without any assistance from the social-security system to which she contributed for fifteen years. She has, in effect, been penalized for child-rearing.

2. Women who take time out from their working careers to bear and raise children receive reduced Social Security protection when they reach retirement age. For example, consider a woman who works for fifteen years at an average annual wage of $11,300 and then works at home ten years raising three children. Another person works for twenty-five years at an average annual wage of $11,300. Both have twenty-five years of productive work. Both have received the same level of wages when they have worked for pay. But the woman who has taken time out to raise children will receive a primary social security benefit that is $50 a month less than the individual who has worked for pay for the entire twenty-five years.

3. Couples where both spouses work receive less from Social Security than couples where just the husband works—even if total earnings by the two couples are identical. For example, a couple in which each partner had a lifetime average earnings of $6,000 per year (for a total of $12,000 for the couple) will receive benefits totaling $530 per month. A couple in which one partner had average lifetime earnings of $12,000 per year, and the other partner never worked in covered employment, will receive benefits totaling $636.60 per month. The benefit for the one-earner couple is more than $100 greater than that for the two-earner couple.

Let me list briefly a few other examples:

There are now inadequate benefits in some cases for aged widows.

Benefits are not provided for nondisabled surviving spouses under age sixty unless they are caring for children.

Benefits are not provided for disabled widows and widowers under age fifty.

Benefits are not provided for children of deceased homemakers.

Different benefit amounts may be paid to the children of married couples with the same total average earnings.

None of these inequities is the result of deliberate policy decisions. They reflect the pre–1940s design of the Social Security program, which was based on a pattern of family relationships in American society—lifelong marriages in which women were solely homemakers and men provided economic support—that was much more common then than today.

For example, 47 percent of married women were in the labor force on any given date in 1977, compared with 17 percent in 1940. Of those married persons aged twenty-six to forty in 1940, one in seven eventually were divorced. Today, one in three marriages of persons age twenty-six to forty is expected to end in divorce.

At present, nearly 90 percent of all women work for pay at some period during their lives. It is simply not fair or realistic for social security to treat those women as adult dependents who had never worked when they reach retirement age. If the program is to maintain the public support upon which it depends, women must have better access to benefits in their own right.

The current benefit structure must be changed to make it more equitable. The issue is not whether, but how to change the current structure to correct the inequities while maintaining the strengths of the existing system.

This report begins the difficult but critically important process of identifying the problems and laying out possible solutions. All the issues and alternatives cannot be fully explored in a single document. This report makes no attempt to do so.

Instead, it lays out two broad models for correcting inequities to illustrate the scope of change necessary to address these inequities. There may be other approaches that can and should be discussed, but this report will trigger the full and careful debate that must precede any major changes in a program that touches the lives of nearly all Americans.

The models outlined in this report are described on a prospective basis only. The report does not consider affecting the benefits of anyone now receiving Social Security. However, the report notes that transitional programs could be designed to remedy serious inequities for particular groups of current beneficiaries or for those now nearing retirement. Such provisions would increase short-range costs.

The report also does not address the impact of changes in Social Security on other federal programs, most notably income maintenance programs, such as Aid to Families with Dependent Children or Supplemental Security Income. That impact should be thoroughly explored in the public discussion on the models described in this report, and on any other proposed changes in the social security system.

The models described in the report are designed to address the inequities in the current system without substantially increasing long-range costs. The report makes it clear that this kind of cost constraint would require reducing benefits for some to achieve the desired equity for others.

Over the long run, however, we must recognize that eliminating inequities and improving the adequacy of benefits in the current system will either require increased funding or mean reducing other benefits. The nation must begin to face this difficult choice. Costs are an important issue and must be thoroughly considered, but they should not obscure the central question for debate: how to structure social security benefits to be as fair, equitable, and adequate as possible for all Americans—regardless of sex and regardless of marital status.

The report is a thoughtful piece of work that deserves the widest possible distribution, study, and discussion by Congress and the general public. To assist in that discussion, I am submitting the report to both the Advisory Council on Social Security and the National Commission on Social Security for thorough debate. Their reaction and comments on the models described in the report will be particularly important as this discussion goes forward.

I have also asked Stanford Ross, Commissioner of Social Security, and Martha Keys, my special assistant, to consult widely and solicit comments on these models and other alternatives that address these difficult questions.

The Social Security system has important strengths. Its continued vitality surely is a remarkable achievement in light of the radical transformation our society has undergone since the 1930s. Our challenge is to recognize and correct the inequities within the system while preserving the inherent strengths of a program that has served millions of Americans so well for more than forty years.

Let me now briefly describe the two models for comprehensive change that the report sets out.

Earnings Sharing: This prototype is designed on the general rule that a worker's Social Security benefits would be based on his or her earnings when single, and on one-half the combined earnings of a couple during their marriage. In the event of divorce, each partner's wage record would be credited with one-half the couple's combined earnings during their marriage—regardless of the length of the marriage. Each spouse would get a Social Security retirement benefit in his or her own right.

Earnings sharing would have a significant effect on several major groups:

1. For retired people: There would be no difference in benefit amounts for lifelong married couples with the same total earnings, regardless of whether they were one- or two-earner couples. One-earner couples would receive lower benefits than those that would be provided under current law. For all couples, the benefit of the higher-earning spouse would usually be less than under current law and the benefit of the lower-earning spouse would usually be higher, both in lifelong marriages and in the event of divorce.

2. For survivors: When one member of a couple dies, 80 percent of the total earnings of the couple during their marriage—but not less than 100 percent of the earnings of the higher wage earner—would be credited to the surviving spouse. (This modification of the basic earnings sharing concept

was included to pay benefits that are somewhat comparable to benefits under law.) Survivors of two-earner couples would generally get higher benefits than under present law.

Benefits would be paid to a young surviving parent only until the youngest child reached age seven, rather than age eighteen as under present law; the child's benefit would continue until age eighteen. This modification of present law is based on increased labor-force participation of women when their children enter elementary school and on indications that the current benefit may act as a deterrent to work.

To partially make up for the loss of the parent's benefit, there would be an increase in the benefit for surviving children. In addition, an adjustment benefit equal to 100 percent of the deceased spouse's benefit would be paid for one year after the death of the spouse—regardless of whether there were any children. This benefit is intended to meet the transitional needs of surviving spouses.

3. For disabled people: Benefits would be roughly the same as those under the present law. They would be based on the person's own earnings, taking in account earnings shared with a spouse during a prior marriage or credits acquired on the death of a spouse. Earnings would not be shared with regard to a marriage still in effect at the time of disability.

The particular earnings sharing prototype described in the report would decrease long-range costs of Social Security by 0.06 percent of taxable payroll. If it were applied to the 1979 taxable payroll, the effect would be a decrease of $0.6 billion over present law.

Two-Tier Benefit Structure: The existing benefit structure would be replaced by a two-tier approach. The first tier would be a flat-rate benefit payable to every U.S. resident, regardless of earnings, who meets the age requirements or who is disabled. The second tier would be an earnings-related benefit payable on the basis of employment covered by the Social Security program. The total benefit for an aged or disabled beneficiary would be the sum of both tiers.

The second tier described in the report includes some of the features of the earnings-sharing option: in the event of a divorce, each partner's wage record would be credited with one-half the couple's combined earnings during their marriage. Surviving spouses could inherit earnings credits.

The effects of the two-tier approach on various groups would include:

1. Retired people: Older people who are not eligible for any Social Security benefits under present law would get a tier I benefit. If they had any covered earnings, they would also get a tier II benefit. On average, benefit amounts would be lower than under present law for one-earner couples and roughly the same for two-earner couples.

2. Survivors: In addition to a tier I benefit, surviving spouses would

inherit earnings as they would under earnings sharing. In most cases, benefits for a survivor of a one-earner couple with a lifelong marriage would not vary substantially from those under present law. Benefits of a survivor of a two-earner lifelong marriage would generally be higher than under present law.

A one-year adjustment benefit would be provided for a surviving spouse under age sixty-two. The amount would be 100 percent of the tier II benefit based on all the earnings credits of the deceased person, including those from a previous marriage.

The benefit for a surviving child would be tier I plus tier II based on all the earnings credits of the deceased parent. Where there is more than one surviving child in a family, the total benefits to the children would be a tier I benefit for each child, plus one tier II benefit for the family—but no greater than a specified family maximum benefit amount.

3. Disabled people: Disability benefits would be payable to everyone who meets the definition of disability. There would be no requirement for the person to have worked under the Social Security program. The basic benefit would be a tier I benefit. If the disabled person had earnings credits, whether from his or her own earnings or as a result of divorce or death of a spouse, he or she would also be entitled to tier II benefits. Tier I benefits would be payable to disabled homemakers who had never worked in covered employment. Disabled widows and widowers of any age could receive tier I and tier II benefits, not just those age fifty to sixty as under present law.

Like the earnings-sharing option, the particular two-tier alternative outlined in the report was designed to hold changes in long-range costs to a minimum, compared to the current system. The long-range cost of this particular two-tier option would depend heavily, however, on the method used to adjust the tier I benefit for changes in wages and prices. Depending on the assumption used, the cost of the two-tier plan could range from an increase of 0.5 percent of taxable payroll ($5 billion in 1979) to a decrease of 1.86 percent of taxable payroll ($19 billion in 1979).

References for Part II

American Bar Association. Section of Taxation. *The Tax Reform Act of 1969.* Roger S. Levitan, reporter.

Barter v. United States. 550 F.2d 1239. (1977).

Bittker, Boris. "Federal Income Taxation and the Family." *Stanford Law Review* 27 (1975).

Blumberg, Grace. "Sexism in the Code: A Comparative Study of Income Taxation of Working Wives and Mothers." *Buffalo Law Review* 21 (1972): 49–98.

Break, George F., and Joseph A. Pechman. *Federal Tax Reform: The Impossible Dream?* Washington, D.C.: The Brookings Institution, 1975.

Chapman, Jane Roberts, ed. *Economic Independence for Women: The Foundation for Equal Rights.* Sage Yearbooks in Women's Policy Studies. vol. 1. Beverly Hills, Calif.: Sage Publications, 1976.

Cooper, George. "Working Wives and the Tax Law." *Rutgers Law Review* 20 (1970): 67–75.

Douty, H.M. "The Slowdown in Real Wages: A Postwar Perspective." *Monthly Labor Review.* U.S. Department of Labor, August 1977.

Faraco v. Commissioner of Internal Revenue. 261 F.2d 387. (4th Cir. 1958).

Fund for Public Policy Research. *Reforming the Federal Tax Structure: Commission to Revise the Tax Structure.* Washington, D.C., 1973.

Giraldo, Z.I. "Tax Policy and the Dual-Income Family: The 'Marriage Tax' and Other Inequities: A Family Impact Statement." Duke University Institute of Policy Sciences and Public Affairs Working Paper Series, no. 10781, October 1978.

Giraldo, Z.I., and J.M. Weatherford. "Life Cycle and the American Family: Current Trends and Policy Implications." Duke University Institute of Policy Sciences and Public Affairs Working Paper Series, no. 378, March 1978.

Gray, Oscar S. Testimony before House Ways and Means Committee, 10 March 1978.

Groves, Harold. *Federal Tax Treatment of the Family.* Washington, D.C.: Brookings Institution Report, 1963.

Hoeper v. Tax Commission, 284 U.S. 206, 52 S. Ct. 120, 76 L. Ed. 248. (1931).

Johnson v. U.S., 422 F. Supp. 958 (N.D. Ind. 1976).

Paul A. Mapes and Jane A. Bryson v. United States of America. Memorandum of Points and Authorities in Support of Plaintiffs' Motion for

Summary Judgment. U.S. Court of Claims. Docket no. 403-77. (October 1977).

Mapes and Bryson v. United States, 576 F.2d 896. (1978).

Mapes and Bryson v. United States; Supreme Court, October Term, 1978. Petition for a Writ of Certiorari to the United States Court of Claims. (September 1978).

Poe v. Seaborn, 282 U.S. 101, 51 S. Ct. 58, 75 L. Ed. 239 (1930).

New York Times, 16 October 1979.

Richards, Britten D. "Discrimination Against Married Couples Under Present Income Tax Laws." *Taxes—The Tax Magazine* (Sept. 1971): 526–537.

Sundberg, Jacob W. "Marriage or No Marriage: The Directives for the Revision of Swedish Family Law." *International and Comparative Law Quarterly* 20 (1971): 223–238.

U.S. Bureau of Census. *Historical Statistics of the United States: Colonial Times to 1970.* 1975, part 2.

———. "Money, Income, and Poverty Status of Families and Persons in the United States: 1976 (Advance Report)." *Current Population Reports,* no. 107 (1977).

———. "Money, Income, and Poverty Status of Families and Persons in the United States: 1977 (Advance Report)." *Current Population Reports.* Series P-60, no. 116 (July 1978).

———. "Population Profile of the United States: 1977." *Current Population Reports.* Series P-20, no. 324 (April 1978).

U.S., Congress, House. Revenue Act of 1948, message from President returning without approval bill H.R. 4790. House Document 589. 80th Cong. 2nd sess. 1948.

———. *Tax Treatment of Family Income, June 1947.* House Document 6182. 1948.

———. *Revenue Revisions.* 80th Cong. 1st sess. 1948.

———. *Revenue Act of 1948. Report to Accompany H.R. 4790.* 80th Cong. 2nd sess. H. Rept. 1274. 1948.

———. *Report of Committee on Ways and Means to Accompany H.R. 4473.* 82nd Cong. 1st sess. H. Rept. 586. 1951.

———. *Hearings before the Committee on Ways and Means on Tax Treatment of Single Persons and Married Persons Where Both Spouses are Working.* 92nd Cong. 2nd sess. H. Rept. 781-12. 1972.

———. *Panel Discussions before the Committee on Ways and Means on General Tax Reform.* 93rd Cong. 1st sess. House Document 781-3. 1973, part 7.

U.S., Congress, Senate. *Senate Prints. Tax Reform Act of 1969, H.R. 13270.* Technical Memorandum of Treasury Position. 91st Cong. 1st sess. 1969.

U.S., Department of Labor. Bureau of Labor Statistics. *Employment in Perspective: Working Women.* Report 544. no. 2 (Second Quarter 1978).

———. *New Labor Force Projections to 1990.* 1977.

———. *News Bureau of Labor Statistics*, 77–369. 27 April 1977.

U.S., Treasury Department, *Press Service no S.370,* 18 June 1947.

Part III
The ERA and the
Family: An Analysis of
State Equal Rights
Legislation

10 Introduction to State Equal Rights Legislation

In recent years a great deal of controversy and energy has surrounded a proposed amendment to the federal constitution known as the Equal Rights Amendment (ERA; see appendix 13A). To date thirty-five states have ratified the federal amendment, and even in these states debate continues about the value and effect of the proposed amendment. At the same time that the controversy continues over the federal Equal Rights Amendment, seventeen states have already enacted state constitutional provisions that prohibit sex discrimination (Alaska, Colorado, Connecticut, Hawaii, Illinois, Louisiana, Maryland, Massachusetts, Montana, New Hampshire, New Mexico, Pennsylvania, Texas, Utah, Virginia, Washington, and Wyoming). In nine of these states the wording of the state amendment is very similar to or exactly the same as the proposed federal amendment (Colorado, Hawaii, Maryland, Massachusetts, New Hampshire, New Mexico, Pennsylvania, Texas, and Washington; see appendix 13B for a table of population and appendix 13C for the specific wording of these nine constitutional amendments).

In these nine states 22 million households with approximately 31 percent of the total U.S. population are presently living under state constitutions that guarantee sexual equality in all of the courts functioning within the legal systems of those states. These families are to a large extent living under the ERA. This part examines the impact of equal rights on the families living in the ERA states in order to better understand what is involved in this issue and what might be the potential impact of the federal ERA on all American families if it is finally ratified.

Much of the acrimony generated by the dispute over the ERA revolves around the uncertainty of how it would affect family life in the United States. Critics unfavorable to the federal ERA claim that it would have a destructive effect on the traditional family in which the husband plays the role of breadwinner and the wife that of homemaker. They argue that sex-based protective legislation is needed to provide for the special needs of wives and mothers. Proponents of equal rights argue that the protection offered by such legislation is actually nonexistent. They point out that in the past so-called protective laws have served to restrict women unjustifiably and have often been openly supported by people with the avowed interest of protecting males from competition on the labor market. They also point out that under the ERA, legislation can be enacted to provide support for homemakers so long as it is phrased in sex-neutral language referring to dependent or supporting spouse rather than wife or husband.

Further opposition to the ERA is based on the belief that the very concept of equality between the sexes is antithetical and destructive to marriage and family life. This is a harder issue to address since it is so subjective in nature. Equality is not harmful to family life, and it serves to help today's families and can therefore be viewed as supportive of family life.

When referring to today's families the concern is with 57 million families of which 48 million are headed by a husband and wife. This last figure includes people living in families in which 51 percent of all wives are working. The U.S. family population also includes over 7 million families with only a female head and 1.5 million families with only a male head. Out of 57 million families, 27 million families have no children under the age of eighteen years. All of these families are living in a nation where the number of divorces has reached 50 percent of the number of marriages taking place. If some change, development, or policy is to be labeled "profamily" it must either be supportive of all of these types of families or be flexible enough to help one type of family without hurting the others. To be profamily today one must be sensitive to the changes that have been taking place in society.

In this chapter the term *profamily* characterizes legislation or court decisions that serve to strengthen all families by acknowledging the new realities of family life. When the courts are allowed to recognize the fact that both employed adult heads have rights and responsibilities toward the support of their families they would be moving in a profamily direction. In certain cases this expansion of rights and responsibilities has expanded the physical resources available to those families. Furthermore, the growing prevalence of divorce and the formation of second families is stretching the limits of a profamily orientation and is challenging the courts with complicated issues of equity. The rights of the family that was formed first must be balanced with the rights of a subsequently formed family. This delicate balancing act increasingly taxes the judicial system and cannot be ignored in any discussion of the impact of equal rights on the family.

By relying on the above-mentioned criteria to judge court decisions made in ERA states, the general findings are that the courts in the ERA states have been keeping to this fine line by balancing the needs of family units against the needs and rights of the individuals who are part of these units and the needs of society to maintain and reproduce itself as an institution. Therefore the implementation of the ERA in the various states is definitely a move in the right direction in terms of having an impact on families that is both supportive and flexible.

The methodology followed in this research was that of concentrating attention on those nine states that have legislation most similar to the federal ERA. A total of sixty-four cases in which the state ERA had been invoked were examined. To the best of my knowledge they represent all of the domestic-relations cases involving the ERA in these nine states prior to 1979. The decisions made by the courts of these states should predict to a certain extent the effect that the federal Equal Rights Amendment might have on families in the United States since it will be these same courts that will be charged with implementing the U.S. Constitution if it is changed in this respect. A limitation on using the experience of the state equal rights amendments to help predict the impact of a federal constitutional amendment is that federally regulated areas, such as the armed forces, social-security system, or federal taxation, are not affected by state court decisions. But, since the great majority of cases directly involving family matters are usually state regulated, these court decisions illustrate a substantial portion of the types of issues affecting domestic relationships that might arise under the federal ERA.

A further limitation is that a discussion of every type of case dealing with family-related matters would be too cumbersome to cover in a book of this size. The small number of cases that have taken up the minimum age requirements for marriage, the taking of a married name, and the entire matter of illegitimacy have not been treated because they would require a disproportionate amount of historical analysis not justified by their number and the narrowness of their applicability. Cases involving what appear to be the major family issues presently affected by state equal rights amendments have been considered instead.

Chapter 11 summarizes some of the problems involved with the implementation of equal rights amendments and outlines the courses of action that a court may choose when faced with a law charged with discriminating between people on the basis of sex. Chapter 12 considers court decisions affecting the ongoing marriage in terms of equality of the marital roles, property rights, and economic interdependence. Chapter 13 deals with families undergoing divorce and remarriage and covers alimony, division of household goods, child support, and child custody. Finally, the appendixes provide documentation for a number of assertions made in the chapters in terms of the changing family picture emerging in the United States and in regard to the specifics of the court decisions involving the various state equal rights amendments.

11

Problems of Implementing the Equal Rights Amendment at the State Level

The passage of an equal rights amendment to a state constitution is only a preliminary step toward eliminating sex discrimination within the legal system. Although such an amendment makes women and men theoretically equal before the law, much remains to be done before the ideal becomes a reality.

Because of the continuing pervasiveness of laws based on sex-role differentiation, almost all of the states studied had a variety of sex-based laws, both common law and statutory, which were in effect at the time passage of the equal rights amendment was contemplated by the state. For that reason the impact of the passage of an equal rights amendment within any particular state was greatly affected by what other efforts the state legislature made to render its laws sex-neutral.

With the passage of an equal rights amendment some legislatures viewed the new legislation as an impetus to review their laws for sex bias. For example, when New Mexico adopted an equal rights amendment in November 1972, a legislative committee was appointed to draft changes that were needed in New Mexican law so that these could be made before the amendment's effective date in July 1973. The state bar helped this committee by suggesting changes needed in the community-property laws of the state. They were concerned not only with the changes required by the state equal rights amendment but also with other areas that were confusing or unclear. The combined effort produced a Community Property Act of 1973, which eliminated almost all discriminatory provisions in the law and had the same effective date as the equal rights amendment. In this way the legislative arm of the state government of New Mexico was primarily responsible for making that state's laws sex-neutral.

When the Washington state legislature passed its equal rights amendment, it also amended 120 separate sections of the state laws and repealed four sections to eliminate sex-based provisions. The greatest number of these revisions dealt with family relationships. At least one author has criticized the Washington legislature for its somewhat mechanical approach to these revisions and recommends that a legislature ought to "examine the entire conceptual framework of a statute and rework it to achieve equality by eliminating sex role stereotypes" (Dybward, 1973–1974). That is to say,

For a full listing of legal cases cited in this and the following two chapters, see appendix 13D.

legislators should not content themselves with merely "sex-neutralizing" existing statutory language. Rather they should analyze the rationale behind the law in order to determine its purpose and then judge whether the law can be sex-neutralized, and, if so, how it should be done without violating the ultimate purpose of the law. A good example of how a mechanistic approach to sex neutrality can go wrong is illustrated in the *Einstein Medical Center* case (see chapter 12). Legislators should heed the lesson of that case when contemplating revisions of legal codes.

The procedure followed by the State of Texas was to amend its property laws to make them sex-neutral but not touch the discriminatory provisions contained in its family code. By leaving these discriminatory provisions in effect, the legislature left to the courts the burden of dealing with these laws on a case-by-case basis.

Within the variety of options open to it, each state's individual behavior during and after the passage of its equal rights amendment governs to a large degree what cases are brought to its courts and how the courts react to those challenges. Pennsylvania has left almost all of the implementation of equal rights legislation to the discretion of the courts. Because the state has opted for this approach, cases challenging state laws on the basis of the Pennsylvania ERA account for thirty-seven cases out of the total of sixty-four of ERA-based challenges that have been examined in the area of domestic relations. This amounts to 58 percent of the total. Furthermore, court decisions in this state have been found to be contradictory on at least one legal issue and argueably overly narrow on another issue (see discussion of *Gilman* v. *Unemployment Compensation Board*). Because of the amount of litigation engendered and the wide fluctuation of opinion that could produce contradictory decisions, Pennsylvania is not a good example of how a state ought to implement its equal rights legislation. As Pennsylvania was the first state in the union to enact and implement a state equal rights amendment, the problems it is suffering may have been caused by haste and lack of precedent upon which to base its behavior. For this reason the Pennslyvania approach ought to be studied separately and in depth or in comparison with the approach taken by one or more of the other ERA states. This would promote a better understanding of the technical issue of implementation of equality of rights before the law.

Consider the choices that face a court if it has determined that a law does indeed violate the state equal rights amendment. Normally the court can choose from three options available to it. If, for example, the law being challenged allowed a payment or award to be made to a wife but not to the husband, the court would have to either (1) declare the law unconstitutional and thus not allow either husband or wife to receive such a payment, or (2) extend the law to cover both husband and wife so that either could receive the award, or (3) look at the purpose of the statute and decide rights and obligations in terms of the functions of the individuals rather than their sex. It could then declare that the dependent spouse was eligible for a payment from the supporting spouse without violating principles of equality.

Before a court can make the initial decision of whether or not a law violates an equal rights amendment, it must first decide what standard of review to use when considering the law. The choice of a standard can be crucial to the outcome of cases involving discrimination. The standard of review used by a court in each case effectively determines what evidence becomes relevant and who bears the burden of proof. When a court upholds a sex-based law because it finds that the legislature had a reasonable basis for making the sex classification, the court is using what is termed a *weak standard of review*. By limiting itself to a rationality test, a court could, if it so chose, play a very minor role in regard to the laws it is responsible for reviewing. If, on the other hand, the court decides that under the equal rights amendment only classifications based on sexual differences that are absolutely inherent to the issue at question can be allowed, it is using an *absolute standard of review*. Under an absolute standard, a law that treated women differently from men would not be allowed except in the rare instances where the crucial differentiation in the case was based on sex rather than function or role.

Between these two poles the courts can choose compromise positions on which it decides what evidence can be brought before it and what arguments it chooses to accept. Thus far no consensus has emerged as to a consistent standard of review to be used within those nine states that have a federal-type ERA. The courts in most of these states are in a difficult position when confronted with questions of equality in domestic-relations law. Frequently they claim that they have been given little guidance about what a legislature intended to accomplish with its passage of equal rights legislation. Thus the courts are left to carve out new rules in an area of rapid social change. Since courts are traditionally loath to be in a position of making new laws, it is not unexpected that in some cases they would opt for a standard of review that allows them to maintain the status quo.

This unwillingness to adopt one standard for all areas of domestic-relations law is illustrated by two Pennsylvania cases. In *Conway* v. *Dana* (see appendix 13D) the court ruled that the legal requirement that a father be the one parent held primarily liable for support of his minor children was invalid because it was a sex-based classification. The court did not consider whether there was any rational or compelling reason for the existence of this rule in the state of Pennsylvania and therefore chose not to use a weak standard of review. By using an absolute standard in this case, the court mandated a major change in the responsibilities of parents in that state.

In a case involving interspousal support, however, the Pennsylvania court used a weaker standard of review. In *Commonwealth ex rel. Lukens*

v. *Lukens* the court upheld a statute that allowed a wife to recover support when a husband willfully failed to support his family even though the statute had no provision for a husband to recover support from a wife. Looking to other Pennsylvania court laws, the court reasoned that since there were other statutes that gave support rights for husbands, there was no pattern of discrimination that would make that particular statute invalid. The court held that "while there may not be mathematically precise equality, these statutes create a substantial right to support for both sexes." This kind of reasoning is far removed from an absolute standard of review. Under an absolute standard any individual law that provided a particular remedy for one sex and not the other would be unacceptable no matter how many other sex-neutral laws there were in existence.

It is not clear why the court chose to use a weaker standard of review in the latter case. Perhaps the complexity of the Pennsylvania support laws (seven in all) made the courts hesitant to extend the statute to both sexes and yet unwilling to declare the statute unconstitutional. Also the court may have been aware that the Governor's Commission on the Status of Women was conducting a thorough review of sex-based statutes for legislative action and chose not to interfere with these proceedings at that particular time. In any event, this seeming vacillation is indicative of the limitations inherent in allowing the courts to carry the full burden of implementation of equal rights legislation.

The standard of review is also of critical importance in cases that involve a classification that is sex-neutral on its face but is discriminatory in its effect. A case in point involved a challenge to Pennsylvania unemployment insurance regulations (*Gilman* v. *Unemployment Compensation Board of Review*). Pennsylvania law provided that when the sole or major support of a family leaves a job to join his or her family in a new locality, he or she would be eligible for unemployment insurance. But the law further stipulated that a working spouse in the same situation who was not the major support of the family would not be eligible to collect unemployment compensation. Mrs. Gilman, the claimant in this case, left her position with the Pennsylvania Department of Justice in Philadelphia to accompany her husband to Harrisburg where he had been transferred. She was unable to find employment in Harrisburg and applied for unemployment compensation. She presented statistical evidence that, on a national basis, the class of major family earners was one-fifth female and four-fifths male. The court accepted her argument that a much greater number of men than women were eligible for benefits under the statute, but nonetheless ruled that the numerical difference alone was not sufficient to warrant characterizing the classification as sex-based. The court did acknowledge that it was aware of a California case that overturned an almost identical statute when claimants showed that 99 percent of the persons denied benefits under the statute were women. But in the eyes of the court, the classification under attack was based on economic considerations, not sexual ones, and therefore they ruled that the state equal rights amendment was not applicable. By making this decision, however, the court allowed Pennsylvania to continue using unemployment compensation in certain instances as a form of public-welfare subsidy, tiding certain families over a major loss of income, rather than an insurance plan available to all who had paid into it. This is a subversion of the underlying structure of the national unemployment compensation system and inherently sex-biased at the present time in favor of male employees over females.

Furthermore, if the court had adopted a stricter standard of review under the equal rights amendment, this case might well have gone the other way. That is, the court could have held that while a functional classification, that of sole or major wage earner, is used in the wording of the law to determine benefit eligibility, because of past sex discrimination the result of the law is still violating the principle of equal rights since substantially more women are excluded from this class than men. Therefore the statute, although giving the appearance of being sex-neutral, could have been found discriminatory in its application. The necessity for strict scrutiny of such classifications has been emphasized by the authors of a leading article on the federal ERA.

> Protection against indirect, covert or unconscious sex discrimination is essential to supplement the absolute ban on explicit sex classification of the Equal Rights Amendment. Past discrimination in education, training, economic status and other areas has created differences which could readily be seized upon to perpetuate discrimination under the guise of functional classifications. The courts will have to maintain a strict scrutiny of such a classification if the guarantees of the amendment are to be effectively secured. [Brown, Barbara, Thomas I. Emerson, Gail Falk, and Ann E. Freedman. "The Equal Rights Amendment: A Constitutional Basis for Equal Rights for Women." *The Yale Law Journal* 80 (1971): 900. Reprinted by permission of The Yale Law Journal Company and Fred B. Rothman & Company.]

Another way that courts can avoid deciding whether or not a sex-based classification is unconstitutional is to find that the person making such a claim has no "standing" to do so. Unless a person can show that he or she is being materially affected by a statute, that person does not have the right to challenge that law in court. In two alimony cases involving the state equal rights amendment, the Maryland courts have taken the position that a person not seeking a benefit under a statute does not have standing to challenge its constitutionality. Thus the Maryland courts refused to invalidate a statute that allowed alimony to women only because the husbands who were challenging the statute were not asking for alimony for themselves (*Colburn* v. *Colburn* and *Minner* v. *Minner*).

Finally, determining the absolute scope of either the federal or the state equal rights amendments is an important aspect of the matter and can only be surmised at present. Opponents to the federal amendment have argued that public bathrooms will be unisex and women will have to march with the infantry. Proponents argue that this kind of interpretation ignores the exceptions that have been accepted previously by the Supreme Court to even the strictest prohibition on sex classifications. There are two exceptions. First, there is the protection of an individual's rights of privacy. Protection of this type would allow a state, for example, to require separate restrooms for men and women. The second exception allows differential treatment based on physical characteristics unique to one sex. Under this exception a state can regulate wet nurses even though such a regulation only applies to women. Some states have upheld rape statutes that applied only to men as also being required by the physical distinctions that exist between the sexes. These exceptions are viewed by the legal system as permissible within a very narrow range. A regulation prohibiting women from engaging in certain physically demanding sports, for instance, would not be an acceptable regulation. However, the establishment of reasonable physical criteria that are directly related to the activity and would have to be met by all participants is likely to be allowed. Thus women could be required to march in the infantry, but only those women who met the physical requirements that would be demanded of all foot soldiers.

Opponents of the federal ERA have taken the view that the present wording of the amendment would not allow these exceptions. Former Senator Sam Ervin argued that "The absolute nature of the ERA will, without a doubt, cause all laws and state sanctioned practices which in any way differentiate between men and women to be held unconstitutional. Then, all laws which segregate men and women, such as separate schools, restrooms, dormitories, prisons, and others will be stricken" (S. Rep. no. 92-689, Senate Committee on the Judiciary, 92d Cong., 2nd sess. 2 [1972]).

These fears are not justified by the cases currently being decided by the courts nor by any trends discernable in the legislative decision-makirg process.

One of the most controversial issues involving the scope of the ERA is whether it would be interpreted to force states to allow homosexuals to marry. The legislative history of the federal ERA clearly indicates that this is not the intention of the Congress. The one state that has considered this issue decided that this was not the intent of the state amendment either. In the 1977 Washington case of *Singer* v. *Hara,* two men appealed a trial court's refusal to order that they be issued a marriage license by a county auditor. The trial court held among other things that the Washington ERA does not require the state to authorize same-sex marriage. In considering whether the state amendment was written with the intention of permitting same-sex marriage, the court weighed the public debate that went on prior to ratification of the amendment and a postelection survey of voters and decided that

> We do not believe that approval of the ERA by the people of this state reflects any intention upon their part to offer couples involved in same-sex relations the protection of our marriage laws. . . . The primary purpose of the ERA is to overcome discriminatory legal treatment as between men and women "on account of sex."

> Prior to adoption of the ERA, the proposition that women were to be accorded a position in the law inferior to that of men had a long history. Thus, in that context, the purpose of the ERA is to provide the legal protection, as between men and women, that apparently is missing from the state and federal Bill of Rights, and it is in light of that purpose that the language of the ERA must be construed. To accept the contention that the ERA must be interpreted to prohibit statutes which refuse to permit same-sex marriages would be to subvert the purpose for which the ERA was enacted by expanding its scope beyond that which was undoubtedly intended by the majority of the citizens of this state who voted for the amendment.

The court also reasoned that marriage is a protected legal institution primarily because our society views marriage as "the appropriate and desirable forum for the procreation and rearing of children." Since no same-sex couple could produce children by their union, "the refusal of the state to authorize same-sex marriages results from such impossibility of reproduction rather than from an invidious discrimination 'on account of sex.'"

Therefore, defining marriage as the legal union of one man and one woman was found permissible by this court because it is based on the unique-physical-characteristics exception to the scope of the equal rights amendment. The court noted that a flaw in this rationale was that not all married couples choose to have children or were capable of having children. It dismissed these as exceptional situations that did not affect the general principle.

12 The Impact of the ERA on Ongoing Marriages

The difference in the sexes and the dominance of the male over the female have been emphasized more in the laws governing family relationships than in any other area of the law. The ancient roots of the present-day legal system are in the remnants of a concept known as *coverture* whereby a wife has no legal personality aside from her husband's. Too often wives remain classed according to this tradition as dependents, along with children, reliant on a male provider.

From this concept of male dominance followed certain presumptions with regard to relations between the couple. These presumptions were particularly evident in exchanges of property between husband and wife. If a wife gave a gift to a husband, because of the presumed lack of equality in the relationship, it was assumed that a subtle form of extortion was present. The court compensated for this by considering such gifts as constituting a trust that the husband held for the wife's benefit. In this way the courts felt that they were protecting wives from having their property taken from them by dominant husbands. Pennsylvania courts, which considered this issue in light of the state equal rights amendment, have held that under the concept of equal rights this presumption no longer holds true. Therefore a contribution by a wife to a joint bank account, for example, in this state is considered to be just that unless some form of coercion can be proven to have taken place (*In re Estate of Klein*). Also in *Butler* v. *Butler* a Pennsylvania court ruled that property owned by both husband and wife is open to contributions by either husband or wife and that the court will only step into the matter "when it appears that the parties are in fact in a relationship with one party enjoying an advantage over the other because of a superior knowledge or influence and that this domination caused a gift of the entireties property to arise."

When examining the question of undue influence in the setting up of a separation agreement between the spouses, the ERA state of Maryland denied the automatic presumption of the husband's dominance. In one of the cases involving a challenge to a separation agreement, the court examined the wife's contention that undue influence by the husband had been exerted. But it noted that during the negotiations for the agreement the wife had successfully negotiated several changes favorable to herself and in the opinion of the court this constituted adequate proof that the wife was not entitled to claim that her husband dominated her in the traditional sense

(*Bell* v. *Bell*). But in another case involving a separation agreement, the Maryland appellate court found that the wife in that particular case was emotionally unstable, penniless, and had believed her husband's threat that she would never see her children again unless she signed the agreement. This was found by the court to constitute valid proof of duress and the agreement was rendered invalid (*Eckstein* v. *Eckstein*). The impact of the state amendment was to remove rules that demanded that the husband's role be viewed with automatic suspicion and instead required that the case be judged on its own merits in terms of what actually occurred between the partners to the agreement.

The historical presumption of dominance by the husband which excused a wife's actions has not been applied only in contractual matters. In criminal cases wives who had performed criminal acts in conjunction with their husbands were presumed by the courts to have been acting under coercion. This presumption has been overturned in Pennsylvania in favor of a case-by-case review of the facts. Citing the state amendment, the court stated: "The independence of women in political, social and economic matters renders the doctrine of coercion outdated and inapplicable to modern society" (*Commonwealth* v. *Santiago*).

This reliance on a determination of the actual situation in the marriage is not only correct under the equal rights amendment, but only seems reasonable given the variety of marriage relationships in society. Some marriages are truly partnerships between persons who have equal control over their lives both economically and socially. In others, one party is the sole wage earner, but both participate in family decision making. In still other relationships one party is dominant economically and in charge in every other way. While it may be a truism to state that equality under the law does not mean equality between the sexes, it is a fact of life that cannot be overlooked or ignored by the courts as they attempt to decide equity issues.

Another legal aspect of the marriage relationship is that matter of domicile. Under common law a wife is expected to live in her husband's choice of residence and she could be found guilty of desertion if she refused to follow him wherever he chose to live. While the legal issue of what will become of the domicile rule under the ERA has not been decided yet, a Washington court tangentially touched on this issue when it decided the effect of a husband's decision to follow his wife on his claim for unemployment compensation in *Ayers* v. *Department of Employment Security*. According to the facts of the case Mr. Ayers, on release from military service, had found a temporary job as a laborer with a landscaping company in Richland, Washington. His wife was unable to find work in Richland but did get a permanent position as a clerk typist in the state capital which was about 250 miles away. Mr. Ayers decided to quit his temporary job and move to Olympia to join his wife. The couple felt that they could neither afford to maintain two residences in separate cities nor to commute and they wanted to maintain their marriage relationship. The Washington Department of Employment Security had decided that Mr. Ayers was not eligible for unemployment compensation because he did not have a "compelling personal reason" sufficient to constitute a "good cause" for having quit his job.

In pre-equal rights amendment decisions this same court had held that the legal duty of a wife to follow her husband to the domicile of his choice constituted a compelling personal reason and good cause for voluntarily leaving employment. This presumption did not, however, apply to Mr. Ayers because he was a male. When faced with the dilemma of how to decide this issue in a state that had passed an equal rights amendment to its constitution, the court went around the issue of what effect the state's equal rights amendment would have on the domicile rule and instead decided the case on the basis of the importance of a couple's desire to keep their family together. According to the majority opinion,

> Many factors may enter into the decision of a family as to where they shall live and work. It is often a substantial factor to be considered that it is desirable for numerous reasons to keep the family together. If employment for the husband and the wife are not available in the same area, it is a compelling personal reason and, therefore, good cause for one of the spouses to leave employment and go to the place of employment of the other spouse in order to keep the family together. The decision as to which place of employment should be accented must not be governed by any arbitrary rule, but should be decided upon a consideration of all relevant factors. It is generally a decision which the spouses should make for themselves, subject to the need to make a reasonable decision. [*Ayers* v. *Dept. of Employment Security*]

In spite of the fact that the court sidestepped the domicile issue by choosing to ignore this arbitrary rule, the decision will probably mean that the domicile rule is defunct in the state of Washington in regard to issues involving unemployment compensation. Instead of relying on the sexual stereotype of male dominance in a marriage relationship, the court will look at the individuals before them and, as it found in this case, will base its decision on whether the justification given by a man for quitting his job in order to be with his wife was reasonable and whether it should or should not disqualify him for unemployment compensation. In this case the court arrived at a decision with which most people would heartily concur under these circumstances.

In addition to the questions of presumed male dominance in contractual matters and choice of domicile, the traditional marriage under common law demands that the husband support the wife and provide her with the necessities of life. A wife, however, does not have a corresponding obligation to provide this minimal support to a husband. *Necessaries* are defined by the courts as food, shelter, clothing, and medical expenses. Inequality of the support obligation in terms of the necessaries doctrine has not been allowed under the state amendment in Pennsylvania, although the courts are in conflict about how to reach equality. In the case of *Einstein Medical Center* v. *Gold* the court held that the marital unit could be held responsible for providing necessaries for the husband as well as the wife. In September of 1973 Charles Gold entered Einstein Medical Center and received $724.50 worth of services for which he did not pay. In August of 1974 the hospital sued both Gold and his wife for the amount of the debt. The hospital based their claim on an expansion of the necessaries doctrine to make it sex neutral. According to the court:

> The case at bar closely parallels the situation as presented in *Conway* v. *Dana,* as regards the legal responsibilities of the husband and wife. In the instant case, rather than support of children, it is liability for the medical expenses of a spouse which had long been presumed to be principally the burden of a husband. The Supreme Court of Pennsylvania in *Conway* clearly stated that presumptions such as these can no longer be followed; in effect, that the distinction between the responsibilities of men and women with respect to certain obligations is no longer effective.
>
> This is not to say that defendant's wife is automatically liable for the amount of the bill. There may be other factual and legal reasons why the plaintiff should not recover, and we do not mean to preclude defendant from making such contentions. We do hold she cannot assert as a defense that a wife is not legally responsible for medical expenses incurred by her husband.

Therefore when faced with having to make a decision to either eliminate this doctrine of support altogether or extend it to the wife, this court opted for the latter choice. However, another lower Pennsylvania court chose to eliminate the necessaries doctrine rather than to extend it to cover both spouses. In the case of *Nan Duskin, Inc.* v. *Parks* the court of common pleas in Philadelphia refused to hold a husband liable for the cost of goods purchased and accepted by his wife alone. The conflict in these decisions will have to await a definitive decision by the Pennsylvania State Superior or Supreme Court or legislative action.

A fundamental consideration of the question of whether or not the necessaries doctrine ought to be continued under the ERA is the recognition that most people agree that obligations for support are one of the responsibilities of family life. Eliminating that obligation might mean that the burden of support would fall on the state. It is preferable that a dependent spouse be able to obligate the supporting spouse for such things as food, clothing, and shelter prior to having recourse to the state. The *Einstein* case goes further than this, however, and makes no distinction between dependent and supporting spouse. The court merely sex-neutralized the necessities doctrine without reference to its purpose. By doing so they distorted its original intent. The conflict over the necessaries doctrine in Pennsylvania provides a good illustration of the consequences of legislative inaction after adoption of an equal rights amendment. Passage of a statute that provided that the supporting spouse was responsible for the necessities of the marital unit would have eliminated the sex-based inequality while maintaining this traditional marital right of the dependent spouse.

Some commentators have pointed out that more far-reaching reforms are needed than merely extending the necessaries doctrine and have suggested that each spouse be entitled to one-half the other's income, as is the case in community-property jurisdictions. Although income splitting would make the position of the nonworking spouse more secure, it is highly unlikely that a court would endeavor to make such a major change by judicial decree.

One lower Pennsylvania court has considered the question of whether a married woman has an enforceable property right against her husband for the services she performs in the home but came up with an answer clearly in the negative. In *Keenan* v. *Pennsylvania Hills School District* a school district attempted to tax non-wage-earning housewives on the basis of their husbands' incomes. The housewives claimed that they were exempt from the tax because it applied only to persons earning over $2,000 income per year. Since these women had no earnings of their own they claimed entitlement to the exemption. The school district differed and claimed that the exemption was specifically meant to give relief only to people in poverty and that these women had the "right of support" from their husbands and therefore did not meet the poverty criterion.

The court rejected the school district's contention and held that neither the legislature nor the courts had interpreted the state equal rights amendment (or any other piece of legislation) as conferring upon married women a property right enforceable against their husbands for the value of their labor performed within the home. The court stated that "While lip service has been given to the role of the wife-mother-housekeeper-nurse-laundress-cook-chauffeur-teacher and all of the other occupations included within the anomalous term of 'housewife' neither the appellate courts nor the legislature has recognized any right to compensation for these services other than the equally anomalous 'right to support.'" Therefore, while the amendment was not used to provide housewives with an enforceable property right, something for which it was never intended, it was also not used to deprive homemakers of their right to support. The idea that the ERA will force housewives out of their homes is a ludicrous one and is receiving no support from the courts. But the ERA does not have to be totally neutral in the way it affects the property rights of homemakers. While the passage of the equal rights amendment in Pennsylvania did not provide housewives with a right to claim the value of their labor in the home, the passage of such an amendment in Georgia would more than likely eliminate the law that a married couple's home belong only to the husband. In Wisconsin the law that puts a woman's earnings from labor performed for her husband under the control of the husband would not be allowed to stand under the ERA. The husband-management principle is still operative in North Carolina and would also have to be eliminated under an equal rights amendment. The passage of a federal Equal Rights Amendment would also most likely eliminate miscarriages of justice such as occurred when a Nebraska widow was found liable for $25,000 in inheritance taxes for a farm on which she had lived and worked for 33 years with her husband. According to the federal government the farm was not hers unless she could prove that she provided funds toward its purchase or improvement (U.S. Commission on Civil Rights, 1978). In all of these instances existing laws that purportedly serve to protect wives are more likely to harm them and should be eliminated from the system of justice.

Nothing detrimental to family life in the United States has been brought about by the various equal rights amendments in terms of family structure or the individual members of the family unit. No case was found where a traditional (male-breadwinner) family was harmed by an equal rights law while, on the other hand, two-earner families and egalitarian families were helped by a more responsive, less restrictive attitude on the part of the courts, as in the *Ayers* case. Where families differed in their structure from the more traditional pattern, the courts judged contested issues among those family members with flexibility and tolerance instead of tying them down to outdated sex-role concepts that were inappropriate in light of the facts of the case.

Passage of equal rights amendments legislation is more a ratification and acceptance of the profound changes that have taken place in our society due to the new status of women and their new place in the American economy than a factor causing such a change. With the passage of equal-rights legislation the courts have been charged with recognizing that the role of a married female has undergone substantial changes in this century, particularly in the last few decades, and that married women must be viewed in terms of these new developments and norms. That would seem to be the fair way to treat everyone concerned.

13

The Impact of the ERA on Families in Transition

With the high incidence of divorce and remarriage, many families are making transitions to new family structures. Since cases involving families in transition frequently involve issues distinct from those of an ongoing marriage, they are discussed in this chapter covering spousal support (alimony), division of household goods, child support, and child custody.

Spousal Support

The practice of granting alimony as an incidence of divorce had its origins in the ecclesiastical law of England. It allowed no absolute divorce but permitted divorce from bed and board, which enabled a couple to live apart although they remained legally married. Alimony granted in these circumstances was simply a continuation of the husband's obligation to support his wife. If the wife's fault caused the separation, however, she was viewed as having failed in her marital obligations and hence the husband no longer owed a duty of support, and alimony would not be granted. These concepts of support and fault carried over to grants of absolute divorce even though they were premised on the obligations of a continuing marriage relationship. Because of this inconsistency, there has been confusion about the purpose of alimony.

The controversies surrounding the alimony question have been long-standing and acrimonious. The trend in the twentieth century, independent of the entire issue of equal rights, has increasingly moved away from treating alimony as a form of punishment applied to a man who wanted a divorce to viewing it as a form of support owed to a former wife who had been left in a position of being unable to support herself adequately.

The traditional argument in support of alimony has been that a woman who entered marriage with the understanding that her husband would provide for her support and she, in return, would provide for his well-being is entitled to continued support if the marriage contract breaks down and leaves her with no salable skills to provide for her own support. Many women find themselves in exactly the position of being divorced by their husbands at a point in their lives where they have no hope of replicating the life styles of their marriage on their own. And in many ways these women can be viewed as victims and certainly deserve more than mere sympathy.

Opponents of alimony, however, tend to emphasize the high awards some-times made to the wives of wealthy men which are designed to allow the exwife to continue living in the same high style of life she enjoyed while married. They pay scant attention to the argument that these cases are few in number and do not cover those persons for whom the bare necessities of support are at issue. When a team of researchers studied alimony and support payments granted mothers and children in the United States they found that only 3 percent of those involved received enough alimony and support payments to bring them up above the official poverty line (James et al., 1976, table 4, p. 74). In those cases where women have given up careers or advancement on account of marriage, it would seem apparent that upon divorce they should not have to live in poverty simply because their most productive years were devoted to the home. In addition, it is not fair to watch former husbands continue to live at the same economic level as when they were married while the situation of their wives deteriorates markedly.

The current trend in both ERA and non-ERA states in the treatment of alimony is decidedly away from judgments involving assignment of punish-ment and fault and toward the concept of alimony as a maintenance pay-ment to a dependent spouse determined on the basis of need. This approach is very much in keeping with the concept of equality embodied in the ERA. Partners in a marriage would be viewed according to their individual char-acteristics instead of having their position and responsibilities defined by their sex. The Uniform Marriage and Divorce Act, which has attempted to devise a norm suitable to all states in the hopes of achieving more uniform-ity in the laws, provides for maintenance for either spouse where the spouse seeking support: (1) lacks sufficient property to provide for his reasonable needs; and (2) is unable to support himself through appropriate employ-ment or is the custodian of a child whose condition or circumstances make it appropriate that the custodian not be required to seek employment outside the home (Uniform Marriage and Divorce Act, 308).

The approach taken by the Uniform Marriage and Divorce Act in determining the amount of a support award is representative of the current trend. Under the model act, a court should not consider marital misconduct but should consider factors such as "the financial resources of the party seeking maintenance, the time necessary to acquire sufficient education or training to enable the party seeking maintenance to find appropriate employment, the standard of living established during the marriage, and the age and the physical and emotional condition of the spouse seeking mainte-nance." Naturally, as long as the labor-force participation of wives follows the current pattern, it will be the wife who would normally be expected to require the support.

Thirty-seven states now provide for alimony awards for either spouse. These include seven (Colorado, Hawaii, Maryland, Massachusetts, New

Hampshire, New Mexico, and Washington) of the nine states with equal rights amendments. The other two, Pennsylvania and Texas, provide for no alimony whatsoever after divorce. They do, however, make provision for spousal support during marital separation and divorce litigation prior to the granting of a divorce decree.

Opponents of the ERA claim that alimony will cease to be awarded with the passage of that amendment and thousands of women every year will be deprived unjustly of adequate support because of the failure of their marriages. An examination of the cases in the ERA states shows this is not so. As the New Mexico court noted, the ERA "definitely does not prescribe conditions governing when and why alimony should be granted, beyond the requirement of equal protection . . ." (*Schaab* v. *Schaab*). Therefore, as long as alimony continues to be granted by American courts, it will be affected by the ERA solely to the extent that it be granted on a sex-neutral basis.

It is necessary to point out that when a divorced person is granted alimony, the enforcement of such orders is so poor that, as shown in one study done in 1975, less than half of the 14 percent of wives awarded alimony collected the amounts awarded them with any regularity (Brown et al., 1977). Whether the ERA is passed or not, for the majority of divorced people alimony constitutes an unreliable form of support that has been gradually disappearing from the legal system and will continue to disappear at an even greater pace in the future as fewer and fewer women remain wholly dependent on their spouses. And given current divorce rates, it would be foolish for women to remain ignorant of this fact. The passage of a state equal rights amendment only raises the issue to a higher plane and concentrates on dependency and need. By itself it will not make any substantive change in what is happening with regard to alimony.

Division of Household Goods

Another area in which reform is needed and in which the ERA will have an impact is that dealing with household property. To put the question of such property in perspective, consider the doctrine of coverture again. Under coverture, when a woman married, her husband gained control of her personal property and real estate, although she would regain control if he predeceased her. The husband's rights in a deceased wife's property were more extensive than those of a wife to her husband's holdings. Many of these inequities were corrected by Married Women's Property Acts passed during the nineteenth century in all of the states. These allowed a wife to keep control of her assets when she married and keep her own earnings. For the women who filled the traditional role of homemaker and had no assets or wages, these reforms made little difference in their position. Normally in common-law states, property is considered owned by the person whose assets paid for it.

The problem of household property was considered in the common-law state of Pennsylvania in a case involving the division of household goods of a couple who were divorced after a ten-year marriage. The husband in the case claimed to be covered by the common-law doctrine that "ownership of household goods used and possessed by both spouses is in the husband." When this case was taken to trial the conclusion of the trial court was that the household goods of this couple had been donated to the marital unit and were held by the couple as "tenants-in-common." This finding, however, meant that when the property was divided, each piece would revert to its actual purchaser. Therefore, while the court eliminated the presumption that the husband was automatically the owner of the goods, many wives could still find themselves deprived of what they considered to be their possessions by the husband simply proving that his money paid for them. In this way wives, whose contributed services probably freed the resources necessary to pay for their household property, could find themselves suddenly and inexplicably dispossessed of this property at the end of their marriage. The appellate court of Pennsylvania disagreed with this lower-court decision and presented its reasons for doing so in a very straightforward manner. According to Chief Justice Jones:

> . . . we cannot accept an approach that would base ownership of household items on proof of funding alone, since to do so would necessitate an itemized accounting whenever a dispute over household goods arose and would fail to acknowledge the *equally important* and often substantial non-monetary contributions made by either spouse. [Emphasis in the original]

> With the passage of the Equal Rights Amendment, this Court has striven to insure the equality of rights under the law and to eliminate sex as a basis for distinction. . . . Furthermore, having found that the husband is no longer necessarily the "sole provider" and noting that even where he is, it is likely that both spouses have contributed in some way to the acquisition and/or upkeep of, and that both spouses intend to benefit by the use of, the goods and furnishings in the household, we will not burden either party with proving that such household items were donated to the marital unit. We conclude, therefore, that for the purpose of determining title of household goods and furnishings between husband and wife, the property that has been acquired in anticipation of or during marriage, and which has been possessed and used by both spouses, will, in the absence of evidence showing otherwise, be presumed to be held jointly by the entireties. [*DiFlorido* v. *DiFlorido*]

The distinction between ownership as tenants-in-common and as tenants-by-the-entireties is that with the latter there is no need for proof of purchase and in the event of death the survivor would have sole right to the property. This distinction is an important step forward in equalizing the marriage relationship because it acknowledges the fact that a wife's services make a contribution toward goods purchased during the course of a marriage. By emphasizing both marital equality and economic unity, the *DiFlorido* case is another example of the ERA functioning according to the definition of profamily. Of course this decision also means that in Pennsylvania couples who do not intend to share all of their household goods in common will have to show proof of this fact if the issue comes into question. Although this aspect of the application of a state equal rights amendment might be considered an example of how the ERA would serve to introduce legal considerations into the making of a marriage and therefore deromanticize marriage, it would apply only to special situations that should be governed by legal agreement to protect the parties involved from misunderstanding.

Child Support

In a majority of states, the father is the parent primarily liable for support of his children and the mother is liable only if the father is unable to support them. In these jurisdictions the mother's assets and earnings are not considered when the amount of child support payable by a father in a separation or divorce action is determined. Under the Equal Rights Amendment such a rule would not be allowed to stand. Instead, parents would both be liable for support of their children. Some jurisdictions provide for joint liability of parents by statute. Many of these laws are similar to the child-support provision of the Uniform Marriage and Divorce Act which states that

> In a proceeding for dissolution of marriage, legal separation, maintenance, a child support, the court may order either or both parents owing a duty of support to a child to pay an amount reasonable or necessary for his support, without regard to marital misconduct, after considering all relevant factors concluding:
>
> 1. the financial resources of the child;
> 2. the financial resources of the custodial parent;
> 3. the standard of living the child would have enjoyed had the marriage not been dissolved;
> 4. the physical and emotional condition of the child and his educational needs; and
> 5. the financial resources and needs of the noncustodial parent.

Two main issues have been raised regarding equality in support of children. The first is whether it is fair to require a working woman to contribute to the support of her children. The imposition of support obligations on working mothers may strike some as unfair in that it takes income away from women who may still be suffering the effects of employment discrimination. The case of *Commonwealth ex. rel Buonocore* v. *Buonocore* shows the kind of careful consideration that should be given by a court in determining the amount of support due from each parent. In that case the court weighed such factors as ability to pay, contributions in kind, and the property settlement to determine the amount of child support required. The court found that the husband, who had actual custody of the two minor children in the case, had an average net income of $166 per week; that the wife had net earnings amounting to $140 per week; and that the expenses for the care and maintenance of the two minor children were approximately $113 per week. The court ruled that the lower court's requirement that the wife pay child support of $30 per week to her husband was not excessive. The court noted that the wife's income represented 46 percent of the combined net income of the parties and that the support order represented 21 percent of her net income and only 26 percent of the financial needs of the children. When it assigned a smaller portion of the upkeep of the children to the mother in this case it took into consideration that she had turned over the family home to her former husband and that this represented a substantial asset, justifying the lack of mathematical balance of the award.

A case such as this in which the court gave careful consideration to the relative abilities of both parties to pay child support does not place an unfair burden on working mothers. Additionally, making both parents liable for child support to the extent of their abilities maximizes the resources available for the care of the dependent children and could therefore be considered a development that provides for children of divorce better than the older system.

The second main issue concerning child support revolves around the question of whether equality means that parents have to contribute equal monetary shares to the support of their children. Clearly this would be unfair and unworkable because it would deprive children of custodial parents by forcing a nonworking parent into the labor force to acquire earnings to pay amounts equal to that of the wage-earning parent. Carried to its logical conclusion, the courts would be placed in the idiotic position of ordering a woman to find a job that paid her a salary equal to her exhusband's salary. The image of having a court order that a divorced woman find a job that, for instance, paid $22,340 within sixty days should immediately reveal the inherent ridiculousness of this contention. The courts in the ERA states have recognized their position in the matter and reiterated that there can be no mathematically equal formulas established in such matters. In Maryland, for example, the appellate court ruled that the requirement that parents share responsibilities of the support of children does not mean equal contribution but rather that "the amount of each parent's obligation varies in accordance with their respective financial resources" (*German* v. *German*). The courts in the ERA states continually shy away from mathematical formulas or ratios and instead have treated the question of child support in terms of providing for all of the needs of the individual child according to the individual standards of the family in question. In the case of *Cooper* v. *Cooper* the Texas court found that

> If "equality under the law shall not be denied or abridged because of sex," it must be presumed that the legislature intended that the duty of the spouses to support their minor children is equal. This does not mean, however, that the court must divide the burden of support of the minor children equally between the parties. The court's order in this respect should reflect a due consideration of the respective abilities of the spouses to contribute. The duty to support is not limited to bare necessities. The court may consider the standards of living which the parties have maintained in the past as an indication of the standard which they will strive for in the future. The court would be justified in requiring the parents to provide a standard of living for their children commensurate with that which they have and will continue to enjoy for themselves.

The question of forcing a mother out of the home to provide money toward the support of her children has been considered in Pennsylvania which, according to statute, measures parents' support obligations not only by actual earnings but also by earning capacity. The case of *Commonwealth ex rel. Wasiolek* v. *Wasiolek* involved a petition for increase in child support brought by the mother of three children, aged seven, nine, and eleven. She was not employed but testified that before she was married she had worked as a secretary and had earned $500 per month. She stated that she was not seeking employment because she needed to be home in order to care for her children. The lower court had increased the child-support payments but not to the amount requested by the mother because the court took the position that she had an obligation to help support the children through employment. In holding that the lower court was not obligated to consider the earning capacity of the custodial parent, the court noted that the purpose of the support order was to guarantee the welfare of the child. The court reasoned that

> Once custody of a very young child is awarded, the custodial parent, father or mother, must decide whether the child's welfare is better served by the parent's presence in the home or by the parent's full-time employment. Hence, permitting the nurturing parent to remain at home until a child matures does not run afoul of the ERA—our holding is based on sexually neutral considerations and on the best interests of the child. Of course, a court is not strictly bound by the nurturing parent's assertion that the best interest of the child is served by the parent's presence in the home. It is for

the court to determine the child's best interest. But the court must balance several factors before it can expect the nurturing parent to seek employment. Among those factors are the age and maturity of the child; the availability and adequacy of others who might assist the custodian-parent; the adequacy of available financial resources if the custodian-parent does remain in the home. We underscore that, while not dispositive, the custodian-parent's perception that the welfare of the child is served by having a parent at home is to be accorded significant weight in the court's calculation of its support order.

An earlier decision by a Pennsylvania appellate court had already held that when a custodial parent who had been unemployed begins working, it could be considered a valid reason for a reduction in the amount of support paid by the other parent. The case in point is the previously cited *Conway* v. *Dana* in which a father appealed a lower court's denial of his petition for reduction of an order of support for his two minor children. The father, Warren B. Dana, had suffered a decrease in his income from approximately $12,400 per year to $10,600 per year. Additionally, since the entry of the support order, his former wife had secured employment and earned a net salary of $700 per month. Mr. Dana argued that the state equal rights amendment abrogated the presumption that the father was primarily liable for support of a minor child. He won his argument and the court ruled that

> Insofar as these decisions suggest a presumption that the father, solely because of his sex and without regard to the actual circumstances of the parties, must accept the principal burden of financial support of minor children, they may no longer be followed. Such a presumption is clearly a vestige of the past and incompatible with the present recognition of equality of the sexes.
>
> . . . Thus, when we consider the order to be assessed against the father, we must not only consider his property, income and earning capacity but also what, if any contribution the mother is in a position to provide.
>
> . . . combining the decrease in the father's income along with the additional income resulting from the mother's recently acquired employment provides a sufficient change in circumstances to warrant a modification of the original order.

The tendency of the courts seems to be that the need of young children for care in the home must be considered within any analysis of the question of child support. Any mother with young children will not be required by any court enforcing the ERA to leave those children in the care of others in order to contribute a salary to that family's resources. As the home situation changes, however, the courts have shown themselves willing to make adjustments according to the changed circumstances. These changed circumstances can include remarriage, at least in the state of Washington. In the 1975 case of *Smith* v. *Smith* both parents had remarried and the mother's new husband, a doctor, had an income of $35,000. A Washington court held that in determining whether or not there had been such a substantial change of circumstances as would warrant a modification of the child-support provisions of a divorce decree, the trial court must consider the income available not only to both parents but also to their respective new marital communities. This is an especially important consideration in this society where the chances for a second marriage for a divorced person in the United States are at present very high. According to the U.S. Census Bureau, four out of five divorced persons remarry, with men showing a significantly higher remarriage rate than that of women (see appendix 14E). For parents in a position of supporting children from more than one marriage, considering the assets of a new marital community could be of great importance in relieving some of the strain placed on new marriages by former marriages. The *Smith* case, however, skirts a matter that was specifically dealt with in the *Pennsylvania Hills School District* case; namely, the issue of a wife's rights to a husband's income. This court chose not to address it directly and, therefore, did not establish on what basis a second husband's income could be attached to provide for the children of a wife's earlier marriage. But if other courts follow the Washington State pattern, this question will undoubtedly have to be dealt with at some level and yield results that cannot be predicted with any certainty at this time.

One last consideration involves cases where fathers have attempted to use the ERA to rid themselves of responsibilities for child-support arrears. Here the courts have shown themselves to be decidedly unsympathetic. Back payments of child support are typically viewed as a vested right that the court has no power to modify. In a case where a father attempted to excuse his noncompliance with alimony and child-support requirements by claiming that the court ought to reexamine this issue "in light of contemporary concepts on the obligations of husband and wife" to pay support, the court ruled that these considerations were not relevant to the issue of past-due support payments (*Slavis* v. *Slavis*).

In a Colorado case in which a Denver district court declared the felony-nonsupport statute of that state unconstitutional because it applied only to fathers, the charges against a man who had violated a support order prior to the enactment of the equal rights amendment were dismissed by the trial court. The appellate court overturned that trial court's decision and held that

> In our opinion, the court erred in applying the Equal Rights Amendment to prohibit the prosecution of the alleged criminal conduct which, as noted above, occurred prior to the effective date of the amendment. The presumption is that a constitutional amendment is to be given only prospective application unless the intention to make it retrospective in operation

clearly appears from its terms. . . . There is no language in the Equal Rights Amendment from which an intention appears to make the amendment retrospective in its operation. [*People* v. *Elliot*]

All indications are that when faced with difficult questions concerning child support, the courts will adhere to the principle of "best interest of the child" and minutely examine all of the issues in each case in order to allocate responsibility for the care and maintenance of each child on the basis of the individual family situation. A father attempting to flee his share of the responsibility by claiming that the ERA has absolved him from it is not likely to have much success.

Child Custody

The main impact of the ERA in the area of child custody would be in disputes between fit parents. Under English common law, fathers had an almost absolute right to custody of their children. This rule gradually lost favor in America, and by the late nineteenth century mothers began to have a superior claim, especially to young children, under the "tender years" presumption. This presumption is based on the belief that a mother is the natural custodian of a young child and her care and love is superior to that of any other person. Although this doctrine has fallen into disfavor in recent years, it was still the rule in Maryland when that state adopted an equal rights amendment. The Maryland court's treatment of the presumption gives an interesting picture of the way judicial attitudes toward the meaning of equality under the law developed.

In 1929 Maryland had adopted a law which stated that "neither parent has any right superior to the right of the other concerning the child's custody." In spite of this law, courts continued to use the maternal preference in custody cases. In 1972, Maryland adopted its equal rights amendment. In a custody case heard on appeal after the passage of the state equal rights amendment, the implications of the maternal-preference doctrine were discussed even though the issue had not been raised directly by the plaintiff or the defendant. The presumption was allowed to stand by the court although its use was limited to that of a tie-breaker: The court justified this decision by stating:

Any possibility of a denial of equal rights properly gives us especial pause since "equality" is the very foundation of this society. The term itself has a ring, as do ritualistic incantations, and well it should, for it occupies a most exalted position in a democracy's scale of values. The awe it inspires should not, however, cause us to forget that the "self-evident truth" of equal creation of all persons was not meant to describe human congenital endowments, but rather their political and legal rights.

Suffice to say that if the presumption of "maternal preference" is utilized within the restrictions articulated in the case espousing it, a proper application neither denies nor abridges the equality of rights of either party. The "rights" of the parents are not the issue. They have been overridded by the singular interests of the child. . . . [*Cooke* v. *Cooke*]

According to the court, after the basic principle of best interests have been applied when all else is found to be equal, then the "presumption is obviously intended to serve the limited function of a 'tie-breaker.'" The maternal preference presumption would be applicable in only "those limited instances where it would be impossible to decide upon the evidentiary facts."

Clearly, this decision would be erroneous under the state equal rights amendment if the amendment were strictly interpreted by the courts. A strict interpretation would not allow sex to be as a factor in the decision. Allowing maternity per se, rather than those factors associated with child-rearing practices, to serve as a decision maker would mean that sex alone could decide a case. Although only women can give birth to offspring, it is obvious that fathers as well as mothers can nurture and rear them. In line with this recognition, approximately five weeks after the *Cooke* decision, the Maryland legislature adopted a new law regulating child custody which stated that "in any custody proceeding, neither parent shall be given preference solely because of his or her sex" (chap. 181, art. 72 A, sect. 1, 1974). This law was effective in finally abolishing the maternal-preference doctrine. In the 1978 decision of *McAndrew* v. *McAndrew,* the Maryland appellate court overruled a lower court's use of maternal preference as a tie-breaker and held that the 1974 law abolished the presumption. The court did not consider the effect of the amendment and concluded that the new legislation by itself was sufficient to decide the issue.

Some concern has been expressed that without the maternal-preference rule, the balance would tip in favor of fathers who typically would have better-paying jobs than would mothers. The father, in effect, could buy the custody of his children by proving his greater monetary worth. That this could be a problem is shown by the Illinois case of *Marcus* v. *Marcus.* In that case the young mother had no means of support and could not provide a stable home for the child, but the father was employed and living with his sister's family. In giving custody to the father the court noted:

There is today no inflexible rule which requires that custody of child, especially of tender age, be vested in the mother. Equality of the sexes has entered this field. The fact that a mother is fit is only one facet of the situation and, standing by itself, it does not authorize a denial of custody to the father, when this appears necessary because of other considerations.

When this matter was heard, the mother did not know, and could not determine, whether she would return to her parent's home in Texas . . .

when she last attempted this she found herself obliged to leave the parental home after approximately two weeks. As regards the choice of another place of residence, this mother had no assets of any consequence, no profession, no education or experience which could enable her to earn her own way and to provide a proper home for the child apart from basic support. No amount of good intentions by themselves can suffice to overcome these insuperable handicaps. . . . It seems basically essential for this child to have the benefit of a stable and secure home. . . .

Although the decision in this case is justified by the other facts in the matter, this court appears to have put a great deal of weight on the mother's lack of means to provide for a conventional home. Courts must continually guard against the temptation to use relative financial worth as an easy test for a custody award. Relative financial worth should be considered only when determinations about child support are being made and not when custody is being determined. It goes without saying that parenthood involves more than merely providing adequate resources for a child's material needs. The courts have long recognized this and the passage of the ERA should not change the reality of this situation. However, since the courts are held responsible for determining custody in accord with the needs of the child, a court could easily find itself confusing material well-being with the best interests of the child. Behind the benign-sounding doctrine of "best interests" lie a whole set of standards and preconceptions about child-rearing. As arbiter of what is best for the child, the court is placed in a position of imposing its own viewpoint on those before it. The judicial system must be required to see to it that all of its courts dealing with custody disputes remain as impartial as possible under the circumstances and that they arrive at their decisions on the basis of a close examination of the particulars of each case presented them. Each court should make the decision about who is the best guardian with an open mind and a recognition that equal rights does not mean that both parents are equal in their abilities as parents.

Appendix 13A:
Full Text of the Equal
Rights Amendment

This is the full text of the proposed amendment XXVII to the U.S. Constitution passed by Congress on 22 March 1972.

Section 1. Equality of rights under the law shall not be denied or abridged by the United States or by any State on account of sex.

Section 2. The Congress shall have the power to enforce, by appropriate legislation, the provisions of this article.

Section 3. This amendment shall take effect two years after the date of ratification.

Appendix 13B:
Population Table

Households and Husband-Wife Families in E.R.A. States and Regions, with Figures for Percentage of Region and Percentage of U.S. Total (1975)

	1975 Households	1975 Husband-Wife Households
United States Total	71,537	47,200
Northeast total	4,029	2,656
New Hampshire [a]	266	184
Massachusetts [a]	1,936	1,236
Connecticut	1,024	697
Subtotal	3,226	2,117
ERA% of Northeast	80.1	79.7
ERA% of U.S. total	4.5	4.5
Middle Atlantic total	12,701	8,137
Pennsylvania	3,980	2,634
ERA% of Middle Atlantic	31.3	32.4
ERA% of U.S. total	5.6	5.6
East-North Central total	13,498	9,142
Illinois	3,745	2,436
ERA% of East-North Central	27.7	26.7
ERA% of U.S. total	5.2	5.2
West-North Central total	5,660	3,830
ERA% of West-North Central	0	0
South Atlantic total	11,205	7,438
Maryland [a]	1,324	891
Virginia	1,592	1,085
Subtotal	2,916	1,976
ERA% of South Atlantic	26.0	26.0
ERA% of U.S. total	4.1	4.2
East-South Central total	4,367	2,986
ERA% of East-South Central	0	0
West-South Central total	6,870	4,623
Louisiana	1,183	774
Texas [a]	4,011	2,718
Subtotal	5,194	3,492
ERA% of West-South Central	75.6	75.5
ERA% of U.S. total	7.3	5.3
Mountain total	3,158	2,143
Montana	253	169
Wyoming	126	88
Colorado [a]	859	569
New Mexico [a]	358	243
Utah	358	259
Subtotal	1,954	1,328

	1975 Households	1975 Husband-Wife Households
ERA% of Mountain	61.9	62.0
ERA% of U.S. total	2.7	2.8
Pacific total	10,050	6,245
Washington [a]	1,248	817
Alaska	97	69
Hawaii [a]	246	168
Subtotal	1,591	1,054
ERA% of Pacific	15.8	16.9
ERA% of U.S. total	2.2	2.2
Total households in ERA states	22,177	14,766
ERA% of total household population	31.0	31.3

Source: U.S., Bureau of the Census, *Statistical Abstract, 1977.* 1978.

Note: Northeast: Maine, New Hampshire, Vermont, Rhode Island, Connecticut, Massachusetts.

Middle Atlantic: New York, New Jersey, Pennsylvania.

East-North Central: Ohio, Indiana, Illinois, Michigan.

West-North Central: Minnesota, Iowa, Missouri, North Dakota, South Dakota, Nebraska, Kansas.

South Atlantic: Delaware, Maryland, District of Columbia, Virginia, West Virginia, North Carolina, South Carolina, Georgia, Florida.

East-South Central: Kentucky, Tennessee, Alabama, Mississippi.

West-South Central: Arkansas, Louisiana, Oklahoma, Texas.

Mountain: Montana, Idaho, Wyoming, Colorado, New Mexico, Arizona, Utah, Nevada.

Pacific: Washington, Oregon, California, Alaska, Hawaii.

[a]States that have passed constitutional amendments similar or exactly in accord with the wording of the proposed federal amendment.

Appendix 13C:
Text, Date of Adoption, and Effective Date of Nine State Equal Rights Amendments

State	Text of Constitutional Provision	Date of Adoption	Effective Date
Colorado	Equality of rights under the law shall not be denied or abridged by the state of Colorado or any of its political subdivisions on account of sex. [art. 2, sect. 29]	November 1972	January 1973
Hawaii	Equality of rights under the law shall not be denied or abridged by the state on account of sex. [art. 1, sect. 21]	November 1972	November 1972
Maryland	Equality of rights under the law shall not be abridged or denied because of sex. [Declaration of Rights, art. 46]	November 1972	November 1972
Massachusetts	. . . Equality under the law shall not be denied or abridged because of sex, race, color, creed or national origin. [Declaration of Rights, (sect. 2) art. I]	November 1976	November 1976
New Hampshire	. . . Equality of rights under the law shall not be denied or abridged by this state on account of race, creed, color, sex or national origin. [part I, art. 2]	1974	1974
New Mexico	No person shall be deprived of life, liberty or property without due process of law; nor shall any person be denied equal protection of the laws. Equality of rights under law shall not be denied on account of the sex of any person. [art. 2, sect. 18]	November 1972	July 1973
Pennsylvania	Equality of rights under the law shall not be denied or abridged in the Commonwealth of Pennsylvania because of the sex of the individual. [art 1, sect. 28]	May 1971	May 1971
Texas	Equality under the law shall not be denied or abridged because of sex, race, color, creed, or national origin. [art. 1, sect. 3a]	November 1972	November 1972
Washington	Equality of rights and responsibility under the law shall not be denied or abridged on account of sex. [art. 31, sect. 1]	November 1972	November 1972

Note: All the above states that have passed state Equal Rights Amendments have also ratified the federal Equal Rights Amendment as follows: Hawaii, 22 March 1972; New Hampshire, 23 March 1972; Texas, 19 April 1972; Colorado, 21 April 1972; Maryland, 26 May 1972; Massachusetts, 21 June 1972; Pennsylvania, 26 September 1972; New Mexico, 28 February 1973; Washington, 27 March 1973.

Appendix 13D:
Domestic Relations
ERA Decisions in Nine
States

State	Domestic Relations in ERA Decisions
Colorado	*People* v. *Elliot*, 525, P.2d 457 (Sup. Ct. 1974). Felony nonsupport charge for past payments upheld even though statute applied to men only; no retroactive application of state equal rights amendment.
	In re marriage of Franks, 542 P. 2d 846 (1975). (application for stay denied, 423 U.S. 1043, 96 S. Ct. 766 [1976]. Uniform Dissolution of Marriage Act upheld against father's claim of sex discrimination in custody awards.
	In re marriage of Trask, 580 P.2d 825 (Colo. App. 1978), (cert. denied 3 July 1978). Evidence failed to show that trial court discriminated on basis of sex against appellant in child-support hearing by awarding attorney's fees to his former wife and refusing to order her to work so that she might be required to contribute support of child on parity with its father.
Hawaii	*Cragun* v. *Hawaii and Kashimoto,*[a] Civil No. 43175 (1st Cir. Ct. 1975) [cited in *Women's Law Reporter* 1(162 (1 March 1975)]. Gave married women right to use birth name to vote.
Maryland	*Minner* v. *Minner,* 19 Md. App. 154, 310 A.2d 208 (Ct. Spec. App. 1973). Husband, who was not seeking alimony or counsel fees, had no standing to challenge the constitutionality of Maryland statutes concerned with alimony and award of counsel fees to a wife.
	Colburn v. *Colburn,* 20 Md. App. 346, 316 A2d 283 (Ct. Spec. App. 1974). Issue of standing decided as in *Minner.*
	Cooke v. *Cooke,* 21 Md.App. 376, 319 A.2d 841 (Ct. Spec. App. 1974). Use of "maternal preference" as a tie-breaker in custody cases does not violate the state equal rights amendment.
	Rand v. *Rand,* 280 Md. 508 (1977) 365 A.2d 587. Parental obligation for child support is not primarily an obligation of the father but is the responsibility of both parents in accordance with their respective financial resources.
	German v. *German,* 37 Md. App. 120, 376 A.2d 115 (1977). Requirement that both parents share responsibilities for child support does not mean that amount charged is to be equally divided; rather the amount of obligation varies with parents' respective financial resources.
	Foster v. *Foster,* 33 Md. App. 73, 364 A.2d 65 (1976). Award of counsel fees to wife was based on need and therefore does not violate the state equal rights amendment.
	Bell v. *Bell,* 38 Md. A.10, 379 A.2d 418 (1977), (cert. denied 23 Jan. 1978). Presumption that the husband is dominant figure in the marriage is sex classification which is no longer permissible, therefore husband's dominance is a question of fact in each case.
	Eckstein v. *Eckstein,* 38 Md. App. 506, 379 A.2d 757 (1978). Presumption that husband is the dominant figure in a marriage has been abandoned

159

State	*Domestic Relations in ERA Decisions*

since the adoption of the equal rights amendment so whether the wife was under duress is a question of fact in each case.

Coleman v. *State*, 37 Md. App. 322, 377 A.2d 553 (1977). Statute that made it a crime for a husband to desert his wife and fail to support his wife but not vice versa establishes a distinction solely on the basis of sex and is unconstitutional under the state's equal rights amendment so that defendant's husband's convictions for nonsupport and desertion were reversed.

Massachusetts   No cases

New Hampshire   No cases

New Mexico   *Schaab* v. *Schaab,* 87 N.M. 220, 531 P.2d 954 (App. Ct. 1974). Sex-neutral alimony statute upheld as applied to appellant husband; ERA does not proscribe conditions as to when and why alimony should be granted as long as it is sex neutral.

Pennsylvania
1972   *Corso* v. *Corso*[a], 59D and C.2d (Allegheny Co. Ct. C.P. 1972). Allowing bed-and-board divorce for women only no longer constitutional. Thus this cause of action is no longer recognized in this county.

DeRosa v. *DeRosa,*[a] 60 D. and C.2d 71 (Delaware Co. Ct. C.P. 1972). Statutes allowing alimony and counsel fees to women without adequate resources do not violate the ERA (Statutes now sex-neutralized.)

Kehl v. *Kehl,*[a] 57 D. and C.2d 164 (Allegheny Co. Ct. C.P. 1972). Statutory provisions allowing alimony and counsel fees to women only violate the equal rights amendment. (Provisions are now sex neutral.)

Rogan v. *Rogan,*[a] Civil No. 1934 (Luzerne Co. Ct. C.P. October term 1972). Neither husband nor wife should be allowed counsel fees under statutory scheme allowing such awards to women upon divorce. (provisions are now sex-neutral.)

1973   *Frank* v. *Frank,*[a] 62 D. and C.2d 102 (Lebanon Co. Ct. C.P. 1973). Upheld statute allowing alimony *pendente lite* for women. (Now statute is sex neutral.)

Greén v. *Freiheit,*[a] Civil No. 1015, Docket No. 260259 (Family Div., 1st Judicial Dist., October term 1973). Child-support responsibility rests equally with both parents according to ability. Presumption charging father with primary obligation no longer valid under equal rights amendment.

Lukens v. *Lukens,*[a] 224 Pa. Super. 227, 303 A.2d 522 (Super. Ct. 1973). Discrepancy in support provisions for wives and husbands does not violate the equal rights amendment because both spouses have a reciprocal and substantial right to support, despite the lack of mathematical equality.

Murphy v. *Murphy,*[a] 224 Pa. Super. 460, 303 A.2d 838 (Super. Ct. 1973). Upheld alimony and counsel fees for women only. (Statute is now sex neutral.)

Wiegand v. *Wiegand,*[a] 226 Pa. Super. 378, 310 A.2d 426 (Super. Ct. 1973), revised on other grounds, 337 A.2d 256 (Sup. Ct. 1975). Appellate court invalidated statutory provisions allowing bed-and-board divorce for women only. However, supreme court said the equal rights amendment challenge not properly raised, so status of bed-and-board divorce remains in question in Pennsylvania.

State	Domestic Relations in ERA Decisions
1974	*Conway* v. *Dana*,[a] 456 Pa. 536, 218 A.2d 324 (Sup. Ct. 1974). Parents have equal responsibility for child support according to their capacities. Presumption that fathers alone are responsible is no longer valid. Court should assess financial abilities of both.
	Hakes v. *Hakes*,[a] 67 D. and C.2d 25 (Sullivan Co. Ct. C.P. 1974). Real estate conveyed to wife in her own name did not create tenancy by entirety or constructive trust in favor of husband. Wife used no undue influence against husband and should not be bound by old presumptions about the marital unit.
	Henderson v. *Henderson*,[a] 458 Pa. 97, 327 A.2d 60 (Sup. Ct. 1974). Found statutory provisions allowing alimony *pendente lite* and counsel fees for women only to use impermissible sex classification. Noted that statute had now been sex-neutralized by legislature. Held that support rights and obligations depend not on sex but on relative financial circumstances of spouses.
	Hopkins v. *Blanco*,[a] 457 Pa. 90, 320 A.2d 139 (Sup. Ct. 1974). Extended right to sue for loss of consortium to women.
	Kaper v. *Kaper*,[a] 227 Pa. Super. 377, 323 A.2d 223 (Sup. Ct. 1974). Must consider mother's income and actual needs of child in assessing father's support obligation.
	Keenan v. *Pennsylvania Hills School District*,[a] 65 D. and C.2d 764 (Allegheny Co. Ct. C.P. 1974). Equal rights amendment creates no new rights of one spouse in income of other during marriages. Thus it is proper for wives without outside income to be covered by school tax exemption, regardless of income of husbands.
	Norris v. *Norris*,[a] 63 D. and C.2d 239 (Phila. Co. Ct. C.P. 1974). Equal rights amendment does not require precise equality in relationship to a substantial right to support for both sexes. Not unconstitutional to allow statutory *in rem* action for support by deserted wife but not by deserted husband.
	Percival v. *City of Philadelphia*,[a] 317 A.2d 667 (Cmwlth. Ct. 1974). Exempting married women from arrest under writ of *capias* action to recover city wage taxes from nonresident employees violates the equal rights amendment.
1975	*Com. ex. rel. Buonocore* v. *Buonocore*,[a] 340 A.2d. 579 (Super. Ct. 1975). Child-support order against wife upheld since husband's income was inadequate and children were living with him and wife had an ability to contribute—otherwise, children would have become "indigent" under "poor law."
	Butler v. *Butler*,[a] 2 Family L. Rep. 2092 (Sup. Ct. 1975). Presumption that wife does not intend husband to benefit from her contributions to entireties property no longer valid. Court held that entireties property should be divided equally at divorce.
	Commonwealth v. *Santiago*,[a] 340 A.2d 440 (Sup. Ct. 1975). Common-law doctrine of coercion of wife in crime by husband and wife not longer legitimate defense since wife's identity will no longer seem to merge with husband's on marriage.
	DiFlorido v. *DiFlorido*,[a] 331 A.2d 174 (Sup. Ct. 1975). Presumption favoring ownership of all household goods by husband is invalid. Nonmonetary as well as monetary contributions to household must be con-

State	Domestic Relations in ERA Decisions

sidered. Proper presumption in dividing goods on divorce is one of joint ownership.

Einstein Medical Center v. *Gold*,[a] 66 d. and C.2d 347 (Phila. Co. Ct. C.P. 1975). Improper for wife to defend against payment of husband's medical expenses by relying on outmoded doctrine that only husbands are responsible for the necessaries of their spouses.

1976   *Adoption of Walker*, 468 Pa. 165, 260 A.2d 603 (1976). Statute which requires consent of mother only for adoption of illegitimate child is unconstitutional because it creates a distinction between unwed mothers and unwed fathers.

Smith v. *Smith*, Pa. Super. 1976, 361 A.2d 756 (1976). Doctrine of interspousal immunity from court action does not violate the Pennsylvania equal rights amendment.

1977   *Commonwealth of Pennsylvania ex rel Spriggs* v. *Carson*, 470 Pa. 290, 368 A.2d 635 (1977) (plurality opinion). Declares use of tender-years doctrine in custody disputes unconstitutional.

Gilman v. *Unemployment Compensation Board of Review*, 28 Penn. Commonwealth 630, 369 A.2d (1977). Category of sole or major support of family in unemployment compensation law was economic classification and not sex discriminatory.

Burchanowski v. *Co. of Lycoming,* 32 Pa. Commonwealth, 207, 378 A.2d 1025. Plaintiff lacked standing to appeal lower court's ruling that housewife is an occupation within the meaning of the local Tax Enabling Act since the court had enjoined collection of the tax ruling that taking housewifes, an exclusively female class, and providing for collection of wife's taxes from husband's earnings but not vice versa violated the Pennsylvania equal rights amendment.

In re Estate of Klein, 474 Pa. 416, 378 A.2d 1182 (1977). Wife created tenancy by the entireties when she used her funds to create joint bank account with her husband. Pennsylvania equal right amendment had abolished sex-based presumptions about interspousal transfers.

Commonwealth ex rel Wasiolek v. *Wasiolek*, Pa. Super, 380 A.2d 400. Permitting nurturing parent to remain at home until child matures does not run afoul of the equal rights amendment.

Margurite v. *Ewald*, Pa. Super. 381 A.2d 480. Presumption that husband and wife take property as tenants by the entireties does not violate the Pennsylvania equal rights amendment.

Commonwealth of Pennsylvania ex rel. Peterson v. *Hayes*, Pa. Super, 381 A.2d 1311. Standard applied to father seeking right to visit his illigitimate child should be the same as that applied to the mother.

1978   *Guinn* v. *Comm. Unemployment Compensation Board of Review,* 382 A.2d 503 (1978). Same as *Gilman*, 1977.

Commonwealth ex rel Berry v. *Berry*, Pa. Super, 384 A.2d 1337 (1978). Equal rights amendment requires that a court assess each parent's overall capacity to discharge his or her obligations of child support, not just compare their respective incomes.

Gulas v. *Gulas*, Pa. Super., 386 A.2d 69 (1978). Same as *Commonwealth of Pennsylvania ex rel Spriggs*, 1977.

Kurpiewski v. *Kurpiewski*, Pa. Super., 386 A.2d 55 (1978). Order directing husband to pay wife's medical bills without limit was improper since wife had not established she was entitled to support after leaving her husband and order placed no limits on amount of obligation.

State	Domestic Relations in ERA Decisions

	Nan Duskin, Inc. v. *Parks,* 4 FLR 2309 (Pa. Common. Pleas. Ct., Phila. Cty (1978). Rule of law that husband is liable to a third party for necessities suppled to his wife violates the state equal rights amendment.
Texas	*Felsenthal* v. *McMillan,*[a] 493 S.W.2d 729 (Sup. Ct. 1973). Tort of criminal conversation, available at common law to husbands only, must be made available to women, too.
	Scanlon v. *Crim,*[a] 500 W.S.2d 554 (Ct. Civ. App. 1973). Equal rights amendment extends right to action for common-law breach of marriage promise to men as well as women.
	Cooper v. *Cooper,*[a] 513 S.W.2d 229 (Ct. Civ. App. 1974). Unequal division of community-property and child-support obligations favoring wife on divorce does not violate the equal rights amendment because court must consider sex-neutral factors such as wife's lower earning capacity.
	Perkins v. *Freeman,*[a] 501 S.W.2d 424 (Ct. Civ. App. 1973), revised and remanded on other grounds, 518 S.W.2d 532 (Sup. Ct. 1974). Upheld award of custody and attorney's fees to father because it was in best interest of child and attorney's fees were necessaries for child. Like women, men should be awarded fees in proper situations under the amendment.
	Friedman v. *Friedman,*[a] 521 S.W.2d 111 (Ct. Civ. App. 1975). Family Code requires both parents to support children but does not require mathematically equal contribution. Services as well as money should be assessed.
	Lipsky v. *Lipsky,*[a] 525 S.W.2d 222 (Ct. Civ. App. 1975). Upheld award of attorney's fees to wife as part of property settlement because her financial need, apart from her sex, justified such an award.
	Miller v. *Whittlesey,* 562 S.W.2d 904 (1978). A wife does have a cause of action for negligent impairment of consortium because the amendment modified the common law to such an extent that it would be improper to deny a cause of action based on the sex of the party bringing the action.
Washington	*Hanson* v. *Hutt,*[a] 83 Wash. 2d 195, 517 P.2d 599 (Sup. Ct. 1973). Unconstitutional to deny unemployment benefits to a woman automatically between the seventeenth week before childbirth and the sixth week subsequent.
	Singer v. *Hara,*[a] 11 Wash. App. 247, 522 P.2d 1187 (1974). Statute prohibiting same-sex marriage upheld under the equal rights amendment as not being sex discriminatory as between men and women.
	Smith v. *Smith,*[a] 13 Wash. App. 381, 534 P.2d 1033 (1975). Equal rights amendment requires equal responsibilities of parents for child support. Trial court erred in not considering income of both new marital units in assessing child support obligations from previous marriage. The amendment does not require fifty-fifty breakdown, however.
	Ayers v. *Employment Security Deparment,* 85 Wash. 2d 500, 536 P.2d 610 (Sup. Ct. 1975). Husbands as well as wives should not be denied unemployment benefits for leaving work to follow their spouses to a new location under appropriate circumstances.
	In re Hanson's Welfare, 15 Wash. App. 231, 548 P.2d 333 (1976). Father's contention that court's decision to terminate his parental rights was based on his sex in violation of the amendment was not substantiated by the facts.
	State v. *Wood,* 89 Wash. 2d 97, 569 P.2d 1148 (1977). Statute requiring natural father of illegitimate child to contribute to support which did not

State	*Domestic Relations in ERA Decisions*

state similar requirement for mother was not violation of the equal rights amendment because under whole statutory scheme both parents were responsible for support.

[a]Indicates a case description taken from table 2-1 in Brown, Barbara A., Ann E. Freedman, Harriet N. Katz, and Alice M. Price. *Women's Rights and the Law: The Impact of the ERA on State Laws.* New York: Praeger Special Studies, 1977. Copyright © 1977 by Praeger Publishers. Reproduced by permission of Praeger Publishers.

Appendix 13E: Wives and Mothers in the Labor Force: What This Implies for the Courts

Because of the overriding importance of the changes that have occurred in the female role, some demographic data is presented here in order to gain a better perspective on what the courts are coping with and will have to cope with in the future. The primary and all-embracing change that has affected the status of married women in the American society is the large-scale entrance of wives into the labor force. Out of 47 million American wives in 1977, 22 million were employed with over 70 percent working at full-time jobs. These figures represent a very substantial change in female employment patterns over the past twenty years. During this time the number of married females on the labor force actually doubled (table 13E-1). Therefore, American courts have had to deal with the fact that in many of the cases brought before them the wife may be employed and have earnings in her own right. In the ERA states these earnings would have to be taken into consideration in an attempt to decide issues of support or alimony. Although in over three out of four married couples where both husband and wife were employed, the husband made at least $1,000 more than his wife, in 21 percent of these marriages the wife made as much as or more than her husband.

Table 13E-1
Labor-Force Status, Participation Rate, and Annual Growth Rates of Married Females, 1956–1976

Year	Number	Participation Rate (%)	Annual Growth Rates per Five-Year Period (%)
1956	11,126,000	29	
1961	13,266,000	33	3.6
1966	15,178,000	35	2.3
1971	18,530,000	41	4.1
1976	21,554,000	45	3.1

Source: Giraldo, Z.I. and J.M. Weatherford, "Life Cycle and the American Family: Current Trends and Policy Implications," Duke University, Institute of Policy Sciences Working Paper, no. 378 (March 1978), pp. 3–4.

Table 13E-2

Comparison of Husband and Wife Earnings in 1975

(numbers in thousands)

Earnings of Husband	All Families with Husband and Wife Earners	Wife Has More Earnings Than Husband by		Wife and Husband Earning Within $1,000 of Each Other	Wife Has Less Earnings Than Husband by	
		$2,000	$1,000		$1,000	$2,000
Total number	22,335	1,641	800	2,171	2,625	15,098[a]
Percent of total	100.0	7.3	3.6	9.7	11.8	67.6
$1 to $999 or less	629	405	61	162	—	—
$1,000 to $1,199	527	285	44	83	113	—
$2,000 to $2,999	570	223	60	84	76	129
$3,000 to $3,999	636	204	62	75	77	217
$4,000 to $4,999	768	175	72	98	107	317
$5,000 to $5,999	874	143	82	93	103	453
$6,000 to $6,999	1,024	109	61	109	114	632
$7,000 to $7,999	1,276	75	81	97	139	885
$8,000 to $9,999	2,830	22	195	317	241	2,055
$10,000 to $15,999	6,917	[b]	82	752	809	5,276
$15,000 and over	6,283	[b]	[b]	301	846[c]	5,134[d]
Median earnings of husband	11,370	2,585	6,311	9,795	12,117	12,711

Source: P.C. Glick and A.S. Norton, "Marrying, Divorcing and Living Together in the U.S. Today," *Population Bulletin* 32(October 1977), p. 12. Courtesy of the Population Reference Bureau, Inc.

[a] Besides these 15,098,000 earning wives with perceptibly less earnings than their husbands, an additional 23,367,000 wives had no earnings. The total number of wives with perceptibly less earnings than their husbands was 38,465,000 or 81.3 percent of all 47,318,000 husband-wife families in 1976.

[b] Separate information not available; included with "wife and husband in same interval."

[c] Wife earns $10,000 to $14,999.

[d] Wife earns less than $10,000.

Only 10.9 percent of married females made $1,000 or more above the salaries of their husbands (table 13E-2). Where the wife is earning $2,000 or more than her husband, his mean earnings only amount to $2,585 per annum. Therefore, it is apparent that the great majority of employed wives are on the labor force out of economic necessity. It can also be seen from table 13E-2 that there are 2.4 million women who are providing more toward the support of their families than are their husbands. Conversely there are 17.7 million employed women who are earning less than their husbands. They, combined with the 22 million nonemployed wives, guarantee that the preponderance of support cases facing the courts will involve the traditional posture of wife seeking support from her husband.

While the figures solely in terms of income indicate that wives have not achieved a high level of economic independence, studies of attitudes indicate that wives are perceived by the general public as playing a strong leadership role within the family. In a survey conducted by the Bureau of the Census in 1975, a sample of the population was asked whether or not the husband of the household ought to be always counted by that bureau as the head of the family. The results showed that 52 percent of the married couples who responded reported that the husband was the family head, 34 percent reported that both husband and wife constituted a joint head of family, and 14 percent of married couples reported that they considered the wife as the head of the family (Glick and Norton, 1977, p. 12). Therefore, a sparse majority of 52 percent still continued to view their families in the traditional manner, while 48 percent perceived the wife as holding a more instrumental role than formally. This perception could account for the fear expressed by some that the courts in the ERA states will provide inadequate protections for housewives. It may be based on an awareness that wives are family heads and a fear that they might be forced out of their homes by the courts in order to make them conform with the way the role of family head is viewed by Americans. No case of this type has been found. Each case brought before a court has to be treated on its individual merits and no woman has been asked to behave according to generalized concepts of how she has changed.

In those instances where the courts have changed the traditional responsibilities and rights that inhere in a marriage, the changes reflect current norms that have become widely accepted in American life. Again this is acceptance of the fact of change, not inducement to change.

One final point is that egalitarian marriages are becoming the norm in the United States. The older view of the marriage relationship was essentially nonegalitarian in that while the husband owed a duty of support, and the wife owed services to him and the family in return for this support, the relationship was never viewed as an agreement between equal partners. The married couple was perceived as a unit with the husband in control. The trend is definitely away from the older view and toward equality of roles and responsibilities within marriage. This trend is doubtlessly developing more quickly because of the growing numbers of women opting for both marriage and employment. At one time studies tended to blame many of society's ills on the lessened role of the homemaker and on the fact that this role had lost its honored status in society. More recent studies have begun to revise this assessment.

These findings and conclusions are optimistic and auger well for the nation. While families are presently undergoing a period of strain and stress, equality may bring equanimity. The great changes in marriage relationships that have caused concern for the well-being of the family in the United States may be producing stronger, healthier relationships that better serve the needs of today's individuals. If that is the case, those states experimenting with treating marriage as an egalitarian relationship are on the crest of a new wave.

Appendix 13F:
Divorce Statistics

Although cases involving divorce appear at first glance not to be specifically addressing the issues of families but only the dissolution of families, all of these cases are family-related. They concern support for family dependents and, given the high incidence of remarriage occurring in the United States at present, are very much involved with the maintainance of family members as they make their transitions from one family to another. Table 13F-1 summarizes the numbers of marriages, divorces, and remarriages that had taken place in the United States up to the year 1975. Seventy-nine percent of all married persons in 1975 were still living with their first spouses, while 21 percent of marriages that had occurred up to that year were between one or two persons who had been previously married. Although these figures are not terribly shocking, particularly when viewed in terms of age categories, what has emerged as an issue of particular concern is that the divorce rate reached 50 percent in 1978 when computed on the basis of the number of divorces and marriages taking place during that year. Obviously if this high rate continues it will fundamentally change the demographic profile of the

Table 13F-1
Husband-Wife Households: Number of Times Each Has Married,
According to Age of Husband, June 1975
(*numbers in thousands*)

Subject	All Husband-Wife Households	Husband-Wife Each Married Once	Percent of All Husband-Wife Households	All Other Husband-Wife Remarriage Combinations	Percent of All Husband-Wife Households
Total	44,302	35,077	79	9,225	21
Husband's age					
Under 25	3,030	2,800	92	230	8
25 to 29	5,376	4,614	86	762	14
30 to 34	5,131	4,192	82	939	18
35 to 44	8,971	7,001	78	1,883	21
45 to 54	9,345	7,225	77	2,052	22
55 to 64	7,677	5,810	76	1,866	24
65 to 75	4,771	3,435	72	1,336	28

Source: Computed from the U.S., Bureau of the Census, Series P-20, no. 312 (Washington, D.C.: Government Printing Office, 1977).

nation in terms of marital stability. However, the jump in the number of divorces per the number of marriages began in 1970 and may reflect factors that will not continue to exert their force over the long run (table 13F–2). But it is undeniable that the slower but steady growth in the numbers of divorces occuring in this country is a long-range trend that cannot be ignored.

A more specific development is likely to have an important impact in terms of the ERA. Table 13F–3 shows percentages of married persons who are likely to divorce in the future, computed according to birth cohort. People who are now entering their thirties have the highest expectations of having their marriages end in divorce. And since the current number of remarriages occurring among divorced persons has reached the level of four out of five, it is obvious that the courts of this nation will be faced with a growing number of divorce, support, and custody cases among those categories of the population most likely to bring up equal-rights issues. The reason for this is that these marriages will involve females with occupational training and work experience who would be more likely to have remained employed after marriage or who could be expected to return to the workforce and resume careers with less of a disadvantage than that of older women. Therefore, the existence of equal-rights legislation is likely to affect this birth cohort more profoundly than persons born earlier.

The major problem involving these families in transition concerns the painful question of child custody. At the present divorce rates, over a million children a year are involved in marriage dissolutions. Table 13F–4 depicts the total number of children affected annually and the average number of children affected per family over a twenty-year span.

Table 13F–2
Total Numbers of Marriages and Divorces, 1950–1975
(*numbers in thousands*)

	1950	1955	1960	1965	1970	1975
Total number of U.S. marriages per year	1,667	1,531	1,523	1,800	2,159	2,153
Total number of U.S. divorces per year	385	377	393	479	708	1,036
Divorces as a percent of marriages	23	25	26	27	33	48

Source: Computed from the U.S., Bureau of the Census, *Statistical Abstract* (1977).

Table 13F-3
Percent of Ever-Married Persons Whose First Marriage May Eventually End in Divorce, by Years of School Completed, Year of Birth, and Sex, June 1975

	Year of Birth									
	1945 to 1949	1940 to 1944	1935 to 1939	1930 to 1934	1925 to 1929	1920 to 1924	1915 to 1919	1910 to 1914	1905 to 1909	1900 to 1904
Men ever married										
All educational levels:										
First marriage ended in divorce by 1975	13.1	16.9	20.1	18.4	18.1	18.4	17.4	16.7	14.9	13.3
May eventually end in divorce	34.1	31.5	29.5	24.0	21.8	20.4	18.4	17.2	15.2	13.3
Women ever married										
All educational levels:										
First marriage ended in divorce by 1975	17.2	19.9	21.5	20.6	21.0	18.0	16.4	15.8	14.9	12.8
May eventually end in divorce	38.3	34.4	30.7	26.2	23.8	19.5	17.2	16.2	15.1	12.8

Source: U.S., Bureau of the Census, Series P-20, no. 312 (Washington, D.C.: Government Printing Office, 1977).

Table 13F–4
Estimated Number of Children Involved in Divorces and Annulments: United States, 1954–1975

Year	Estimated Number of Children Involved	Average Number of Children per Decree
1975	1,123,000	1.08
1970	870,000	1.22
1965	630,000	1.32
1960	463,000	1.18
1955	347,000	0.92

Source: U.S., Department of Health, Education and Welfare, *Monthly Vital Statistics Report,* Advanced Report Final Divorce Statistics, 1975.

When both parents are fit and custody is raised as an issue, the courts face their severest challenges. The attention that has been recently focused on the growing number of divorced fathers seeking sole custody of their children must not, however, blur the realization that the vast majority of children in the custody of only one parent still remain under the supervision of the mother. It is important to be aware of the fact that in 1976 close to 800,000 children lived in the sole custody of their fathers, however, this hardly compares with the fact that over 10 million children lived only with their mothers.

The figures for the past sixteen years show that the number of children living with divorced mothers doubled while it only rose 1.1 percent to 1.2 percent for fathers during that same period (table 13F–5). Yet viewed solely in terms of the courts, the spurt in demand for child custody by divorced men has brought this particular issue into prominence. The attitude of the courts a generation ago might be characterized as one of viewing the fit mother as the parent with a better claim to the custody of her child, especially during the phase of life defined by the courts as the "tender years," however, the courts in both the ERA states and in the non-ERA states have been moving away from that presumption of late. Without this traditional legal paradigm to rely on, custody cases severely test the court's ability to discern all of the relevant aspects of a matter so that it can render impartial decisions that best serve all of the parties involved.

The number of persons involved with the entire matter of alimony is much smaller. In 1975, 248,304 income-tax returns indicated receipt of alimony payments. This indicates the existence of an approximately equivalent number of alimony papers, so slightly less than 500,000 persons, representing an extremely small segment of the total population, are concerned with the giving or receiving of alimony payments. The average payment amounted to $2,900 per year and only began to reach a significant dollar level for persons in the $50,000 income bracket and above (table 13F–6). In

Table 13F-5
Living Arrangements of Children Under Eighteen in the United States,
1960, 1970, and 1976

Living Arrangements	Year			Ratio 1976/1960
	1960	1970	1976	
All children under 18	64,310,000	69,523,000	65,129,000	1.01
Percent living with				
Two parents	87.5	83.1	80.0	.91a
Both married once	c	68.7	68.8b	c
One parent	1.1	13.4	17.0	1.87
Mother only	7.9	11.5	15.8	2.00
Divorced	1.9	3.5	6.2	3.26
Married	3.7	4.5	5.8	1.57
Separated	2.3	3.4	4.9	2.13
Widowed	2.0	2.4	2.1	1.05
Single	0.3	1.1	1.7	5.67
Father only	1.1	1.9	1.2	1.09
Divorced	0.2	0.3	0.6	3.00
Married	0.5	1.0	0.4	.80
Separated	0.2	0.2	0.3	1.50
Widowed	0.4	0.4	0.1	.25
Single	0.0	0.2	0.1	——
Other relatives only	2.4	2.3	2.3	.96
Nonrelatives only d	1.0	1.2	0.7	70

Source: P.C. Glick and A.J. Norton, "Marrying, Divorcing and Living Together in the U.S. Today," *Population Bulletin,* v. 32, (October 1977), p. 28. Courtesy of the Population Reference Bureau, Inc.

a This ratio is the result of dividing 80.0 by 87.5.

b Based on data for 1975.

c Base less than 75,000 children.

d For 1976 exludes children living in institutions: in 1979, 0.4 percent lived in institutions.

Table 13F-6
Alimony Income in 1975

Size of Adjusted Gross Income	Number of Returns with Alimony Income	Total Amount of Income	Average Amount of Alimony (Dollars Divided by No. Returns)
Under $2,000	9,089	5,030,000	550
$2,000 under $4,000	11,859	25,475,000	2,150
$4,000 under $6,000	28,879	49,055,000	1,700
$6,000 under $8,000	25,474	56,010,000	2,200
$8,000 under $10,000	38,403	109,030,000	2,840
$10,000 under $12,000	31,679	84,304,000	2,660
$12,000 under $14,000	22,067	89,739,000	4,070

Table 13F–6 continued

Size of Adjusted Gross Income	Number of Returns with Alimony Income	Total Amount of Income	Average Amount of Alimony (Dollars Divided by No. Returns)
$14,000 under $16,000	20,564	51,608,000	2,510
$16,000 under $18,000	16,773	78,872,000	4,700
$18,000 under $20,000	13,245	40,868,000	3,090
$20,000 under $25,000	13,250	61,758,000	4,660
$25,000 under $30,000	5,976	7,480,000	1,250
$30,000 under $50,000	8,730	31,565,000	3,622
$50,000 under $100,000	1,874	21,299,000	11,370
$100,000 under $200,000	364	9,372,000	25,750
$200,000 under $500,000	62	2,011,000	32,440
$500,000 and above	16	1,258,000	78,630
All returns, total	248,304	724,736,000	2,900

Source: Computed from U.S., Internal Revenue Series, *Statistics of Income, 1975*, No. 79 (May 1978).

this upper bracket only 2,316 persons received alimony payments, although these persons probably received a disproportionate share of publicity surrounding their alimony grants.

There is no doubt that under the ERA alimony will continue declining in usage following much the same pattern it was showing prior to the issue of the ERA. As fewer and fewer women require it, those women, their exhusbands, and society in general will be much better off. Alimony may have served a valid function at a time when women were socialized to dependency but, as society rejects this attitude, alimony will fall into disuse.

References for Part III

Booth, Alan. "Wife's Employment and Husband's Stress: A Replication and Refutation." *Journal of Marriage and the Family* 39 (1977): 645–650.

Brown, Barbara, Thomas I. Emerson, Gail Falk, and Ann E. Freedman. "The Equal Rights Amendment: A Constitutional Basis for Equal Rights for Women." *The Yale Law Journal* 80 (1971): 871–984.

Brown, Barbara A., Ann E. Freedman, Harriet N. Katz, and Alice M. Price. *Women's Rights and the Law: The Impact of the ERA on State Laws.* Praeger Special Studies: New York, 1977.

Dybward, Linda H. "Supplementing Washington's ERA: Problems with Wholesale Legislative Revisions." *Washington Law Review* 49 (1973-1974): 571–573.

Freed, Doris Jonas, and Henry H. Foster, Jr. "Divorce in the Fifty States: An Overview as of August 1, 1978." *The Family Law Reporter* 4 (1978): 4FLR 4033–4041.

Giraldo, Z.I., and J.M. Weatherford. "Life Cycle and the American Family: Current Trends and Policy Implications." Duke University Institute of Policy Sciences and Public Affairs Working Paper Series, no. 378 March 1978.

Glick, Paul C., and Arthur J. Norton. "Marrying, Divorcing and Living Together in the U.S. Today." In *Population Bulletin,* v. 32, Population Reference Bureau, Inc. Washington, D.C.: October 1977.

Kanowitz, Leo. *Women and the Law: The Unfinished Revolution.* University of New Mexico Press, New Mexico: 1969.

Kurtz, Paul M. "The State Equal Rights Amendments and Their Impact on Domestic Relations Law." *Family Law Quarterly* XI, 2 (1977): 101–150.

James, Carol Adair, Nancy M. Gordon, and Isabel V. Sawhill. "Child Support Payments in the U.S." The Urban Institute Working Paper 992-03, 1976.

Ramsey, Sarah. "Constitutional Protection for the Private Realm of the Family." Duke University Institute of Policy Sciences Working Paper Series, no. 11781, 1978.

U.S. Bureau of Census. *Marriage, Divorce, Widowhood, and Remarriage by Family Characteristics.* Series P-20, no. 312, 1977.

U.S. Bureau of Census. *Statistical Abstract, 1977.* 1978.

U.S. Commission on Civil Rights. *Statement on the Equal Rights Amendment.* Clearinghouse Publication 56, 1978.

U.S., Department of Health, Education and Welfare. *Monthly Vital Statistics Report.* Advanced Report Final Divorce Statistics, 1976.
U.S., Internal Revenue Service. *Statistics of Income.* no. 79 (5-78), 1975.

**Part IV
The Impact of
Employment on Family
Life in the United States**

14 Recent Trends and Studies on Two-Job and Two-Career Families: How They Have Changed and Where They Are Heading

As of March 1978 (the latest available figures) the participation rates for married women with school-age children reached 57 percent and for married women with preschool-age children, 42 percent. For divorced women the rates are 81 percent and 67 percent respectively (U.S., Department of Labor, 1978, table F). These growing numbers of working women are the main reason so much interest has been generated by the question of how employment affects the family. As long as the majority of mothers remained at home to supervise their children and care for the residence, the impact of employment on families tended to be overlooked and, particularly for the upper and middle classes, even discounted.

And what about the future? Are we at a point in time where we can look ahead and begin to discern what American families will look like in the 1980s? There are four relatively foolproof predictions I would like to make.

1. The number of two-job families will continue to rise steadily from 40 percent of all families in 1978 to 50 percent of all families (U.S., Department of Labor, 1978, table 1).
2. Women comprise 42 percent of the total civilian labor force and will soon be 50 percent of the labor-force (U.S., Department of Labor, 1978, table 2).
3. The percentage of family income contributed by wives, which rose from 19 percent in 1974 to 26 percent in 1978, should also begin heading perceptively toward the half-way mark (U.S., Department of Labor, 1974, 1978).
4. The percentage of women enrolled in colleges rose from 39 percent in 1968 to 49 percent in 1978. This figure is projected to rise to 52 percent by 1986 by the National Center for Educational Statistics.

In a survey of attitudes conducted among 188,000 college students in the class of 1980, 96.6 percent of the women felt that "Women should have job equality" (*Chronicle of Higher Education,* 1978, 1979). I predict that this will be achieved.

What these statistics emphasize is the fact that men and women are heading toward an equal share in the financial responsibility of providing for American families. On some unheralded day during the decade of the seventies women crossed an artificial barrier that had been holding them back from a full share of responsibility for their own lives and that of their families and began heading toward the natural barrier—the half-way line.

But the realization and acceptance of this occurrence by society still lags behind the figures. This means that policies toward families in the private and public sectors are not responding as supportively as they could to the new needs of families. They must do their share also. Because they have not, two-job families have found themselves coping single-handedly with all of the extra adjustments required to lead their daily lives. At the same time they have to cope with the outdated stereotypes that make them feel unconventional and depict their life styles as destructive of the social fabric. These stereotypes still view the two-job life style as harmful to the growth and development of children, particularly young children, and adolescents. Concern continues to be voiced about the deleterious impact of a wife's employment on her husband's and on her own health. Fears are expressed that the family is being rent apart or twisted out of shape by the demands of trying to balance two employment schedules and a full family life without a full-time mother. Even thoughtful people who recognize that American families are not going through the final throes of destruction find themselves caught up in a media-heightened atmosphere of fear. There is growing evidence that the American family has survived the initial shocks of a great upheaval and, although it is still rocking, it remains basically stable.

This chapter surveys recent studies that have attempted to look at problem situations with a relatively open mind and measure them fairly in order to determine the specific causes of the problems. Since the literature is quite large I have drawn certain arbitrary boundaries. One of the limiting principles was a recent publication date. The rationale for this is that things are moving very swiftly and material, no matter how interesting, loses its relevance almost before it is published. I have also tried to limit myself to reports on surveys administered rather than deal with the literature that attempts to develop theories explaining the present state of affairs. There is actually very little of that type of scholarship being done, probably because the situation is still too fluid to pin down. Finally, I have avoided covering areas examined in other chapters of this book.

One of the first aspects of the problem that everyone is interested in is determining what the effects are on children that have been brought about by these changes in family living. According to a study prepared by Mary Rowe at the Massachusetts Institute of Technology, in the 1980s at least half of all American children will spend at least two years of their childhood in a nontraditional family; that is, a family that has gone through divorce or is a two-job family (Rapoport and Rapoport, 1979). The findings of recent surveys of UNCO National Childcare Consumer Study and the Institute for Survey Research, as reported by Rowe show that only 3 percent of all households rely solely on the mother for all childcare within the family. But about a third of all families use childcare for only about an hour a week. In about 75 percent of all homes with children under fourteen, the mother remains the principal caretaker (Rapoport and Rapoport, 1979). Of the other 25 percent being provided with care for ten or more hours per week, only one-third of these mothers were on the labor force. The conclusions were that "all formal child-care arrangements . . . comprise not more than 8 to 10 percent of all arrangements, and not more than 20 percent of all major arrangements (those over 10 hours per week)" (Rowe, 1976, p. 93). Therefore, formal day care is not prevalent in our society.

The major types of childcare arrangements relied on by two-job families were provided by a relative or a private individual. This was true for a total of 70 to 81 percent of all the arrangements. While the studies indicate considerable satisfaction with this type of childcare, they also indicate "substantial potential demand for more care, for better care and for different options" (Rapoport and Rapoport, 1979).

Therefore, at the present time, children continue to be cared for substantially within a homelike environment. Although this development is not considered detrimental to the well-being of the child, some of the problems faced by parents because of the informality of the arrangements, or for other reasons, have led to widespread interest in providing them with more options. This leads to the consideration of what would be the impact of greater reliance on outside forms of day care. Is there any evidence that children are harmed by spending their days in a day-care center? According to other studies: "Above the level of child abuse, it is almost impossible to find lasting differences among children who have experienced different arrangements. . . . [S]uch evidence as exists suggests that children thrive best when their parents are satisfied with their work lives and child-care arrangements, and when the caretaker is stable and responsive" (Rowe, 1976; Howell, 1973).

A basic consideration about the impact of employment on children concerns the drop in birthrates. In a recent study involving a sample of sixty-three professional and sixty nonprofessional women living in the Los Angeles area, the researchers found that employed women view work and family as competing with each other and "that high perceived role conflict . . . is associated with lower fertility" (Beckman, 1978). This study conforms in its findings in general with fertility research in the United States. However, research in less-developed countries where child-rearing is more the responsibility of the extended family indicates a lack of such a conflict (Clifford and Tobin, 1977). Also, the data are not as conclusive among rural American females, low-income populations, and blacks. What they all

point to is that white urban women, particularly professionals, are responding to the strain of combining employment and family life by curtailing the
size of their families. These women do not appear to have as many support
resources available to them as do women from rural areas with low population mobility, which presumably provides them with more kin on whom to
rely, or as black women who have had much greater experience with combining employment with family responsibilities on the basis of higher labor-
force participation rates over a much longer period. If this is not perceived
as a desirable social development, policies to relieve some of the causes of
conflict between employment and parenting could be devised.

A study done in 1976 claimed that husbands of working wives were in
poorer health and less contented with their marriages than were husbands
married to homemakers (Burke and Weir, 1976). Struck by this result,
another researcher looked into the matter and found that the sample used in
the survey was very peculiarly chosen and rather limited in that its entire
population consisted of engineers, accountants, and their wives. He then
redid the survey with a sample representative of an urban population and
had very different results (Booth, 1977). This new study consisted of the
administration of a questionnaire, physical examination, and general psychiatric impairment test. The ailments tested for included hypertension,
angina pectoris, acute myocardial infarction, irritable colon, infectious dis-
eases, and the use of tranquilizers, sleeping pills, and alcohol.

The findings of this battery of tests showed that the only statistically
significant findings (at the .05 level) were that (1) husbands of employed
women were less likely to have an infectious disease, (2) they scored better
on the psychiatric test, and (3) they reported a better, more relaxed, less
demanding relationship with their wives than did husbands of homemakers.
Other less statistically significant differences included a somewhat higher
rate of stress disease for these same men but lower consumption of alcohol
and sedatives.

Among the women who participated in the test, little difference was
found between those working full-time for over a year and the homemakers. However, women who had just begun to work full-time and current housewives who had left the labor force showed more signs of stress
than the other wives. It appears that the stress was caused by the transitional
state and the modification of schedules rather than the effects of employment. The researcher is moved to optimism by these findings and states:
"While there is no doubt that wives, and probably husbands, go through a
period of adjustment . . . when a woman first joins the labor force, our evidence suggests that it is short-lived. The added income and the greater personal fulfillment the wife and probably her husband eventually enjoy far
outweigh the short-term disadvantages which female employment may
bring the couple" (Alan Booth, "Wife's Employment and Husband's

Stress: A Replication and Refutation," *Journal of Marriage and the Family* 39 (1977): 649. Reprinted by permission.)

While the studies are tending to show that children and husbands are not suffering dire consequences of having a mother and a wife on the labor force, studies concentrating on other factors are showing more pessimistic results. When surveying the impact of employment on women with family responsibilities, two types of women can be identified as being adversely affected in different ways. Women who place a high priority on companionship with their children were found to view the cost of work as a high one which was not sufficiently compensated for by the rewards of employment. Women who value their careers, on the other hand, are faced with difficult choices over whether or not to have a child (Beckman, 1978, pp. 226–227). If they do decide on children they are then faced with the decision of postponing a child until their careers are well-launched, but this may put them into the at-risk maternity category. Finally, for all women who choose motherhood, there are many crucial dilemmas brought on by role conflicts.

Without exception all of the studies reaffirm that women still carry a larger share of the burden of child-rearing than fathers. Because of the continuation of the emphasis being placed on the mother role, women who choose to work or who have to take a job tend to follow two different "patterns of accommodation" (Weingarten and Davis, 1978). In the "sequential pattern" women either have their children first and enter the workforce later or vice versa, while women following the "simultaneous pattern" attempt to combine employment with child-rearing. The first pattern continues to have the effect of lessening a women's chances of moving up the employment ladder because of preconceptions still governing many personnel decisions by corporations and firms. The second pattern puts considerable strain on a woman attempting to do it all. Furthermore, as this woman tends to be career-oriented and ambitious, role conflict is bound to cause her a great deal of strain.

In spite of all of the changes that have been brought about within today's family, the tendency to offer careers to men and jobs to women is affirmed by the latest studies. For example, a study was conducted in 1974 and 1975 among 160 couples with advanced degrees, both of whom were on the job market at the same time. The results show that while over half of the couples attempted to accommodate each other's career needs, eventually three-quarters of the couples were forced to revert to the traditional pattern of wife following husband (Berger and Foster, 1979). And this occurred in spite of the fact that the couples were genuinely committed to an egalitarian relationship in terms of their careers. The reason was simply that in the majority of couples only the male was offered a career and the wives followed their husbands under duress—a stressful situation for all of them. All of this, in turn, reinforces employers' beliefs that women are not as committed to careers as men. This vicious circle undoubtedly harms career-minded women and their families. Furthermore, in the rare cases where the opposite occurred (he following her) the couples reported that they were stigmatized socially by their colleagues, thereby affirming again the pressures brought to bear on families thought nonconventional in their life styles.

Among the remedies that have been suggested to help cope with the problems encountered by two-job, dual-career families are an increase in the status and benefits derived from part-time jobs; an acceptance on the part of business that today's career-oriented female is serious about her work and ought to be treated as such; an elimination of outmoded concepts applied to both males and females about what constitutes a normal career path; and the extirpation of agism as a barrier to the advancement of otherwise suitable males and females. One option that has not received as much attention in the United States is job sharing. In a survey of twenty-one couples in fields such as the clergy, academe, and journalism, positive results were reported for experiments with job sharing accompanied by some negative aspects that should be mentioned here (Arkin and Dobrofsky, 1979). The main problems revolved around the stigma placed on the couples by their colleagues who considered them part-time workers and, therefore, lacking the dedication that would be expected from full-time workers. Also, the couples tended to feel that each was contributing more than one-half of a job and indicated that they would prefer to share one-and-a-half jobs.

The federal Civil Service system has already been modified to provide policies and benefits for permanent part-time employees by the Part-Time Career Act of 1978. According to the *Federal Personnel Manual* (1979), "Part-time career employment means part-time employment of sixteen to thirty-two hours a week under a schedule consisting of equal or varied numbers of hours per day, whether in a position which would be part-time without regard to this section or are established to allow job-sharing or comparable arrangements. . . ." A system of prorated retirement, insurance, and health benefits accompanies this policy and establishes a genuine attempt to implement the part-time career concept in the federal government. Wesleyan University has also devised a set of guidelines to describe the variety of possible permanent appointments that could be made under a permanent part-time system and to set out the rules to be followed in regard to prorating salary, insurance coverage, tenure, work load, and title considerations for these so-called "Sunlighters" (Wesleyan University, 1975). Similar policies have also begun emerging in the private sector and should become universal with large employers as attitudes change and general recognition of the scope of the need becomes more widespread.

The general attitude that families need from all employers is that of acceptance of the changes wrought in familial patterns by social and economic pressures. Employers cannot continue to insist on setting outmoded standards for their employees. Flexible work arrangements are necessary to allow all employees to choose work patterns that best suit their needs. Also, employers, while acknowledging the pressing needs of parents of young children, ought not to limit the options they offer solely to that group. All employed persons should be allowed to choose from a greatly expanded list of available schedule and benefit options so that they can find an acceptable combination of employment and private life demands that will enable them to integrate their lives into a unified whole.

As the second millenium draws to a close it has become apparent that the results of changes that have taken generations are beginning to make themselves felt. The policy guiding the American educational system long ago gave into pressure and ceased educating girls and boys for different roles in life in terms of classes, activities, and sports. It would appear that by the end of this century the fruits of this policy will have been gathered in the job market—the marketplace for the products of our educational system.

Business, which greeted females with open arms during World War II and continued to welcome them somewhat more grudgingly in the fifties, sixties, and seventies, is very reluctant to acknowledge that the business world would collapse without the labor of millions of women. It is long past time that the business community make this acknowledgment and reform its practices to better conform with the society in which it exists.

Government, which has sometimes lagged behind and sometimes led the rest of the nation in securing equality of rights for all of its citizens, committed itself officially to equality of rights for women on the labor force in 1963 and continues to move haltingly in that direction. It is the right time for government to take a stronger supportive stand on behalf of all employed parents.

Women have been doing their share by dutifully preparing themselves for full membership in the labor force by earning more high-school diplomas than men and almost as many college degrees. Men will have to learn to take up their share by recognizing that they have for too long been deprived of enjoying the richness of family life because of unnatural social and economic forces that have tried to turn them into machines. Men need families as much as do women. Social attitudes should begin to reflect this and encourage men to seek out more fulfillment in their children and in their families.

It appears on the surface that all of the changes that have taken place in business, government, among large numbers of women and some men can only be the result of a commonly agreed on purpose that set this whole process in motion and has kept it on the tracks for about a century. But unless we are witnessing the operations of Adam Smith's invisible hand, all of this activity seems to be neither concerted nor planned. It has happened haphazardly and against the wishes of a large segment of the population who still view women as essentially nurturers whose proper place is in the home. It is this segment that appears to be dragging its feet in terms of the passage of the ERA in the hopes of somehow reversing the process and returning to a golden age that never was. However, no matter what happens with the ERA, there is no way to reverse the process, uneducate women, take them out of the job market, and make them contented homemakers. We have long since passed the point of no return.

Basically humanity is not threatened with the prospect of becoming an endangered species, not from its women anyway. All the evidence indicates that women intend to continue raising families even while working outside their homes. How then do we help families in ways that are meaningful for today's problems? How do we get people all working together, accepting the new realities, applauding the efforts of men and women to do the job while rearing the next generation? These are the questions which will be examined in chapter 15 in light of some aspects of family life and employment in a county of North Carolina.

15 Employment and Families in Mecklenburg County, North Carolina: A Survey

Introduction

Although U.S. labor-force statistics do not emphasize that 29 percent of the parents on the labor force have children under the age of eighteen and that the vast majority of wage earners are parents or expect to be parents, it is not an overstatement to say that it is the labor of parents which powers the U.S. economy. (See Department of Labor, 1978.) It is also the labor of parents that is raising the next generation of American workers. For all of their importance in society, however, relatively little attention has been focused on the special problems and needs of employed parents. Until two decades ago when almost two-thirds of American homes could claim the presence of a nonemployed female to care for the family, these problems and needs were considered private matters best cared for within that sphere. But when that crucial number of mothers shrinks as it did in 1978 to under 50 percent, or less than half of all mothers with children under the age of eighteen, the strain begins to show. People are becoming alarmed about the consequences of this development.

One manner in which this concern manifests itself is by the growing number of persons studying these developments and trying to chart their impact. In doing so, many scholars are challenging old accepted truths about society and asking people to consider the realities of the present situation. Two recent studies have attacked the "myth of separate worlds" that divides society into the workplace and the home and pretends that they are not connected to each other, and the "myth of the self-sufficient family" that pretends that parents have more control over their lives and their families than they actually do (Kanter, 1977, pp. 8–21; Keniston, 1977, p. 13).

There is widespread agreement that the great majority of American families are being subjected to forces beyond their control. These forces are causing fundamental changes in family living patterns. The most important of these changes is that, whether by choice or because of economic neces-

Extracted from a working paper of the same title which was prepared as a joint project of the Center for the Study of the Family and the State and the Junior League of Charlotte, Inc.

sity, millions of mothers spend part or all of the working day or night out of their homes and at their place of employment. According to the director of the Women's Bureau, Alexis M. Herman, 60 to 65 percent of women hold jobs out of economic necessity (*The New York Times,* 1978). And this appears to be a very conservative estimate.

One underlying impetus for change affecting many factors of family life is the impact of inflation on families. The shockingly swift erosion of the value of the dollar is cutting the resources at the disposal of families and depriving them of choices about how they want to live. This same inflation process intrudes on government spending and shrinks programs that should be providing more, rather than fewer, services to the growing number of families who need them. As more mothers enter the labor force there is a greater need for good, dependable, day-care services for young children in need of supervision. At the same time, federal and state dollars which could be subsidizing a variety of types of day care for low-income families and paying for studies and experiments to develop more acceptable forms of day care, particularly for the very young, are being cut back. A study published in 1977 estimated that a $20 million cut in day-care funding by New York State would affect 7,500 low-income families and lead to an increase of at least $18.8 million in welfare benefits and other program costs (*The New York Times,* 1977). Not paying attention to day-care needs is a short-sighted policy that eventually affects all society.

All of these factors combined lead to the conclusion that private enterprise must begin to take on a greater role in dealing with the present situation. Employers can no longer claim that they are not directly involved with the family. The workplace and the homeplace impinge on each other. Family life is greatly affected by what happens to parents in the labor force, and parents cannot completely isolate themselves from the demands of family life while functioning as employees. Many American business firms have acknowledged this and taken a greater share and responsibility for helping their employees deal with the increased burdens affecting families in the seventies and eighties that were not present in the fifties and sixties. Often this has only required small schedule changes that cost little or nothing but that enable an employee to adjust a work routine to family demands. According to a study by The American Management Association, 13 percent of all private employers in the United States who have over fifty workers in their employ offered flextime options in 1978.

Sometimes it might mean adjusting a career path to the birth of a child. Proctor & Gamble presently gives both men and women employees the option of taking a six-month unpaid childcare leave when they either adopt or have a baby.

Other times it might mean job sharing to enable families with young children to continue on the labor force at a time when their family responsibilities are highest. For example, while no statistics are available on job sharing, media coverage of the many types of jobs and people involved in job sharing indicate that it is being tried out all over the U.S. with considerable success. The key attitude required of today's business firms is flexibility and a willingness to adjust. Employers must learn to work with the demands faced by their workforce if they want to maintain stable relations with it.

The basic problems facing employers considering making adjustments in their procedures are (1) assessing what are the policies needed by their own employees, and (2) deciding how to implement them at a feasible cost. This chapter concentrates on detailing employees' needs and leaves the implementation in the hands of businessmen themselves. The needs of various individuals within Mecklenburg County, the most populous county in the state of North Carolina, are noted. Charlotte, the major city, is the largest in the state. Its population is estimated to reach 430,000 in April of 1980 by the Charlotte-Mecklenburg Planning Commission and it has the highest per capita income in North Carolina, an estimated $6,995 in 1976. In terms of its population mix, Mecklenburg is approximately one-quarter black and over 40 percent of the labor force is female. The city of Charlotte is an acknowledged leader in the state and its progressive policies concerning the social welfare of its citizenry are well-known in the region. It is hoped that this concern will lead to the formulation of policies that ever better address the changing needs of its family population. The key to policy changes that will help employed parents is a recognition that different types of families require different approaches. Single parents have needs and stresses that differ significantly from parents who share the parenting role with another person. Single parents with low incomes have greater needs than single parents with adequate incomes. Parents with children under the age of six have greater and different needs and stresses than parents with no children under the age of six. Older parents have different needs than do younger parents.

The limitations on the data presented in this chapter are that in spite of distributing the questionnaires to a representative sample of the Mecklenburg workforce, the returned questionnaires do not represent the entire workforce. Certain populations and employment sectors did not respond to the survey. Because of this fact all of the recommendations and findings are carefully considered and worded to avoid misrepresenting the data. The technical problems concerning representativeness are dealt with in detail within the methodology section of the original version of the report (Giraldo, Z.I., Robert Kelly, et al., 1979). This original version also includes a section on work/family stress measured via regression analysis. This was the first attempt to my knowledge, to take the pulse of a county by concentrating on the needs of the parents on its workforce. Their special needs and those of their children ought to figure in the plans of corporate and city officials. None of the results detailed in this chapter appear individual to Mecklenburg or Charlotte. The problems encountered by different segments of the sample reflect the problems reported in the media and in the literature on a nationwide scale.

Summary of Cross-Tabulation Analysis

There were patterns among the answers to individual questions given by certain groups of persons who answered the questionnaire. A main interest was the types of answers given by respondents who belonged to certain family types and whether or not their families contained children under the age of six. The impact of income, race, sex, work schedule, and occupation on the answers to any particular question or group of questions was also important. By reporting the answers that subgroups of the sample gave that differ substantially from what would be expected among the whole sample, it was possible to concentrate on areas where the subgroups gave unique answers. All of the cross-tabulations reported here have been tested and the large majority of the patterns reported would have occurred by chance only one time in a hundred ($p < .01$) or one time out of 1,000 ($p < .001$) and, therefore, are in the highly significant range. No finding that could have occurred by chance more than five times out of a hundred ($p < .05$) is reported.

Family Type

The replies to the survey were divided by family type into three major categories: female-headed families, dual-income families, and male-major-earner families. For purposes of this analysis this division was deemed most relevant in studying the impact of employment on family life because these three categories represent the most tangible distinctions among family styles relating particularly to work and family life. Of 465 replies determined to be useable for this portion of the analysis, 62 percent or 288 of the families reported both heads of family as having an occupation, 26 percent or 120 replies reported the male head as the sole wage earner in the family, and 12 percent or 57 respondents indicated that they were female-headed families with no male present in the household. Therefore, 74 percent of the mothers in the sample were employed or reported as having an occupation. Coincidently, this figure agrees with state estimates indicating that 75 percent of mothers in North Carolina are employed. It is believed by officials of the state that North Carolina contains the highest proportion of working mothers of any state in the union.

Famile Life Cycle

A further factor that enters the picture in terms of dividing the responses by family type is whether or not individual families contain children under the age of six or not. Of the families in the survey 35 percent (N = 165) reported having children under the age of six, and 65 percent (N = 303) reported having only children above that age. As with income, family life cycle was deemed an essential element to be examined.

Income

When viewed in terms of income, the figures show that 46 percent of the female-headed households had annual incomes of under $10,000 with 35 percent of them clustered in the $7,000 to $9,999 range. On the other hand, 42 percent of the male-major-earner households had incomes of $25,000 and over. In the dual-income category 55 percent of these families had incomes of less than $15,000 per year. Over one-half of the families who answered the survey and who had both adult heads on the workforce had incomes below the national median family income, which stood at $17,106 in 1977 (table 15-1). It is apparent that income by family types tends to bifurcate with over 50 percent of the female-headed and dual-income families tightly clustered below $15,000 and over 50 percent of the male-major-earner families ranging above $20,000. Two of the family types dominate the bottom of the income scale and the remaining type is strongly represented in the top.

Race

In addition to the income skew, a racial skew is discernable among the family types. In terms of race, 32 percent of the female-headed households were black, only 10 percent of the dual-income category and 7 percent of the male-major-earner category were black (table 15-2). Since the latter two categories showed a very small difference in terms of race, the only family type where race might play a role in connection with the way questions for that family type were answered was in the female-headed category. However, when the replies of only the female-headed families were run to determine significant differences on the basis of race, no statistically significant differences at the .05 level or higher were found. Therefore no reportable differences appear in the answers given by black single female heads of households and similarly situated whites to the questions on childcare needs, housework, role satisfaction, attitudes toward employment, self, or family.

Table 15–1
Respondents' Income by Family Type

	Female-Headed		Dual-Income		Male-Major-Earner	
	Number	Percent	Number	Percent	Number	Percent
Under $10,000	25	46	73	29	9	9
$10,000 to $14,000	14	26	66	26	17	17
$15,000 to $19,999	8	15	43	17	12	12
$20,000 to $24,000	6	11	44	17	21	20
$25,000 and over	1	2	27	11	44	42
Totals	54	100	253	100	103	100

Note: These figures only include respondents who answered the question on income. $p < .001$.

Table 15–2
Family Type by Race

Female-Headed Families	Dual-Income Families	Male-Major-Earner Families
32% (18) black	10% (28) black	7% (8) black
68% (38) white	89% (253) white	92% (109) white
0% (0) other	1% (3) other	1% (1) other

Note: $p < .001$.

Only 12 percent of the total survey sample was black and only 2 percent identified themselves as belonging to other racial categories, which means that 85 percent of the respondents classified themselves as white (table 15–3). Because of the small representation of persons other than white and because the sample only included responses by eleven black men and only four persons choosing "other" as a racial category no cross-tabulations were run by race except those already noted.

Sex

The 277 female respondents in the survey formed 60 percent of the pool compared with 40 percent of 183 male respondents. A significant difference appeared in terms of their place of employment with a large share of females working in the service sector (table 15–4).

In terms of the sex breakdown of the dual-income respondents by the sex, 194 or 69 percent of the respondents were female versus 89 or 31 percent males (table 15–5). Therefore the perceptions reported as being held by

Table 15-3
Race of Respondents by Family Type

	Black	Percent of		White	Percent of		Other	Percent of
	No.	Black	Total	No.	White	Total	No.	Other	Total
Female-headed families	18	52	6	38	10	8	0	0	0
Dual-income families	28	33	4	253	63	54	3	75	1
Male-major-earner families	8	15	2	109	27	24	1	25	1
Totals	54	100	12	400	100	86	4	100	2

Note: These figures only include respondents who answered the question on race. $p < .001$.

Table 15–4
Workplace Type by Sex

	Female		Male	
	Number	*Percent*	*Number*	*Percent*
Construction	4	1	8	4
Manufacturing	18	7	30	16
Transportation, communication	65	24	43	23
Wholesale and retail trade	19	7	9	5
Services	135	49	44	24
Government	32	12	47	26
Finance, insurance	1	—	2	2
Total	274	100	183	100

Note: The responses of three females did not indicate workplace type. $p < .001$.

dual-income families are weighed in favor of the viewpoint of the female head of the family. The overrepresentation of females in the survey testifies to the continuing strength of the belief that the sphere of the family is still the major responsibility of wives and mothers.

Work Schedule

Additional frequencies and cross-tabulations were run in terms of one further category directly related to employment. (Although it was the intention to use a seventh category of analysis which would have shown up differences among the respondents by workplace type the very uneven nature of the response according to work sector (as shown in table 15–4) precluded continuing with that analysis.) On work schedule the 444 replies which could be used for this part of the analysis were divided into five groups. These are (1) 215 regular day-time work schedules commencing between 8 and 9 A.M. lasting for at least seven hours of work a day and finishing between 4 and 6 P.M.; (2) 181 full-time day workers who worked at least seven hours a day but did not start or end at the usual hours; (3) four full-time evening night workers who worked at least seven hours a day and commenced work after 2 P.M.; (4) thirty-five part-time workers who were employed less than thirty-five hours a week; and (5) nine irregular workers who reported that they did not have a regular beginning and ending time but who worked thirty-five or more hours a week.

Table 15-5
Occupation by Sex

	Number	Percent of Females	Total	Number	Percent of Males	Total
Professional and technical workers	86	32	19	71	39	16
Managers, officials, and proprietors	17	6	4	56	31	12
Clerical	135	49	29	8	4	2
Salespersons	11	4	2	5	3	1
Crafts, foremen	3	1	1	9	5	2
Operatives	5	2	1	14	8	3
Service workers	13	5	3	13	7	3
Laborers, nonfarm	3	1	1	5	3	1
Totals	273	100	60	181	100	40

Note: These figures only include respondents who answered the question on income. $p < .001$.

Results of Cross-Tablulations: The Questions Answered by the Survey

Are There Differences among Family Types in the Survey in Terms of Childcare Arrangements?

In regard to reliance on childcare provided by older children, relatives, neighbors, and paid care by private individuals, no statistically significant differences at the .05 level or higher appeared among the three major family groups. The category where arrangements differed significantly was in the actual use of day-care centers. When asked about how much use is made of licensed day-care centers for preschoolers, 81 percent of the female heads of families who replied reported some use of day-care centers compared with 64 percent for the dual-income families and 30 percent for the male-major-earner families (table 15-6). These figures conform to the general expectations, however, it was surprising that over a quarter of the male-major-earner families, that is, those who report the presence of a full-time home-maker to look after the family, reported some use made of day-care centers. This high usage of day-care centers is related to income. Six out of the ten male-major-earner families who reported what they spent on day care were in the $20,000 and above salary range.

Table 15–6
Use of Licensed Day-Care Centers for Preschool-Age Children

	Female-Headed		Dual-Income		Male-Major-Earner	
	Number	Percent	Number	Percent	Number	Percent
Use a lot	0	0	9	0	1	2
Use a little	13	81	60	64	11	28
Do not use	3	19	34	36	28	70
Total	16	100	103	100	40	100

Note: $p < .001$.

Is There a Need for More Day-Care Centers?

From the survey it appears that it is the female-headed families who are most in need of more day-care centers to provide for their child-care needs. When asked: "If more day-care centers were available, how much would you use them for your preschool-age children?" twelve out of the fourteen female sole heads of family who replied to this question indicated that they would use more day care if it were available. This compared with forty-four out of seventy-nine of the dual-income families and thirteen out of forty-three of the male-major-earner families who also indicated that they would use day-care centers more if they were available ($p < .01$). The answers to this question were also significant in terms of the family life cycle. Forty-six families with children under six claimed that they would make more use of day care if there were more centers as opposed to ten families with children over age six who reported they would also use these centers if more of them were available ($p < .01$).

What Do Nonusers Think of Day Care?

When the approximately 300 families who did not use day care were asked if they disapproved of the idea of their child being in a day-care center, of the fifty-one who replied that they did no significant differences showed up in the answers divided by family type or income. However when divided by family life cycle, 35 percent of respondents with children under age six did not approve of the idea of day care and 16 percent of parents with no children under age six answered similarly ($p < .001$). This type of response conforms to other studies that have shown that parents tend to prefer more home-like, informal arrangements for their younger children. When answers to this same question were run by family life cycle, no significant differences in attitudes appeared among the three types of families when controlling for the absence or presence of children under the age of six. Therefore the age of the children involved rather than the needs of the families for day care appears to govern the attitudes of all the parents.

What Problems with Day Care Are Reported by Persons Participating in the Survey?

Question 30 of the survey listed ten types of problems associated with day care and asked respondents who have had experience with day-care centers to circle all the problems they experienced. Only two of the ten problems show statistically significant differences in the answer patterns. These two problems involved the cost of day care and the number of hours of available day care.

Are Day-Care Centers Operating a Sufficient Number of Hours? In the sample 12 out of 40 of female-headed families replied "yes" to the question: "Center isn't open during some or all of the hours that I work?" Twenty-five out of 185 dual-income families and 3 out of 47 male-major-earner respondents reported a similar problem. Table 15-7 summarizes the responses to this question by family type. Table 15-8 shows the significant difference when respondents' working schedules were considered. The largest number of employees who report problems with day-care hours are those workers who put in a full day of labor but who do not start or end at the regular hours. However, proportionately it is irregular workers who report the highest amount of conflict between their day-care needs and the hours that such care is available. If adequate day care is to be provided for all employed persons needing it, some attention will have to be paid to the special needs of employed persons in these two categories.

Table 15-7
Day-Care Hours Inconvenient in Terms of Work Schedule by Family Type

	Female-Headed		Dual-Income		Male-Major-Earner	
	Number	*Percent*	*Number*	*Percent*	*Number*	*Percent*
Yes	12	30	25	14	3	7
No	28	70	160	86	44	93
Totals	40	100	185	100	47	100

Note: $p < .001$.

Table 15-8
Working Schedules of Respondents Who Reported Day Care Was Lacking During Work Hours

	Numbers	Percent of All Who Reported Problems	Percent Reporting Problems Compared to All Workers in Category
Full-time day workers	22	55	12
Regular day-time workers	14	35	7
Irregular workers	3	8	33
Part-time night workers	1	2	3
	0	0	0
Totals	40	100	

Note: $p < .001$.

Are Day-Care Costs Too High? Although no difference of statistical significance showed up among day-care users on the above question in terms of family type, when cross-tabulated by income, eight out of eleven families with incomes under $10,000 reported that their costs of day care were too high ($p < .01$). When the average weekly cost of day care was computed for the families reporting usage of centers, the eleven female-headed households reported spending $29.12 per week, the seventy-six dual-income families reported $26.83 per week, and the male-major-earner families reported spending $19.83 per week (with a standard deviation of $11.11, $12.05, and $9.48 respectively). When all family types were grouped by income ranges, the families with incomes under $10,000 were found to pay the highest average dollar amount for their day-care services. The reason for this is the high proportion female-headed families in the category.

Day-care costs affect low-income families much more detrimentally than other families in the survey. And yet because these families include so many female-headed families, they are the ones in need of more day-care arrangements to help with their child-raising responsibilities. If these families are to be helped in any way, their day-care costs must be lowered in proportion to their income. Many of the families are overtaxed simply because they are attempting to raise one or two children on low incomes. Alleviating the excessive burden of day-care costs should have a significant impact on the lives of families attempting to raise the next generation.

Who Cares for Sick Children?

As would be expected, female heads of households have a significantly higher responsibility for caring for sick children than the other two family types. Eighty-three percent (43 out of 52) female-headed families replied that they take time off from work to care for a sick child; 43 percent (109 out of 253) dual-income families and 9 percent (8 out of 94) male-major-earner families reported similarly. When a frequency was run to see how many dual-income families reported sharing sick-child care with their spouses, only 84 or 29 percent reported such an arrangement. Among the dual-income families as among the other two family types the female carried the major responsibility for sick childcare.

For women in low-income brackets this means a further loss in pay since many of these women are not paid when taking time off to care for a sick child. When pay for child sick leave is run according to income, over 40 percent of the parents in the sample reported that they did not receive pay for staying home to care for a sick child (table 15-9).

In terms of the family cycle a significant difference in the number of days taken off from work to care for a sick child appears between parents of children under the age of six and other parents ($p < .001$). Six parents with children under six reported taking more than ten days off from work due to a child's illness, but no parents of older children reported similarly. However, when the actual days taken off for the care of a sick child are averaged out according to the family life cycle the results are almost identical for the two groups. In spite of this fact, a statistically significant difference in responses to the question: "Regardless of your company's policy, do you feel guilty or irresponsible if you take time off to care for a sick child?" emerged when cross-tabulated by family life cycle. In answer to this ques-

Table 15-9
Families Receiving Child Sick-Leave Pay by Total Household Income

	Under $10,000		$11,000 to $20,000		$20,000 and Above	
	Number	Percent	Number	Percent	Number	Percent
Yes	8	44	34	43	146	62
No	9	50	44	56	78	34
Do not know	1	6	1	1	9	4
Totals	18	100	79	100	233	100

Note: $p < .001$.

tion 50 percent (79 out of 158) of parents of younger children acknowledged some feelings of guilt or irresponsibility as opposed to 44 percent (107 out of 246) of parents of older children ($p < .05$). Here the overriding factor appears to be age of child as no statistically significant differences are noted in the answers of families divided into the three major types nor by sex of the employee.

Parents of young children ought not to feel guilty for taking time off to care for a sick child. These are duties that cannot be ignored by parents nor by society. Employers who allow time off for this reason should emphasize that they understand the necessity for this absence. Employers who do not allow such absences ought to recognize that parents of young children, particularly children under the age of six, need time off to care for a sick child and when necessary will have to take it no matter what the company policy may be. The average number of days of sick leave taken on account of a child's illness by 165 families with children under age six equaled 9.6 (with a standard deviation of 25.2). The average number of days taken by 303 families with children ages six to eighteen amounted to 9.8 (with a standard deviation of 26.6). All employers should consider granting ten days of paid sick leave for sick-child care. Employers should be expected to recognize that families with children need to take time off to care for sick children.

What Child-Care and Home-Care Differences Are Noted Between Female-Headed, Dual-Income and Male-Major-Earner Families?

The female respondents in the survey who cared for their families on their own had the lowest median income of the three major family types. Low income combined with lack of help in the household make the female sole heads of families the most hard-working in terms of family responsibility, the most put-upon in terms of family and employment problems, and the most vulnerable to insecurities in regard to themselves as parents.

When the amount of housework on work days reported by the respondents was measured, 24 of 48 of the female-headed families reported four or more hours of after-work chores as compared to 110 of 264 of members of dual-income and 12 of 109 of male-major-earner respondents who reported that many hours of household chores performed in their families on work days ($p < .001$). On nonwork days, 69 percent of female-headed families reported doing six or more hours of housework as compared to 54 percent of dual-income and 35 percent of male-major-earners doing a similar amount of weekend work ($p < .001$).

Childcare on work days is also a more demanding activity for these women as 17 of 41 of them report providing more than four hours of after-work care for their children as opposed to 65 of 236 and 14 of 94 respectively for the other types of families ($p < .001$). Only in childcare on non-working days did no significant difference appear in the study among the three major family types.

What About Role-Conflict?

When measuring the amount of conflict normally felt by the respondents in regard to the obligations they felt as parents and workers, 19 of 56 of female sole heads of families reported "a lot" of perceived conflict between these two roles, while 68 of 281 of dual-income and 20 of 117 of male-major-earner families reported that they too felt "a lot" of conflict between their roles as employees and parents ($p < .05$). As these figures indicate, problems of role conflict affect two of the major family types and rightly so when such high percentages of families in the study found themselves responsible for such a great number of hours of after-work home and childcare.

Who Are the Dissatisfied Parents?

It is also the female sole-head-of-a-family who demonstrated a significantly greater dissatisfaction with herself as a parent. Twenty-five percent (N = 14) of female heads of households claimed they were dissatisfied with themselves as parents compared to 10 percent (N = 25) and 9 percent (N = 8) respectively for the other two famlily types ($p < .01$). And as these same females revealed no significant difference in their responses to the question of how much activity the family had together as a group, it would appear that they are either being hard on themselves or asking too much of themselves. The female head-of-family works harder than the average individual in a dual-income or male-major-earner family while perceiving that she is providing her family with less than they need or deserve. This bind on these women is very apparent in the survey. If any projects are undertaken in Charlotte to provide more services to families of employed persons, the female-headed family would be the most obvious target for help of all of the families. Since the largest percentage of persons who reported some use of the services of community-helping agencies were female sole-heads-of-families, it is likely that increased services provided to the community via the already established local service networks could affect the lives of those families most in need of help.

*How Do Dual-Income Families in the Survey Differ from
the Other Major Family Types?*

Dual-income families in the sample stand somewhat between the female-headed families and the male-major-earners in terms of income and home-employment-childcare problems. Their needs and problems appear greater than those experienced by male-major-earner families but less than those of female sole heads of families. The dual-income families stand closer to female-headed families in terms of the use they make of day-care centers and the money they spend on them but move much closer to the male-major-earner families in terms of how much more they would use day care if more were available. Therefore, while their day-care needs are considerably greater than those of male-major-earner families, they also are better provided for than the female sole heads of families—or at least perceive themselves to be so. Since the income differential is not the most significant factor explaining these differences, it must be attributed to the presence of another adult in the household to share the burden of providing the family with its material and nurturant needs. As female sole heads of families have no other adult to rely on and since dual-income families have only a part of another adult, it is these two types of families that have the most difficult time juggling the demands of work and family life.

*How Do Female Employees Differ from Male Employees
in the Survey?*

In terms of hours of employment, significant differences appear between male and female employees with more females working less than forty hours per week compared with more males working more than forty hours (table 15-10). Therefore the Mecklenburg sample does not differ in respect to work patterns in the nation as a whole where females still hold more part-time jobs than do males. And while many mothers hold part-time jobs to enable them to continue to bear the larger share of family responsibility, other findings of this study indicate that whether or not a female works part-time or full-time she continues to bear the larger share of responsibility for this role.

In terms of attitudes, no significant differences appear between male and female employees on questions about job satisfaction, pay satisfaction, satisfaction with hours worked, work schedule, or work duties. The regression analysis, however, does indicate some differences. They include the finding that "women as a group, regardless of whether they are in single or two-parent households, experience a much greater amount of work-related time pressure than do men" when other factors are controlled (Giraldo,

Table 15–10
Work Hours by Sex

	Females		Males	
	Number	Percent	Number	Percent
Less than 30 hours per week	36	13	3	2
Between 31 and 39 hours per week	63	23	15	8
40 hours per week	146	53	78	43
Over 40 hours	29	11	87	47
Totals	274	100	183	100

Note: $p < .001$.

Table 15–11
Housework on Work Days by Sex

Number of Hours of Housework	Female Workers		Male Workers	
	Number	Percent	Number	Percent
No housework at all	6	3	28	17
1 to 2 hours	118	46	118	71
3 to 4 hours	110	44	18	11
More than 4 hours	16	7	2	1
Totals	250	100	166	100

Note: $p < .001$.

Z.I., Robert Kelly, et al., 1979). The indication is that in general women have a greater need than do men for policies that reduce time pressure conflicts related with responsibilities outside of the job.

The highly significant differences that do appear in the cross-tabulations between female and male employees cluster around the matter of housework and childcare. The families in the survey continue to follow the pattern followed by the rest of the country in demanding more family care from the female heads of household than from the male heads (table 15–11). Fifty-one percent of females do three or more hours of after-work housework as compared to 12 percent of the males (table 15–12). While this differentiation is made up for to a certain extent during the weekends on nonwork days, the female workers continue to carry a disproportionate share of the home-care burden. On nonwork days the percentage of males who work three or more hours on home chores jumps up to 79 percent. This still does not mean much in terms of the female employees, 96 percent of whom are also putting in that many hours of their own.

Since the females in the study tended to include more part-time workers and fewer persons working over forty hours per week, the replies were checked to see what impact the number of hours of employment had on household work. There is a relationship between the number of hours worked per week and the number of after-work housework hours put in by females, but males consistently worked fewer hours at home than females, no matter what the work schedule (table 15–13). The highest number of hours of housework put in by the males did not match the lowest number of hours of housework contributed by the females.

The impact of marital status on workday housework was checked to see if the presence of a husband in the home lessened the number of hours of work that females performed after-work hours. There is practically no difference discernable between mothers with spouses and mothers without spouses in terms of the amount of housework that they are responsible for doing every day (table 15–14). Forty-four percent of mothers with spouses work three to four hours in the home in the same way that 44 percent of mothers without husbands do; in the other categories there are negligible differences between the groups. Because of this continuing pattern of sexual division of household labor, an employed female derives no benefit from having a spouse in terms of lessening the burden of work on her shoulders when she gets home from her own job. While he, on the other hand, can claim that he has not added to her labor, it is to be hoped that husbands of employed females would be more embarrassed than defensive over these statistics. Mothers should not be expected to work more total hours per week than fathers. The stressful effect on this pattern becomes even clearer in the regression analysis.

How Does Overnight Travel on Company Business Affect Families?

In the survey eighty-nine males (49 percent of all male respondents) and forty-four females (17 percent of all female respondents) stated that they traveled overnight on company business ($p > .01$). As would be expected, these travelers were mainly in the professional and managerial occupational groups.

No significant difference appeared between male and female travelers concerning family acceptance of travel as part of the job and acceptance of weekend travel. Nor were there any differences manifested over interference with the planning of family activities nor with regard to the attitude of the respondent's spouse. The only area where a significant difference was found was in the number of respondents who circled the statement: "The entire family is bothered by my travel." Here 24 percent of the females indi-

Table 15–12
Housework on Nonwork Days by Sex

Number of Hours of Housework	Female Workers		Male Workers	
	Number	Percent	Number	Percent
No housework at all	3	1	5	3
1 to 2 hours	7	3	31	18
3 to 4 hours	51	20	52	31
More than 4	192	76	83	48
Totals	253	100	171	100

Note: $p < .001$.

Table 15–13
Mean Number of Daily Hours of Housework by Weekly Hours of Employment and by Sex

	Hours	Number of Respondents
Females who work less than 30 hours per week[a]	3.2	36
Females who work less than 40 but over 30 hours[b]	2.9	63
Females who work 40 hours[c]	2.5	146
Females who work more than 40[d]	2.1	79
Males who work less than 30 hours[a]	1.7	3
Males who work less than 40 but over 30 hours[b]	1.4	15
Males who work 40 hours[c]	1.5	78
Males who work more than 40[d]	1.3	87

[a] $p < .05$ (T test difference of means)
[b] $p < .001$ (T test difference of means)
[c] $p < .001$ (T test difference of means)
[d] $p < .01$ (T test difference of means)

Table 15–14
Housework on Work Days for Mothers by Marital Status

	Married Mothers		Single Mothers	
	Number	Percent	Number	Percent
No housework at all	5	3	1	2
1 to 2 hours	95	46	23	48
3 to 4 hours	88	44	21	44
More than 4 hours	13	7	3	6
Totals	201	100	48	100

Note: $p < .001$.

cated that this was so compared to 9 percent of the male respondents (table 15-15). When this question was analyzed by occupation it appears that it is the female travelers among the managers and officials and not the females in the professional or technical occupations who have this perception ($p <$ .01).

When answers to the questions on travel were run by family life cycle, no significant differences occurred among families with children under age six and those without younger children in regard to the amount of travel, frequency, and family problems. Only one question revealed a statistically significant difference and that was concerning overnight travel on weekends. Seven of the families with children under six indicated a problem as compared to four of the other families ($p < .05$). This is probably caused by the unavailability of weekend day care and the greater need of younger children for supervision.

The answers to the questions on company travel lead one to believe that regardless of the sex of the employee, persons traveling for their companies tend to perceive this aspect of their jobs as not being greatly disruptive to family life. Women who travel on business by-and-large appear to have adapted themselves and their families to the exigencies of the situation. Not one woman (and only two men) circled the statement: "I'm not sure how they [their families] feel," which would indicate that 98 percent of the company travelers felt sure about their perceptions of how their families were reacting to this aspect of their employment. The only group that appeared to feel some stress about their travel on company business were the female managers and officials. Since this feeling was not shared by females in professional or technical work, it is likely that female managers and officials have not been as prepared to accept travel as part of their job as professionally trained females. They in turn, either have not prepared their families for this aspect of their lives or, because of guilt feelings, perceive greater interference of travel with their families' lives.

Is There Interest in Parent Education?

When responses to question 72: "If parent education classes were available to you at a reasonable cost and at a time and location convenient for you, would you consider attending such classes?" were counted, 208 (44 percent) of the parents participating in the survey replied that they were interested in parent education classes and 56 percent were not interested. When the responses were run by life cycle the following pattern emerged (table 15-16).

When the responses to the question: "How much would you be willing to pay for a parent education course that met once a week for two months?" were cross-tabulated by household income for those who indi-

Table 15-15
Families Bothered by Company Travel

	Female		Male	
	Number	*Percent*	*Number*	*Percent*
Yes	11	24	7	9
No	35	76	75	91
Totals	46	100	82	100

Note: $p < .05$.

Table 15-16
Interest in Parent-Education Courses by Life Cycle

	Families with Children Under Age 6		Families with No Children Under Age 6	
	Number	*Percent*	*Number*	*Percent*
Yes	93	56	115	38
No	29	18	101	34
Not sure	1	1	5	2
Other replies	42	25	79	26
Totals	165	100	300	100

Note: $p < .001$.

cated that they were interested in such a course the results appeared as in table 15-17.

The results of the question on parent education courses indicate that parents with children under the age of six show the most willingness and interest in parent education courses. If such a course were offered the price would have to be scaled by income in order to be accessible to families with incomes under $10,000. Since 55 percent of the 379 parents who gave an estimate of what they thought such a course would cost thought it would be priced at $50 or higher, if such a course were offered free or on the basis of an income scale, publicly stressing this fact should have the effect of encouraging participation by members of families with low incomes. All efforts to reach low-income families and families with children under the age of six would probably be worthwhile in terms of the potential impact on these families and the apparent need and interest demonstrated by the sample. However, any attempts made to establish a program of parent education courses should keep in mind the fact that "research on parent education in past decades does not provide grounds for much optimism about the

Table 15-17
Dollar Amount Persons Willing to Pay for a Parent-Education Course by Household Income

	Up to $9,999		$10,000 to $19,999		Over $20,000	
Price of Course	Number	Percent	Number	Percent	Number	Percent
$10 and under	2	100	11	39	32	31
$11 to $20	0	0	12	43	28	27
$21 to $49	0	0	4	14	32	31
$50 and over	0	0	1	4	12	11
Totals	2	100	28	100	104	100

Note: $p < .001$.

power of this approach to make significant changes in the family life of large numbers of people'' (Keniston, 1977, p. 8). Full cognizance of the reasons for past failures is an essential ingredient of any approach to help families to have better parents by offering parent education courses.

Summary

Only during the past decade has the true size and scope of a major problem in the United States been made manifest. The attempt to combine employment and family responsibilities is keeping the American family under pressure. This pressure is building steadily as more and more families attempt to deal with life patterns that differ from the traditional one. And yet little is being done by governmental policymakers to address the specifics of the issue.

One of the most obvious needs revolves around the question of day care. The day-care services presently offered under governmental auspices are mainly for that segment of the population receiving some form of public assistance. Part of the rationale for this limited response on the part of government is based on a tendency by policymakers to assume that the problems of working parents should only be considered problems to be addressed by government policy when they affect a group that has traditionally received government aid, such as the poor. But the problems of combining employment with family life are not solely the problems of the poor. It is apparent now that growing numbers of families need two paychecks in order to survive at a decent level in the face of inflation and persistent international pressures on the value of the dollar. These two paychecks often cannot provide for the loss in services the family must suffer when its homemakers are employed outside the home for eight or more hours a day, five or more days a week. This income is often strained as it is stretched to pay for food, shelter, clothing, transportation, and medical care without much, if any, leeway to pay for the childcare, house care, and personal care that families would normally be expected to provide for themselves. Large numbers of families are not in a position to choose whether or not they want a homemaker or an additional salary check. They have to have the additional income and simply must do without essential services. As this situation becomes more universal there is less and less reason to pretend that these families are exercising their options to choose their own life styles. The irony is that up until the present the more universal a problem becomes, the less inclined policymakers are to specifically address it. If a majority of the population needs expanded childcare services that makes it a private matter; if a small sector of the population needs the same service, it then becomes incumbent on policymakers to seek a method to supply it.

In addition to the fact that many persons consider the problems of employed parents to lie, by definition, outside the purview of government policy, another deep-rooted attitude is preventing governmental remedies from being implemented. The attitude continues to hold, in spite of all evidence to the contrary, that women belong at home and should be offered no encouragement to seek employment. It is this mentality that believes it is unnatural for females to be employed outside of the home. Yet all recent scholarship investigating the matter has found that the historical roots of the separation of the workplace from the family hearth are shallow and, therefore, it is no more natural for a male householder to seek employment outside of the home than it is for a female to do likewise. It is long past time for people to acknowledge that depriving families of essential services will not stop females from seeking employment. The only purpose accomplished will be to make life more difficult for that entire family.

A further rationale that seems to support persons opposed to having government policymakers move toward providing services, particularly day care, is the belief that government-provided services will be tainted. It will smack of federalism and of *1984*. Children will be brainwashed to think federal thoughts rather than reflect the attitudes of their community, kin, and parents. These arguments are rooted in a recognition based on the historic interference with private life that marred the good intentions of the reformers of the Progressive Era. Too often services provided by agencies have attempted to impose themselves on the recipients and make choices that should have been allowed to be exercised only by individuals. Therefore, if attempts are to be made to apply remedies to the present problems, these remedies cannot be manufactured in one central workshop. They must emerge from those directly affected by the problem, that is, from the parents themselves and from their employers. And while everyone readily acknowledges that employed parents are involved with this problem, little recognition is given the fact that employers are also parties to the problem and share many of the concerns that have been discussed in the text. They, too, are concerned with sick childcare; regular, reliable day-care arrangements; overworked employees; and achieving the benefits of obtaining a stable workforce. Parents and employers share interests that make them ideal partners in attempting solutions that stand a chance of truly resolving these issues.

Such a partnership appears to be emerging but in a very hesitant, tentative manner because of old fears about never breaking the barrier that separates the world of business from the private realm of the family. Although this is a permeable barrier when it allows parents into the business world, it is impenetrable in the other direction. The reluctance of business to breech this barrier and respond to the family needs of its employees is based on fears of opening a Pandora's box that would sap the vitality of the American enterprise system. But this fear is certainly exaggerated if not groundless. Companies that have experimented with a variety of flexible options that would better accommodate the needs of their employees tend to report satisfactory results. Often a policy that starts out as an attempt to provide for family needs, such as flextime, is found to have a positive impact on productivity. Many business firms have acknowledged this and yet are afraid to generalize to the larger question.

Individual firms and individual business leaders are incapable of generating an overall direction that would set guidelines for the entire business community. The only agency capable of performing that task would be the federal government. But calls for government regulation of the private enterprise system are normally viewed as attacks on the fundamental operations of the market economy, with only dire consequences foreseen as the result of such hubris. Any institutional attempt to regulate business is implemented only after much soul-searching and is never supported in any case by some segments of the population.

Yet in spite of the sacred quality that has been attributed to the rights of employers, in the course of history a large number of regulations have been imposed on employers in order to protect the citizenry from harm at the workplace. The recent stance taken by actions of the government indicate that a new attitude has made some inroads on the older, laissez-faire policy toward the private sector. A whole new quality can be discerned in the Equal Pay Act of 1963, in Title VII of the Civil Rights Act of 1964 and in the Age Discrimination in Employment Act of 1967. By these acts public policy enjoined private (and as amended later, public employers) from practicing discrimination based on the sex, race, or age of an employee. The quality of perception on the part of public opinion that allowed these regulations to be imposed on the private sector has taken a quantum leap from the more obvious public interest in protecting the health and welfare of citizen employees. These acts accomplish a much more high-minded purpose in that they hold employees responsible for the social consequences of their employment practices. Employees are no longer allowed to apply arbitrary criteria to the decision concerning who does and who does not receive employment. In effect, the federal government has held that fair treatment on the job market is a legal right that the regulatory agencies are empowered to enforce and courts are empowered to uphold if necessary. The big question is how far are we now from a recognition that the public interest is affected in a very serious manner when approximately 15 million children under the age of fourteen have two parents on the labor force, more than three-quarters of whom are employed full-time? Would it be possible to institute a public policy that required all employers to have a written family policy that would attempt to provide flexible options to all of their employees so that they would be able to better function as parents while meeting their responsibilities to their employers?

If U.S. policymakers were to institutionalize such a requirement, it would be interesting to speculate on some approaches that could be taken by a company drafting a policy to address the family needs of its own employees. Perhaps a company would decide to extend the work day in both directions so that parents could stretch the time that at least one of them is at home with children or so that a single parent could choose which end of the day they would prefer to be with their children. It might choose to allow parents to borrow paid time while they have children under a certain age that could be paid back later as time demands decreased. Other options might be to allow parents to form work pools to cover for each other when they have to be away at school meetings or children's dental appointments, and so forth. Or a company could offer parents the option of earning less by working a nine-to-three day but promise them full advancement according to their merits so that they need not sacrifice career goals while caring for young children. Possibly large companies would be encouraged to develop more on-premises day-care centers, if their employees indicated that there was such a need, while other companies could help arrange for childcare pools similar to helping their employees arrange car pools. Perhaps an insurance plan similar to unemployment insurance could be devised to make up for lost wages because of sick-child care, and all parents would contribute to the plan along with the employer. Or parents could be offered different insurance options and plans in addition to those offered all employees so that they could choose benefits that more closely approximate their needs. Some of the options mentioned here might appear far-fetched and visionary and possibly outside of the realm of public policy. Yet public policy can take on many guises and work through many agencies. Public policy that has anything at all to do with families must be designed to work through the most direct agencies possible and have the greatest flexibility possible in order not to strangle one family with the lifeline thrown to another family.

The federal government, as the largest employer, should be the first to adopt such a policy. It has already taken steps in the right direction with its Part-Time Careers Act and recognition of the need to comply with its own Affirmative Action regulations as described in the Uniform Guidelines on Employee Selection Procedures adopted in 1978 by the EEOC, the Civil Service Commission, the Department of Labor, and the Department of Justice. It should continue to lead the way by adopting guidelines for providing employees with flexible options to deal with the variety of family needs that affect employees during work hours. The experience gained by designing and implementing such a system could then be offered to the private sector to help it come into compliance with a federal policy directing employers to deal with specified areas of need as indicated by the individuals employed by that particular employer. The principle of providing guidelines to govern voluntary compliance has many possibilities for the future.

But it is clear that we are a great distance away from achieving anything like a policy just discussed. And many Americans would say amen to that. They do not believe that families need help from outsiders and are suspicious of any attempt to design such help. But because of this reluctance to set policy directing employers to address family problems engendered by job demands, large groups of citizens performing a vital social function, along with a large population of children, find themselves caught in the coils of a social problem under the pretense that it is a private affair.

References for Part IV

Arkin, William, and Lynn R. Dobrofsky. "Job Sharing." In *Working Couples,* edited by Robert Rapoport and Rhona Rapoport, pp. 122–135. New York: Harper Colophon, 1979.

Beckman, Linda J. "The Relative Rewards and Costs of Parenthood and Employment for Employed Women." *Psychology of Women Quarterly* 2 (1978): 226–227, 231.

Berger, Michael, and Martha Foster. "Finding Two Jobs." In *Working Couples,* edited by Robert Rapoport and Rhona Rapoport, pp. 23–25. New York: Harper Colophon, 1979.

Booth, Alan. "Wife's Employment and Husband's Stress: A Replication and Refutation." *Journal of Marriage and the Family* 39 (1977): 645–650.

Burke, R., and T. Weir. "Relationship of Wives' Employment Status to Husband, Wife and Pair Satisfaction and Performance." *Journal of Marriage and the Family* 38 (1976): 279–287.

The Chronicle of Higher Education. 13 November 1978.

The Chronicle of Higher Education. 22 January 1979.

Clifford, William B., and Patricia L. Tobin. "Labor Force Participation of Working Mothers and Family Formation: Some Further Evidence." *Demography* 14 (1977): 273–284.

Giraldo, Z.I., Robert Kelly, et al. "Employment and the Family in Mecklenburg County, North Carolina: A Joint Project." Duke University Institute of Policy Sciences and Public Affairs Working Paper Series, no. 11791, November 1979.

Howell, M.C. "Effects of maternal employment on the child-ll." *Pediatrics* (1973): pp. 32F–43.

Kanter, Rosabeth Moss. *Work and Family in the United States: A Critical Review and Agenda for Research and Policy.* New York: Russell Sage Foundation, 1977.

Keniston, Kenneth. *All Our Children: The American Family Under Pressure.* New York: Harcourt Brace Jovanovich, 1977.

The New York Times. 15 March 1977. 40:1.

The New York Times. 17 May 1978. p w, 2:1.

Office of Personnel Management. *Federal Personnel Manual System.* FPM Letter 890-22. advance edition 6 April 1979.

Rapoport, Robert and Rhona Rapoport, eds. *Working Couples,* p. 90. New York: Harper Colophon, 1979.

Olds, Sally Wendkos. "A New Look at the Day-Care Controversy." In *Redbook,* pp. 65–68. November 1978.

Rowe, Mary. "That parents may work and children may thrive." In *Raising Children in Modern America, Problems and Prospective Solutions,* edited by N. Talbot, pp. 286–303. Boston: Little, Brown, 1976.

U.S., Department of Labor, Bureau of Labor Statistics. *Marital and Family Characteristics of the Labor Force, March 1974.* Special Labor Force Report 173 (1974).

——. *Marital and Family Characteristics of Workers, March 1977.* Special Labor Force Report 216 (1978).

——. *Marital and Family Characteristics of Workers, 1970 to 1978.* Special Labor Force Report 219 (1979). table F, table 1, table 2.

Weingarten, Kathy, and Pamela Davis. "Family/Career Transitions in Women's Lives: Report on Research in Progress." Paper presented at APA Symposium on Transitional Experiences in Adult Development, Toronto, Canada, 31 August 1978.

Wesleyan University, Middletown, Connecticut "Part-Time Faculty Policy " 1975, obtained from the Office of the Provost.

Index

About the Author

Z.I. Giraldo received the B.A. and M.A. in history from Queens College, New York, and the Ph.D. in history from The City University Graduate School. In addition, she completed a two-year postdoctoral research program at The Center for the Study of the Family and the State at The Duke University Institute of Policy Sciences.

Dr. Giraldo has been the recipient of a number of fellowships and grants, including a Fulbright Doctoral Fellowship, an NIMH Postdoctoral Fellowship, a Mellon Fellowship, an ACLS/NEH Research Travel Grant, and a Mary Reynolds Babcock Foundation Research Grant.

She is presently manager of special projects for the Affirmative Action Division of the North Carolina Office of State Personnel.